After All These Years

After All These Years

SIXTIES IDEALS IN A DIFFERENT WORLD

Lauren Kessler

THUNDER'S
MOUTH
PRESS

Published by THUNDER'S MOUTH PRESS

54 Greene Street, Suite 4S

New York, N.Y. 10013

First edition.

First printing, 1990.

Library of Congress Cataloging-in-Publication data:

Kessler, Lauren.

    After all these years : sixties ideals in a different world
Lauren Kessler.—1st ed.

          p.   cm.

    ISBN 0.938410.92.X : $13.95

    1. United States—History—1961-1969. 2. United States—Social
conditions—1960-1980. 3. Radicalism—United States—History—20th
century. 4. Social reformers—United States—Interviews.
5. Political activists—United States—Interviews.   I. Title.

E846.K45   1990

973.923—dc20   90-10749

                                     CIP

Designed by Loretta Li.

Manufactured in the United States of America.

Distributed by Consortium Book Sales & Distribution

287 East 6th Street, Suite 365, St. Paul, MN 55101

Contents

Preface

Not all of us survived.

There were the early casualties—those who lived hard, who were too young to know or care about their own mortality: Janis Joplin, Jim Morrison, Jimi Hendrix.

There were the casualties of the seventies, those who seemed to care too much: the folksinger Phil Ochs, Tom Forcade of the Underground Press Syndicate.

Then the eighties began with the assassination of John Lennon and ended with the suicide of Abbie Hoffman. A week after he killed himself, Abbie made the cover of *People* magazine with a photo, circa 1968, of a brooding radical in his infamous American flag shirt and an inset shot from the mid-eighties of a grizzled but broadly smiling middle-aged man wearing an American flag sweater. The blurb on the cover—"He was the madcap firebrand of sixties protest, but when times changed, he didn't"—implied that he should have changed, that it was wrong to remain unchanged, that not changing killed him.

Of course, one doesn't expect *People* to offer sensitive insights about people. But that magazine's rendering of Abbie's life—and by extension, the lives of other sixties veterans—is very much the interpretation one sees in the media in general. When the sixties generation is not being trivialized, as it is almost hourly in advertising campaigns, it is being reviled by turncoats like David Horowitz and Peter Collier or laughed at by younger cynics who can't fathom a time when millions of people felt they had the power to make things happen. "The sixties for me are like one of those stories where nobody laughs, and you say, 'I guess you had to be there,' " wrote one 22-year-old in the *Seattle Weekly*.

Maybe it *was* refusing to change that killed Abbie Hoffman, but not in the way *People* magazine meant. The story presented a "madcap" leader who found himself with no followers. In fact, Abbie had been involved with others in several successful environmental battles. He had forged ties with a number of groups and was certainly not alone in his ecological activism. Perhaps it was the persistence not of his activism—which surely gave him strength—but of his countercultural life, his enduring place outside the comfort of middle-class adulthood, that led him to suicide. Living on the edge for twenty-five years takes its toll. While other fifty-year-old men amassed property and reached the heights of corporate success, Abbie got arrested and gave away whatever money he had. He survived until he couldn't summon the enormous energy demanded by a life outside the mainstream.

Others survive still and have somehow found the energy and optimism to continue. This book is about—and for—them. It is not about those who have managed to make a decent life in some eddy of the mainstream, the artists, artisans and subsistence farmers who create their own mostly self-sufficient world and live happily and invisibly there. And it is not about those who live their lives as if the sixties never happened, or never happened to them. This book is about the people who learned valuable lessons in the sixties and have integrated these lessons into their lives. In rejecting a proposal for this book, the editor at a major New York publishing house wrote: "Although I can sympathize with [the author's] view that not everybody has abandoned the values and activities that the sixties embodied, I'm afraid I feel that most people have. And I feel that there will be small interest in a book about those that have carried on . . . ."

Obviously, I disagree. I believe—and the research I did for this book confirms—that there are thousands, perhaps millions of sixties veterans out there struggling to live decent, socially conscious lives. We are working, perhaps more quietly than twenty years ago, but no less energetically, for social change. I wrote *After All These Years* to help foster a sense of community among these people. Because we're not on the cover of major magazines any more (unless we commit suicide), because we're not easily identifiable by our appearance, we don't know just how many of us there are. Twenty years ago, we felt part of a big family. We could recognize family members wherever they were—Boston, Madison, Boulder, Austin, Berkeley—because their hair was long and their clothes were colorful. They drove VW buses. They listened to rock 'n' roll. Today most of us are indistinguishable from others our age. But that doesn't mean we're not here. Discarding one's bellbottoms is quite different than discarding one's values. So, in large part, I wrote this book to make us visible to ourselves.

But I wrote it also, particularly the essays, to reach out to younger people, those whose view of the sixties and the veterans of that time has been almost completely obscured by media stereotypes. Bombarded with images of the sixties generation as self-indulgent lightweights then and nostalgic self-indulgent lightweights now, many of the next generation see us as sybaritic yuppies, New Age flakes or pitiable burnouts—or perhaps just silly anachronisms. We're not. Most of us are not. The best of what we stood for then—peace, egalitarianism, respect for the earth—is what we stand for now. And these values, as well as the people who continue to take them seriously, are anything but anachronistic.

People speak in this book. They speak about what they believe in and how they've struggled to preserve those beliefs, about aging, about optimism in the face of major setbacks, about how and why they manage to carry on. Almost all of these people were strangers to me. I found out about them through friends of friends or references in books or mentions in faded newspaper articles. I called them, an unknown voice on the other end of the telephone line, and they responded with, I think, astounding candor. They trusted me. We shared a common bond, a common set of beliefs about the power and the potential of human beings, about the kind of future it is possible to build.

I have many people to thank for this book, but first and foremost, I want to thank the people who speak here. They tell the story of the last twenty years better than any historian could. What they do today and for the next twenty years will help determine what kind of society we live in. I particularly want to thank Eliza Schmidtkunz, a friend and consistent supporter of this project, and Charlie Dee, a stranger, for suggesting the names of others who appear here.

A number of people with whom I talked did not make it into the book, although their ideas informed my questions to others and my thinking. I thank Kit Andrews, Andy Stapp, John Woodward, Paul Pappas, Gwen Hamilton, Juliet Wittman, Quito Hernandez, Wayne Koberstein, Jack Noel and Margie Joy. Dan Reece was a wonderful source for interesting people as were Steve Cohen and Steve Clark. Susan Henry and Lesli Mones both contributed names, and Lesli listened patiently and with interest to the ups and downs of the project as we ran together on summer mornings. I owe a debt to Suzanne Braun Levine, currently editor of *Columbia Journalism Review* and one of the founding editors at *Ms.* for clearing a path to Gloria Steinem. And I thank Roberta Goodman for helping me reach Angela Davis, and Sharon Palma for arranging, rearranging and re-rearranging my time with Arlo Guthrie. I am also indebted to these talented social scientists whose insights made me think: Todd Gitlin, Jack Whalen, Richard Flacks, James Fendrich and Alberta Nassi.

This book would never have happened were it not for the assistance of computer wizard Doug Metzler, who solved my far-too-numerous problems with both efficiency and good humor. And I thank Arnold Ismach, dean of the University of Oregon School of Journalism, my home base, who blanched when he saw the phone bills but paid them. Kathy Kroeger did an excellent job transcribing the interviews. She was not only fast and accurate but interested as well. Finally, and most importantly, I want to thank Tom Hager who not only did those things some lucky writers' spouses do—like lend unfailing and good-humored support and encouragement—but also, as a fellow writer, edited every page, and as a co-parent and partner, took up far more slack than I had any right to let out. The neck rubs helped, too.

L.K.
Eugene, Oregon
1989

Introduction

Ken Kesey lumbers through the door of his house, laughing, talking, harumphing, shaking the persistent Oregon rain from his plaid golfer's cap. He's wearing jeans, a fuchsia and yellow tie-dyed T-shirt and, under his work boots, fire engine red socks. Behind him trail Pranksters Zonk, Babbs and Hagen. In the kitchen, Faye is brewing tea.

It could be 1964, when day-glo field marshal Kesey led his psychedelic troops on the cross-country bus trip that both symbolized and heralded the coming counterculture. It could be 1968, when Kesey, fresh out of jail from a marijuana conviction, returned to the family farm, parked the bus alongside the barn, wired the trees for sound and gathered the Prankster survivors around him.

But it isn't. It's 1988. And Ken Kesey—52, balding, with grown kids and a 60-acre farm—is still at it.

"I'm a member of the tie-dye mafia," he says. His grin is at once beatific and goofy. "And my belief is: Ya nevah quits da mob."

Kesey's mob, in fact, is pretty much intact. The key Pranksters moved to Oregon with him twenty years ago, and they're still there, partying, picnicking, planning political stunts, musical extravaganzas and cultural blowouts. And there's plenty of evidence that the larger mob is also still around—in Berkeley, Boulder, Austin, Madison, New England, upstate New York and anywhere the seeds of the sixties rooted and took hold.

"I don't know anyone who has been involved in all this seriously who has ever quit," says Kesey. "All the people I know are working just as hard, and they're becoming very skillful at it." He thinks for a moment. "The Grateful Dead's a good example. These guys have never got off the elevator, saying, 'Okay, here's as high as we're gonna go. We gonna get off at Menswear.' They're still on the elevator, and they're going to go as high as they can."

Kesey tips back in the rickety chair that's usually in front of Faye's sewing machine and puts his feet up on the couch. Through the thin walls of the old house you can hear Babbs and Zonk laughing. "This isn't the throwing Molotov cocktails kind of revolution," he says. "But it *is* a revolution. It's psychedelic Christian philosophy, the belief that love and mercy are the most powerful things in the world, a belief in the old, traditional American dream.

"What the last two decades show is that if something really is beautiful, you can burn it and bury it and put it in jail, but it is more resilient than evil. Finally, the bad stuff does decay and goes back into the earth. Finally, it washes itself out. Listen," he says with his characteristic mixture of sincerity and mirth, "there is in the United States right now a cadre of revolutionaries just waiting for the cause."

That's not what conventional wisdom would have us believe. Conventional wisdom says that privileged young people—be they the flappers of the twenties or the hippies of the sixties—will sow their wild oats but ultimately settle down to become pillars of the established order. It happened to Jerry

1

Rubin, the fun-loving anarchist of the sixties who became the money-grubbing stockbroker of the eighties. It happened to ex-*Ramparts* editors Peter Collier and David Horowitz, now unabashed right-wing apologists. The media tell us it has happened to almost everyone. "Many former radicals or dropouts have become entrepreneurs," a 1978 *U.S. News and World Report* article states with confidence. In another late seventies report, *60 Minutes* reporter Morley Safer, while strolling down Berkeley's Telegraph Avenue, observes, "there seems to be little here that's counter about the counterculture." And Collier and Horowitz, in *The Destructive Generation*, their enthusiastic trashing of the sixties, write: "When the revolution in the streets that the New Left yearned for failed to happen, most of its members disappeared—into health foods, jogging, business school, entrepreneurship and yuppiedom."

On the small and wide screens, sixties hippies are eighties yuppies, yesterday's activists are today's narcissists. In two of the past decade's most popular statements about the fate of babyboomers, *The Big Chill* and "thirtysomething," characters rhapsodize about their romantic radical pasts while living self-centered, apolitical lives. The message is clear: Sixties radicals were just a bunch of kids out to have a good time. The experience was so superficial that they all soon outgrew it and went on to more important things like making money. There's another message out there, one that came through loud and clear when Abbie Hoffman died in 1989: Unreconstructed sixties activists are tragic anachronisms. Demoralization, depression and suicide are the natural consequences of a life committed to political activism and social change.

It may be convenient for economic interests to view the sixties as merely a fad. Trivialized, robbed of its soul, the sixties become no more than a marketing tool. And it may be comforting for mainstream political interests to dismiss the sixties as irrelevant. It makes it easy to forget the important (and still relevant) criticisms levelled against the political power structure during that time. But those who continue to work for social justice and live politically meaningful lives—and there are many who fit that description—know that, to paraphrase Mark Twain, the reports of their deaths are greatly exaggerated. Sociologists know it too. For the past fifteen years, a number of them have been charting the fate of sixties activists. Every few years, a study appears in scholarly journals, and the message is always the same: The sixties changed some people's lives . . . permanently. While few remain as untouched by time and travail as Ken Kesey, many serious activists are still committed reformers today.

Civil rights activists were still "keeping the faith" thirteen years after Freedom Summer, writes a Florida State University sociologist who studied them. Activists accused of burning the Bank of America branch in Isla Vista, California, had not been coopted fourteen years later. "They are not the new narcissists," write researchers Richard Flacks and Jack Whalen. "They want to live socially responsible lives . . . making at least some contribution to the public good." Two Catholic University sociologists who tracked University of Michigan radicals into the eighties conclude, "The activism of the 1960s was not a transitory event. It is associated with long-term values."

What were the values of the sixties that made such a lasting impression on people's lives? "The definitive sixties idea," writes former SDS leader now Berkeley sociologist Todd Gitlin, "was that everything was at stake and anything might, just might, be possible—revolution on the public scale, transcendence on the private scale." Many of those who lived through the sixties and many of those who have since written about the era see the counterculture as neatly segmented into the public and the private, the public representing the political arm of the movement, the private representing the cultural contingent. Those whose major thrust was political—from the Student Nonviolent Coordinating Committee (SNCC) to the Black Panthers, from Vietnam Moratorium to the SDS—valued collective action, self-sacrifice and social responsibility. Much has been written lately about the self-defeating sectarianism of the New Left. But while any one political group may have suffered bloody in-fights that ended in purges and seemingly endless splintering, something more basic than strategy, more basic even than ideology, united them: they saw the world, and their own lives, in political terms. Change to them meant an actual reconfiguration of power. On the other hand, to those compelled mainly by countercultural ideas—hippies, yippies, back-to-the-land utopianists—self-expression, autonomy and personal liberation were at the heart of the movement. The goal was to transcend the rules and roles of a society that labored mightily to manufacture consensus and conformity. Change was internal, a personal struggle to free oneself from the past.

The values of the two contingents may seem contradictory, but in fact, there was amazingly little tension between rank and file "freaks" and "politicos" of twenty years ago. Leaders may have espoused doctrinaire positions, but many of their followers had feet in both camps. Most underground newspapers reported on, and pledged allegiance to, both scenes. But more than that, both contingents shared some very basic beliefs: They were committed to equality, both racial and, at least after the women's movement began to make an impact, sexual. They distrusted authority. They shared a humanitarian sense of social justice. They rooted for the underdog. They rejected what they saw as the moral and intellectual wasteland of American middle-class adulthood.

Twenty years later, many of these people continue to refuse to settle for conventional identities and traditional institutional ties. Those who have married are struggling to redefine what has long been an inequitable institution; those with children are trying to become a new breed of parent. Many of those who work in what used to be called "straight jobs" are laboring from within to reform, restructure and humanize their workplaces. Some have carved for themselves permanent channels outside the mainstream. All of the sociologists who have studied former sixties activists find they have gravitated toward the helping professions, shying away from business, management, large bureaucracies and formal politics. Not surprisingly, they are making significantly less money than their non-activist contemporaries.

Of course, some did "quit the mob": not just media-hyped "turncoats" like Rubin or Eldridge Cleaver, but many investors, developers, corporados and cosmetic surgeons can (perhaps only privately) trace their roots to the sixties. The fashionably cynical "Woodstock Anniversary Calendar" for the year 1989 celebrates these people. The illustration for one month shows a balding, overweight man behind a desk telling his employee: "Not with-standing that we both dropped acid at Woodstock, I'm still going to have to fire you." In another illustration a conservatively dressed businessman sitting behind a desk-top computer has his eyes closed and a peaceful expression on his face. He is chanting to himself: "Buy low, sell high, buy low, sell high." The caption reads: "Update: The Mantra." But even those who moved back into the mainstream with a vengeance may not have completely escaped from or obliterated their ties to the past. In small ways that are sometimes easy to make fun of, their lives may be different: They recycle. They don't buy their kids plastic assault weapons. Maybe they think twice about doing something selfish or manipulative or, to use an old phrase, politically incor-rect. That small voice, which they sometimes listen to, is the link to their past. The very defensiveness of some hard-core yuppies about their cur-rent lifestyles shows that the values of the sixties still hold some sway over their lives.

Collier and Horowitz announce early on in their book that the sixties exist merely as a "nostalgic artifact," and that the only enduring legacy of that time is "a collection of splinter groups, special interest organizations and newly minted 'minorities' whose only common belief was that America was guilty and untrustworthy." They're wrong on both counts. The sixties exist in a very real and very important way as the sum of certain core countercul-tural values that continue to play a vital part in people's lives. The legacy of the sixties is people who have alternative political, social and personal agen-das, and who find the energy to keep on working for them.

This is what a former communard and activist says, referring to the knowledge about self and society she gained during the sixties: "Once you understand, that doesn't mean you're cool. It means you are responsible wherever you are to keep working in whatever way you can. Once you see how things work, you can't unsee it or ignore it. You can get fashionably cyni-cal; you can cover it up with booze, with drugs, or with illness. But you can't forget it."

On some level, ya nevah quits da mob.

SOCIAL JUSTICE
I

More than the Black Panthers, who were sectarian in their politics and often provincial in their goals, Angela Davis symbolized black power and black militance in the sixties. With her trademark Afro, her strong—some said "regal"—presence and her impassioned eloquence, she also embodied the growing notion of black pride. A self-proclaimed revolutionary, a card-carrying Communist, she devoted herself entirely to radical politics in the sixties, organizing, speaking, writing and touring on the behalf of blacks, women and political prisoners.

The eldest of four children, Davis was born in Birmingham, Alabama, and grew up in a segregated, middle-class black neighborhood. Her mother, politically active in the thirties and forties, was a public school teacher who later became involved in the early civil rights movement. Her father was a teacher turned small businessman. In some respects, Davis had a storybook youth. She studied piano, clarinet and dance and was the most decorated member of her Girl Scout troop. In both elementary and high school, she was a straight-A student. She played in the high school band. Every Sunday, she attended church with her family.

But there were also the seeds of activism and discontent in her early life. In the mid-fifties, she and her mother took part in civil rights demonstrations in Birmingham, and as a teenager Davis organized interracial study groups among young people. Police soon disbanded the groups, and white "night riders" terrorized Davis's neighborhood, at one point setting off a bomb across the street from her family's home.

When she was fifteen, Davis went to New York on an American Friends Service Committee scholarship that funded her junior year at a private, progressive Greenwich Village school. Her parents arranged for her to live with the family of Reverend William Howard Melish, a controversial Episcopal minister who had won the 1956 Stockholm Peace Prize and was deeply involved in the civil rights movement. At Elizabeth Irwin High School, she joined a communist youth group, Advance, and studied hard. French, her weakest subject, became her strongest, and in 1961 she enrolled in Brandeis as a French literature major.

Davis spent her junior year abroad at the Sorbonne, as a classmate later put it, "just chain smoking and studying." She did find time to sit in cafes and talk to students from Algeria, who described the revolution against French colonialism and their treatment as second class citizens in France. These conversations contributed to her growing radicalism, as did her reading. "The *Communist Manifesto* hit me like a bolt of lightning," she writes in her autobiography. "I read it avidly, finding in it answers to many of the seemingly unanswerable dilemmas which had plagued me."

Back at Brandeis, her radicalism moved forward under the instruction of radical philosopher Herbert Marcuse, who taught Davis during her senior year (and his last year on the faculty). Profoundly affected by Marcuse's eclectic brand of Marxism, with its powerful and original critique of post-industrial society, Davis moved further to the left. The respect was apparently mutual. "I consider her the best student I ever had in thirty years of teaching," Marcuse once said.

Davis graduated *magna cum laude* in 1965 and headed for Germany to study philosophy with a colleague of Marcuse's at the University of Frankfurt, where she continued her brilliant academic career. But she left two years later, before earning her master's degree because, as one of her teachers was quoted as saying, "she could no longer tolerate the deterioration of the situation in the United States without becoming actively involved."

Back in the States, she enrolled at the University of California, San Diego, where Marcuse was now teaching. Within a year, she finished her master's degree. By 1969, she had all the requirements completed for her Ph.D. except her dissertation, which was to be a study of Kant's analysis of violence during the French revolution. Meanwhile, her radical politics were deepening as her political activism increased. At the university, she helped establish the Black Students Council, devised guidelines for an experimental college for minorities, worked with the militant San Diego Black Conference and, for a while, became involved in SNCC. At an SNCC workshop late in 1967, she was reintroduced to the Communist party and met the woman who headed an all-black communist collective in the Los Angeles ghetto, the Che-Lumumba Club. In the summer of 1968, she formally joined the Communist party.

The next year she was hired to teach philosophy courses at UCLA and, according to student evaluations and faculty review, did an excellent job. A few months later, a letter written by an ex-FBI informer appeared in the UCLA *Daily Bruin*. Without mentioning names, the author revealed that a member of the Communist party was now part of the university's faculty. A week later, Angela Davis was named in a Los Angeles *Examiner* story. Then-governor Ronald Reagan pressured the Board of Regents to dismiss her, against the recommendation of the faculty and the chancellor. A court order reinstated her, and the courses she taught during the 1969/1970 school year were among the most popular on campus. But in 1970, the Board of Regents refused to renew her contract on the grounds that she delivered "inflammatory" speeches outside the classroom.

The speeches the Board was referring to were those she gave in defense of the Soledad Brothers (so named after Soledad Prison, where they were inmates), the most prominent of whom was George Jackson. In jail since 1961 for robbing a service station of $70, Jackson was an organizer of a Marxist-Fanonist revolutionary collective among the prisoners. After a white guard was found murdered in the prison, Jackson and two others were indicted for murder. Davis and others saw Jackson as a political prisoner, not merely a victim of society but a pioneer in the fight against repression.

During Jackson's trial, she legally bought several guns, as she later contended, for self-defense after receiving threatening calls and letters. What happened next was to be the subject of one of the era's most dramatic, most widely publicized court cases. George Jackson's teenage brother, Jonathan, took Davis's guns and used them in an ill-fated attempt to storm the Marin county courthouse where two other black prisoners were on trial. When the shooting stopped, Jonathan and both the black prisoners were dead, and the district attorney was critically injured. Davis, who friends said was shocked by the incident, went into hiding. The FBI, discovering that three of the guns used were registered in her name, placed Davis on its Ten-Most-Wanted list. After a two-month nationwide search, she was arrested in a New York City motel and extradited to California. The resulting "Free Angela" movement inspired protest marches all across America and from Ceylon to Paris. After a lengthy trial in the spring of 1972, a jury of eleven whites and one Hispanic acquitted her on all counts.

After the trial, Davis moved to the Bay Area where she still lives today. She spent most of the seventies immersed in the Communist party, lecturing around the world. In the 1980 general election, she ran for vice president on the Communist party ticket. In the eighties, without cutting back on her speaking engagements, she moved to reestablish herself as an author and academic. In 1982, her *Women, Race and Class* was published by Random House. In it, she traces the historical development of feminism, arguing that the separate and unequal history of black and white women is the basis for their continuing estrangement within the larger women's movement. Currently on the faculty at San Francisco State, she is working on a new book that examines the cultural legacy of women's blues. She continues a rigorous lecturing schedule as an articulate and outspoken proponent of social justice.

"I find young people—students and workers alike—much more politically conscious than twenty years ago, which seems somewhat contradictory because two decades ago we were in the midst of a really powerful activist movement, and we don't see as much activism today. But I think that this is an era during which consciousness will be transformed into activism. I think in particular that people today are much more aware of the need to build bridges between movements, between cultures, between ethnic groups, between issues, in relationship to the movement of the late sixties and early seventies, which had a tendency to be rather compartmentalized. There is the understanding today that, while many of us may be involved in very specific causes, that we should also find ways to link those causes and to link our energies and our power.

"Some of the largest demonstrations in the history of this country have taken place in recent years. We should keep that in mind. It's rather interesting that during the Reagan administration the largest demonstration around peace, for example, occurred. We had a demonstration of a million people in New York [in 1982]. And certainly that played a role in compelling the Reagan government to adopt a different kind of posture towards the Soviet Union with respect to negotiating around nuclear arms.

"The women's movement, I think, is really on the rise, especially the reproductive rights movement. The demonstration that took place in Washington last spring [1989] was extremely impressive. We've never seen a demonstration of that magnitude around the issue of reproductive rights, even during the period when *Roe v. Wade* was handed down by the Supreme Court.

"The Jesse Jackson campaign also indicated at least a will toward activism. And particularly the last campaign indicated the extent to which people are prepared to come together. And then of course we can look at what happened around the nomination of Bork to the Supreme Court. That coalition, which was very rapidly put together, was unprecedented in its breadth and in its intensity. Unfortunately, the effect with respect to the composition of the Supreme Court is not that much different. But we did learn that it was possible to thwart the agenda of the Reagan administration by organizing effectively.

"So I think that the social movements today are a lot more sophisticated than they were in the sixties and seventies, and of course that is to be expected because we've been able to benefit from the lessons that were learned in that movement. And whereas at that time we were willing to simply go out in the streets around any question, in any way, I think now we realize that we have to be more serious about the way in which we organize. It's a lot harder to organize today because we're dealing with more complex issues.

"This is also a period of a great deal of confusion. And it is a period during which it appears that racist violence can be generated in a way that many people had not believed possible. There is also homophobic violence. I don't think that these violent explosions represent the mood of the country as a whole, but they certainly do represent the mood of the government. So that's very frightening. Extremely frightening.

"I still passionately believe in the quest for justice and equality. And even though I may be involved in a different way today than I was in 1968 or '69, that commitment to see that struggle through to the end is unshaken, utterly unshaken. And I would say that I think I understand more clearly today what that commitment entails, but those basic values—I guess I've had them since I was a child. I don't think that that's something that emerged in the sixties. I think that is something that I received as a legacy from my parents, because my mother was active in the thirties and forties, and I grew up with those values and that commitment. And I know that that's something that will never change.

"My mother, when I was very young, told me many times that I should dare to be different, that I should follow the voice within me, what I believed. And over the years it has never occurred to me to forsake a cause in which I passionately believe in order to gain acceptance. So the question of regretting my involvement in the Communist party has never ever occurred to me. Yes, it has been far more difficult. But I wouldn't even say that that was the price I had to pay because I don't consider it as having paid a price. That is what I decided that I have to do with my life. And that decision, that commitment, involved a willingness to accept the consequences, which of course were at some points in my life a lot more difficult than they are today.

"But I do find that over the years there has been an increasing acceptance of those of us who are communists. I am active in the National Political Congress of Black Women, for example, and because I was elected to the board, there was a little resistance. Someone wrote a rather nasty anti-communist letter to Shirley Chisholm, who is the chairperson. I felt very proud indeed when at a national conference she got up and alluded to that letter and challenged the person very aggressively by saying that I was capable of bringing to that organization a large social vision that no one else had brought. I don't think that would have happened—I know that wouldn't have happened—twenty years ago.

"But you know I can look back on the period when I was fired from my position at UCLA because of my membership in the Communist party and reflect on the kinds of responses that came from those who were supporting me, and look at the changed set of circumstances today. This is another example of progress, I think, that has been made in the consciousness of people in this country.

"I can't present a blueprint of the society that I would want to live in or would want the coming generations to live in, but I do know what I don't want. I do know that the continual dominance of the corporate monopoly structure in this country has devastating implications for working class people in general, for people of color in particular, for women, and for all other oppressed groups. I think that what we need to be concerned about now is building a movement that will be capable of resisting the reign of the monopoly. And I'm convinced that we need a socialist United States of America.

"I can't say exactly when that will happen or how that will happen or exactly what it will look like, but I think it's very clear that we are in continual crisis in the society. We are confronting one crisis after the other. For example, the drug crisis now threatens to destroy a whole generation of young people, and especially the black community. That is very much connected to the dominance of the monopolies in this country. The Bush administration makes it appear that the problem is in the community itself with those who use the drugs and those who push the drugs, but we know that very few black people have the means to import the drugs. They don't have the boats and the planes and the hundreds of millions of dollars.

"There has been evidence, documented evidence, that the CIA is playing a role in this, especially with respect to the counterrevolutionary groups in various parts of the world that depend on drug traffic for their funding. Someone who works with young people in the streets here in Oakland said that a lot of the young men, who actually are the small-time drug pushers, say that the CIA is behind the whole thing. As a matter of fact, they say that the initials CIA mean 'Cocaine Importing Agency.' I find it very interesting that young people who are on that level have an understanding of the fact that this is something whose tentacles go into the government agencies of this country.

"I think it is important that we find a way to regenerate some of the excitement that we felt as young people, and the attraction to organized forms. Certainly many of the young people who are unfortunately victims of the drug crisis today would have been attracted twenty years ago to the Black Panther party. So we do have to build a kind of organizational structure that can generate excitement and move people away from the self-destructive antisocial phenomena that exist in our community.

"As a young activist, like most other young activists of that time, I expected the revolution to happen tomorrow. Even though we were talking at that time about what we called a protracted struggle, I don't think that our vision was such that we could foresee that in two decades we would still be fighting a lot of the same battles. But it has been important to learn how to recognize the victories that we have won. I think that sometimes that poses serious problems for people who, because they cannot see that the work they have done has led to any significant change, turn away and become disillusioned and disassociate themselves from those movements. So it is extremely important, I think, to recognize that the work that I have done has led to some very important changes.

"People in this country look at the world very differently today than they did two decades ago. The majority of white people in this country count themselves among the anti-racist forces, and that was not true two decades ago. Of course it's another question whether or not the majority truly understands what racism is and what needs to be done to eradicate it, but the fact is there has been a realignment of forces. And even though we have a Republican government that is quite conservative, the majority of the people in this country are far more progressive, almost across the board.

"For example, when the anti-choice forces became visible, through Operation Rescue and all of the so-called pro-life movements, it was clear to me that they represented only a small minority—even though they were very visible and even though at that time the pro-choice forces were not as organized as we should have been. But of course in the meantime polls have confirmed the fact that the majority of people in this country are in favor of retaining the legalization of abortion. Many people didn't understand this. They assumed that because the so-called pro-life forces were out front and were receiving all of the media coverage, that they were the ones who represented the sentiments of the people of this country. Now as the pro-choice movement becomes stronger and more organized, the real balance of forces becomes apparent. But if we had not been able to recognize the disparity between media projections and the visibility of the conservative forces on the one hand, and on the other hand, the latent progressive forces, then we would not have, I think, understood the possibilities of organizing—which did lead to that very impressive demonstration last spring and this past November. I think that's extremely important, learning how to count one's victories.

"I think it is our responsibility, those of us who are older, to transmit this knowledge to those who are younger. And we have reached the point where generations don't necessarily define involvement in movements, as membership in particular generations did in the sixties. There were very few movements in which you had very young people and very old people and all of the generations in between. As a matter of fact, one of the slogans during the late sixties, was that 'You can't trust anyone over thirty.' I think we've gone beyond that, which I think is absolutely imperative—not just because we're over thirty. It's not important for us—it's important for the younger people.

"But see, what we didn't have that we should have had in the sixties was a clear relationship to the generations that had been involved before us. And we ended up having to make some of the very same mistakes that they had made twenty years before, or thirty years before. And I think now among young people who are activists, there is a reverence and respect for sixties veterans, although I'm not saying that they should necessarily follow our leadership, because I don't think that that would necessarily lead them in the best direction. I think that it is up to those who are older to learn how to follow the leadership of those who are younger, but at the same time provide the wisdom and the experience that we can claim. And that can be very exciting. And of course, as someone who does a great deal of lecturing, I continually find it inspiring that young people on the campuses want to hear what I have to say.

"In fact, I think my energy comes from my continual contact with younger people. In my classes, as I lecture, I am continually inspired to do the things that I do when I realize how thirsty young people are, not only for knowledge, but for models. I recognize that there is a responsibility here that I cannot abdicate. And it is not something that I carry as a burden because it enlightens my life.

"I have come to realize through my involvement with, for example, the black women's health movement, that the nature of my involvement must leave some space for me to take care of myself. I don't want to be a person who ends up having a heart attack at age fifty because I have not taken care of myself. Because that means that the contributions that I might possibly make will have been cut short.

"So through my involvement, particularly in the National Black Women's Health Project, I have come to understand that there is really a dialectical relationship between taking care of my physical and mental and spiritual health and being involved in a movement to bring about social change for masses of people. So that I don't feel, as I once did, that I don't have the right to take time to take care of myself. So that I always find space to do the things that I like to do, that are good for my body and my spirit. There was a time when I would not have considered saying, 'Well, you know, I need to take a run every morning, so there's certain things that I can't do at this time.' I'm actually very physically active. I run, and I'm a mountain biker, and I lift weights and that type of thing. And there was a time when I wouldn't have made time for that. But now I realize that I'm more effective when I do take care of myself.

"Of course, even in the heat of all of the struggles of the sixties, we had fun. We had dances and we did things that made us laugh and that were joyous. We weren't the kind of people who felt that in order to be revolutionaries there could be no joy in life. So we found our sources of joy and happiness at that time too. But I think that at the same time, many of us did push ourselves too much. And that's probably why many people did eventually end up feeling that they could no longer be a part of the movement and did drop out. Because they didn't know how to integrate that involvement into a fuller kind of life.

"I can't really say that I can point to a particular moment where I began to look back on the sixties as an era. I'm often very amazed now when I reflect upon the fact that all of these things happened twenty years or more ago. I just recently had an experience—unfortunate, tragic—the death of Huey Newton, which allowed me to reestablish contact with a lot of the people with whom I had worked during that era, some of whom I had not seen since I left Los Angeles. Well, I had been arrested of course and after I got out of jail, after my trial was over in 1972, I decided to remain in the Bay Area. So at Huey Newton's funeral a lot of the people with whom I was active in Los Angeles from '67 to '70 when I was arrested, were there. And we reminisced. But it wasn't just nostalgic reminiscence. We decided that we would try to organize something like a reunion to begin to do some oral history on what occurred during that period.

"What I found exciting was that many of the people are still active in movements, whether they be electoral politics or whether they be cultural movements, but they're still out there trying to bring about change. And of course the image that has been continually encouraged by the media is that that movement died. It didn't die. I know I'm not the only one who's continued to maintain a relationship to the movement, and who can talk about the continuity in my own life. And that is why I can't say there is a moment when that ended, because for me it still continues, and I see it as a part of a continuum.

"I guess one of the reasons why it has been easy for me to integrate that vision of the long haul into my own life is by virtue of my involvement in the Communist party with people who have been active for, I don't know, sixty years, sixty-five years. And so I don't think there was a single moment where I decided that my involvement was going to have to be different. I think that what happened was I simply grew older. And perhaps a little more patient as a result, and a little wiser."

Angela Davis has committed her life to gaining social justice for blacks, women, the poor, prisoners—victims of what she calls "an oppressive politico-economic order." And although few followed the precise path she took—militant radicalism and allegiance to the Communist party—she was and is far from alone in this struggle. Many who came of political age in the sixties confronted the basic inequities in American life and joined together to do something about them.

They saw the deep contradiction between the promise of America and the reality of many Americans' lives. This was the land of egalitarianism and democracy; yet a century after the Civil War, the South was still segregated and southern blacks were all but disenfranchised. This was the land of equal opportunity, yet women were an underpaid, undervalued underclass; four decades after they won the right to vote, they still had little political or economic power. This was a country that took public pride in its diversity, yet those who by virtue of skin color or sexual preference strayed from the norm were often treated brutally. This was the land of freedom of thought and individuality, yet in schools across the nation, young people were being taught conformity. This was the country whose previous two generations had fought two world wars to "make the world safe for democracy," yet, on the eve of the sixties, with the dual threat of the atomic bomb and the cold war, the world seemed more dangerous than ever.

The ideal of a classless America was always part myth, of course. (The historian Daniel Boorstin once wrote that "America was the first country to begin with perfection and aspire to progress.") But in the years after the second World War, when the United States was assuming a preeminent position as the world's great defender of democracy and human rights, the *mythos* was overwhelming. And so were the contradictions, which the strong postwar economy and burgeoning middle class only served to highlight. Ironically, at the same time, postwar prosperity helped create a generation of people born into comfort, with the time and resources to concern themselves with the struggle for social justice.

That struggle took many forms in the sixties, from Freedom Rides to campus occupations, from peaceful marches to bloody confrontations. Tactics varied not only from group to group—Dr. Martin Luther King, Jr.'s nonviolence to the Black Panthers' armed militance, for example—but also within groups over time, as in the increasing radicalization of the Student Nonviolent Coordinating Committee (SNCC). But more important than their diverse strategies, groups differed in their fundamental aims. Some groups wanted a piece of the American pie: equal access to the goods, services and opportunities the country had to offer. Others wanted to throw the pie back in the face of those who baked it.

These were very significant differences, yet much united the many groups struggling for social justice (although most of them didn't appreciate the similarities at the time). At the most basic level, a growing number of people had a sense of themselves as members of an identifiable group, be they blacks, gays, feminists or radical youth. The teach-ins, consciousness-raising groups, celebratory parades, even fashions (the Afro, for example) fostered group identification and spoke to the common experiences, concerns and goals of those within the group. As individuals, but especially as members of these defined groups, people of color and nonmainstream proclivities shared a deep sense of alienation from mainstream American society. Either they had been forcibly prevented from realizing the American dream or they just as forcibly rejected it. In whatever case, their attitude throughout the sixties became one of questioning, rather than accepting, society's definition and treatment of them as second-class citizens.

Certainly they saw the inequities inherent in the legal system, from the glaring Jim Crowism of the South to the insidious state laws making homosexuality a crime. But they also began to recognize that inequities were part of their own everyday lives: The personal was political too. Feminists examined their relationships with the men and women in their lives. Gays saw their lifestyle as a political statement. Native Americans realized that their physical and spiritual health were essentially political issues. Out of this awareness came fundamental questions about American society and its values, questions central to all groups fighting for social justice: Do we truly believe in the equality of all— men, women, people of color? Is everybody free in "the land of the free"? Are we tolerant of diversity? Can we be appreciative of differences? These questions—sometimes not articulated, but always there—underlay the daily culture shock of living in what some perceived as a self-contradictory society.

But questioning values was more than a philosophic exercise. For those who struggled for social justice in the sixties, values translated into direct action. Equality was worth fighting for. Theoretical discussions were important; certain books and tracts were vital to the intellectual underpinnings of the movements, but in the end it was individuals taking action that sparked the social justice movements of the sixties. Rosa Parks, the Montgomery, Alabama, seamstress who kicked off the now-famous boycott of that city's public transportation system in December 1955, wasn't thinking about the theory of oppression when she refused to relinquish her seat in the front of the bus to a white man. She was bone-tired after another long day of work—and infinitely more weary of her 42 years as a black in the deep South. The men and women who ushered in the Gay Liberation Movement by fighting police in front of Stonewall Inn in Greenwich Village "hadn't read Marcuse to understand the implications of their actions," says Randy Shilts, author of *And the Band Played On*. They just did it.

From the Boston Tea Party on, direct action has been an important part of social change movements, but that action has always existed within a larger context. These movements always began with relatively primitive self- and group-awareness: "There's something very wrong in my life. I am part of a group for whom these same things are wrong." (Feminists coined the phrase "consciousness-raising" to describe this learning process.) After reaching a critical level of awareness, members of emerging social justice movements often went through a stage characterized by irate optimism: "Our situation is monumentally unjust. If only others realized how unjustly we are treated, changes would be made." (Teach-ins, conferences, speeches, the attention to press coverage were all part of this move to educate and inform.)

But this initial optimism proved unfounded in most cases, and the emerging movement—now cemented by its failure as well as its group identity—moved on to another phase of development: confrontation. As the major strategy for social justice movements in the late sixties, confrontation had solid successes: many black voters successfully registered in the South, some urban police forces learned to operate more sensitively within their communities, women won their reproductive rights, many universities changed their policies to empower students. But confrontation also could result in "quick fix" policy changes that did not get at the root of the injustice. And, although a demonstration or sit-in might be organized as a nonviolent protest, it was often met with violent reaction. As heads were bashed (and, occasionally, people killed), positions hardened, and the gap between "them" and "us" opened into a chasm. For those who believed that the country could only be changed through large-scale revolution, the chasm was temporarily comforting. But when revolution didn't happen, what remained was a polarized society with blocked or nonexistent communication channels between groups. Those who wanted change existed outside the system they wanted to change, yet it was becoming increasingly clear that institutional change depended on savvy people within the institution, not just angry people battering at its walls.

To move forward in the fight for social justice, movements not only had to endure, they also had to mature. By the mid-seventies and into the eighties, social justice movements had increased their repertoire of action. People were, in the parlance of the day, "organizing *around*" various issues; that is, they were using diverse strategies to surround a problem. Demonstrations, direct action and confrontation were part of it but so were lobbying, supporting sympathetic political candidates and working within mainstream groups. While the social justice movements discussed here—civil rights/black power, brown and red power, student power, feminism and gay liberation—clearly experienced a heyday in the sixties, all continue their battles today using these more inclusive tactics.

Although all movements for social justice in the sixties were significant, both to American society and to those within the fringe groups fighting for change, the civil rights/black power movement was perhaps the most important. The first mass movement of the sixties—it actually began in earnest in the mid-fifties—it established the precedent for mass action by those outside the mainstream. Both in its early phase when it was dominated by the nonviolent direct action tactics of Martin Luther King, Jr. and in its more militant phase when it was influenced by the aggressiveness of Stokely Carmichael and the Black Panthers, the movement acted as an example to others fighting for social change. The civil rights workers of the early sixties were heroes to the emerging New Left just as, a scant seven years later, the Black Panthers were a source of inspiration for the Weathermen.

The early sixties civil rights movement was quite literally a training ground for young, disaffected white youth. Mario Savio, a Freedom Rider in Mississippi during the summer of 1964, returned to Berkeley that fall to start and lead the Free Speech Movement. The ubiquitous Tom Hayden, one of the founders of Students for a Democratic Society (SDS) and later one of the Chicago Seven defendants, got his political education during the sit-ins and voter registration drives of the early sixties. It was "both a necessary moral act and a rite of passage into serious commitment," writes Hayden in his autobiography. Casey Hayden (Tom's first wife), a tireless worker for SNCC in Atlanta in the early sixties, was one of the first articulators of what would later become the women's liberation movement. Clearly, many of the sixties crusades owed a debt to the civil rights movement.

The modern day movement was really a campaign to regain and restore rights won almost a hundred years before: the right to vote and the right of equal access to public accommodations. As the movement intensified through the 1950s and 1960s, its concerns widened to include better educational and economic opportunities, improved housing, safer and healthier neighborhoods and, especially in the late sixties, a sense of cultural and racial pride.

The civil rights movement always included a wide range of organizations employing diverse tactics, from the venerable National Association for the Advancement of Colored People (NAACP) with its strategy of litigation, to the Congress of Racial Equality (CORE) and the Southern Christian Leadership Conference with their nonviolent direct action, to the "revolutionary violence" of the Black Panther party. But the hallmark of the civil rights movement—at least until after King's assassination in 1968—was nonviolent confrontation, a tactic first used by CORE in the early 1940s when the group staged sit-ins and bus rides in both the North and South.

In the mid-fifties, the landmark *Brown v. Board of Education* decision made segregation, which had been a fact of life in the South, suddenly illegal. For the next decade, blacks, sometimes alone, sometimes with the help of white northerners, tested the decision throughout the South, attempting to integrate public facilities from schools to bus terminals to swimming pools. The other major activity of the early civil rights movement was voter registration. Enfranchised by the Fourteenth and Fifteenth amendments passed after the Civil War, blacks had been effectively prevented from exercising their right in the South by intimidation, specially concocted literacy tests and poll taxes. Blacks made up 43 percent of the population in Mississippi in

1960 but accounted for only five percent of the registered voters. In one of the counties targeted by SNCC in the early sixties, the situation was even worse: 47 percent of the eligible voters were black, but only one black person voted in 1960.

As the direct actions continued, the early optimism and idealism were tempered by a growing list of martyrs to the cause: NAACP official Medgar Evers shot in the back; four black children blown apart by a bomb thrown at a Birmingham, Alabama church; three civil rights workers murdered by Klansmen in Mississippi; and countless others, black and white, brutally beaten for their part in sit-ins, freedom rides, voter registration drives and demonstrations. Later other icons would die, notably Malcolm X, a vitriolic critic of integrationist goals and nonviolent tactics, and Martin Luther King, Jr., who stood as their greatest proponent. The violence escalated and spread, becoming the leitmotif of the later movement. Urban riots—born of frustration and anger rooted in the seemingly permanent ghetto conditions of high unemployment, miserable housing and lack of hope—were the first signs that a new kind of political statement was evolving. That statement stressed black community unity rather than integration and sanctioned retaliatory violence as a legitimate weapon.

Harlem and Philadelphia erupted in the summer of 1964, presaging a series of long, hot summers. For five days in August 1965, rioting shook the Watts section of Los Angeles, leaving 34 dead, 1,000 injured and more than 4,000 arrested. During subsequent summers, riots erupted in Newark, Detroit, Milwaukee, Washington, D.C., Hartford, Connecticut, Providence, Rhode Island and dozens of other American cities. Clearly, the reformist spirit of the early sixties was waning, replaced by the revolutionary anger of men like Stokely Carmichael, who took over SNCC in 1966 and immediately declared the advent of "Black Power," and H. Rap Brown, his successor in 1967, who asserted that "violence is as American as apple pie." Meanwhile, in Oakland, California, Huey Newton and Bobby Seale founded the Black Panther Party for Self-Defense which initially patrolled black ghetto areas with guns and lawbooks to protect citizens from police harassment. At its peak in the late sixties, the Panthers were an army of 3,000 to 4,000 militants, working out of an estimated forty storefront headquarters. While today chiefly remembered for their guns and black leather jackets, the Panthers established free breakfast programs, free health clinics, schools and emergency services in several cities in the late sixties. In 1968, they joined forces with the white radical Peace and Freedom party to run Panther Minister of Education Eldridge Cleaver for U.S. president on a platform of social revolution. But just a few years later, torn apart by internal power struggles and tactical disputes, infiltrated by the FBI (J. Edgar Hoover called the Panthers "the most dangerous and violence-prone of all extremist groups") and decimated by their own and police violence, the Panthers were no longer a force. The reformist civil rights movement, which had spanned the fifties and sixties, died with King in 1968; its replacement, the armed revolution of the Panthers, was dead by the early seventies.

The civil rights/black power movement was a source of inspiration for other people of color in the U.S. It was no accident that Native Americans called for "Red Power" in the sixties or that, borrowing from black American parlance, they dubbed the elders who sold out tribal interests "Uncle Tomahawks." Native Americans learned tactics from both the early civil rights movement and its more aggressive successor. Red power focused on self-determination, the right of Indians to decide programs and policies for themselves, to manage their own affairs, to govern themselves and to control their land and its resources. Like blacks, Indians were in many cases fighting for rights they had already won and had already been guaranteed by the federal government.

The early Indian movement paralleled the civil rights movement in its moderation. In the summer of 1961, more than 400 Indians from 67 tribes met in Chicago to consider the state of Indian affairs. There they drafted a quiet, reasoned statement that stressed the importance of democracy and individuality and called for renewed tribal dignity and preservation of Native American heritage. In the mid-sixties, a whole generation that had left the reservations to get an education came back and tried to improve conditions within the existing system. The author Vine Deloria, Jr. (*Custer Died for Your Sins*) was one of them. He and others met with anthropologists, sociologists, educators, missionaries and a dizzying array of government officials. They wrote letters, circulated petitions, held meetings and organized conferences. Nothing happened.

In desperation and frustration—and with more than a casual look at the strategies of the anti-war and black power movements—younger Indians formed new alliances. In the cities, so-called urban Indians formed radical activist organizations like the American Indian Movement (AIM) and the United Native Indians. In 1969, a new group calling itself Indians of All Tribes seized Alcatraz Island, an abandoned federal penitentiary in San Francisco Bay. Offering to buy The Rock for 24 dollars worth of beads, they demanded that it be turned into an Indian cultural and educational center. Alcatraz opened the door to other less famous confrontations. In Colorado, Indians occupied a Bureau of Indian Affairs (BIA) office to protest gross discrimination within the federal agency designed to help them. In South Dakota, a group camped atop Mount Rushmore, asserting occupation of the site. In California, Indians occupied a site in Lassen National Park and another owned by Pacific Gas and Electric, claiming the land was theirs. In New York, a group attempted to seize Ellis Island.

In 1972, a caravan of Indian protestors organized by AIM arrived in Washington, D.C., with demands for reinstatement of tribal sovereignty and enforcement of treaty rights. Frustrated by the cool reception given them by federal officials, they seized the BIA office on Constitution Avenue, refusing to leave. Threatened with forcible removal, they retaliated by trashing the interior of the building. The next year, in another daring move to dramatize their concerns, AIM members seized the village of Wounded Knee on the Pine Ridge Indian Reservation in South Dakota. There, on the site of the fatal confrontation between Indian ghost dancers and the U.S. Seventh Cavalry, Native Americans staged a compelling presentation as the media, and thus the nation, looked on. Through the sixties and into the seventies, red power strategies were direct, dramatic and, for the most part, nonviolent. Like the confrontational tactics of the civil rights movement, they focused national attention on a problem few white Americans had ever thought about.

To less visible extent, Hispanic Americans waged a fight for brown power, the nomenclature again borrowed from the civil rights movement. A Chicano group called the Brown Berets consciously modeled itself after the Black Panthers, from its espousal of revolutionary violence to its internal hierarchy (with Ministers of this and that) to its garb (berets and leather jackets). Like the Panthers, the Brown Berets formed short-lived alliances with white revolutionaries. Also like the Panthers, they self-destructed—with plenty of help from the FBI and local police.

More moderate in its aims—and far more long lasting in its contribution to social justice for a portion of Hispanic Americans—was Cesar Chavez's United Farm Workers' (UFW) movement. Essentially a poor people's movement not unlike the campaigns of Martin Luther King, Jr. and Ralph Abernathy in the South, Chavez organized migrant farmworkers throughout California, forming a massive, loosely constructed union that began to exert power in the late sixties. The UFW led the fight for such basics as minimum wage and adequate sanitary facilities. Chavez and the union orchestrated several ultimately successful strikes against California table grape growers, in the process winning the support of a wide variety of white liberals. Some of the strikes erupted into violence allegedly perpetrated by the Teamsters, but Chavez's strategy remained creative nonviolence. Through the seventies and into the eighties, he led a series of hunger strikes to bring attention to the deplorable working and living conditions of migrant farmworkers.

The early student movement also owed a debt to the civil rights crusade. It was where a significant number of early sixties student activists were first exposed to what was essentially a foreign culture to them: rural, southern, poor and black. It was where they saw—dramatically, emphatically and for the first time in their sheltered, middle class lives—the failures of democracy. It was where they first experienced the power of civil disobedience and learned to distrust bureaucracies and officialdom. They emerged from the experience with, in Todd Gitlin's words, a "fierce moralism" and a strong sense of purpose, ready to do battle with injustice wherever they saw it.

Not surprisingly, they saw it closer to home—on the campuses they returned to and in the system of higher education they were a part of. They saw the university as hierarchical, anti-democratic and paternalistic, with decisions, actions and communication all flowing from the top down. Those at the bottom, the students, had no power within the hierarchy and no real control over their lives within the institution. They saw the university as elitist in form and function, essentially teaching the already privileged how to maintain and improve their position in society. Those at major centers like Berkeley and Michigan, where the student movement first began, saw the university being swallowed by what was then called the "military-industrial complex." Instead of a place where new visions and diverse ideas could be explored, it seemed to them that the university was becoming the research arm—worse, the lackey—of government and business.

In Berkeley, student power translated first into the Free Speech Movement (FSM), a direct descendant of Freedom Summer 1964. Mario Savio and others fresh from their experiences in the South planned to set up tables on Sproul Plaza to recruit civil rights workers and raise money for the cause. When University of California administrators, bowing to pressure from local right-wing politicians, refused to allow the use of campus space, the FSM was born. At other campuses, other issues emerged. One of the most widespread was the demand for a more relevant curriculum. "Relevant," in fact, became a watchword of the student power movement. Student activists called for new classes in contemporary issues like racism, the power elite, the workings of the military-industrial complex. They wanted to read Camus, Pynchon, Barth and Kesey. They wanted classes to include an appreciation of nonwhite, nonwestern cultural, political and artistic contributions. Part of the call of relevancy included demands for ethnic studies, black studies—and later women's studies—departments that would promote cultural diversity and be a focal point for a new (that is, nonwhite, nonelite) kind of student.

Underlying the demands for curricular change, of course, was the demand for power. Students saw they had no control—in fact, no input whatsoever—over decisions that affected their university lives: what classes would be taught, who would teach them, how tuition money would be spent, who could recruit on campus, how students were to conduct themselves in their daily lives. On many campuses, students were particularly irked by the *in loco parentis* stance of the university. Acting as institutional father figure, the university demanded that women (and on some campuses, men) return to their dorms by eleven every night, that women wear skirts to the dining hall, that men and women not visit each others' dorm rooms. Students— including those with a mature commitment to civil rights and, as the decade wore on, a growing commitment to stop the war—could not abide being treated as errant teenagers. Through the sixties, students staged rallies, sit-ins, walk-outs, strikes, building seizures, teach-ins and all manner of nonviolent protest to bring their message to university officials. Specific in its goals, and largely successful in meeting them, the student power movement was one of the first proving grounds for the New Left. In the mid- and late sixties, as the war escalated, the campus movement increasingly centered on anti-war activities. (Section II: "Political Activism" deals with this time.)

Feminism—known in the sixties as the women's liberation movement—emerged from both the civil rights and anti-war crusades but predated them by almost two centuries. In one form or another, there has been a women's movement in the United States ever since there has been a United States. " . . . in the new Code of Laws . . . I desire you would remember the Ladies," Abigail Adams wrote to her husband John in 1776. "If particular care and attention is not paid to the Ladies, we are determined to foment a Rebellion." John and his colleagues didn't heed Abigail, and women spent the next one hundred and fifty years marching, rallying, leafleting, speechifying and otherwise fighting for the rights of full citizenship. But when finally enfranchised in 1920, women found that the vote did not open the doors to political, social or economic equality. Instead, the discrepancies between their expectations and the reality of their lives continued to grow.

In the early sixties, a new women's movement emerged to challenge the traditional, subservient role to which women had been, it seemed, permanently relegated. Women of the fifties such as Betty Friedan, Simone deBeauvoir and Doris Lessing paved the way, but the impetus came from young women in the civil rights and anti-war movements. Educated, articulate and committed, they had expected to stand on equal footing with men as they waged the battles for civil rights and against the war. But, as Gitlin notes, "men sought them out, recruited them, took them seriously, honored their intelligence—then subtly demoted them to girlfriends, wives and notetakers . . ."

Often the demotion was anything but subtle. In late 1964, two women in SNCC wrote an anonymous memo protesting the fact that women were automatically assigned menial office tasks in the organization. Stokely Carmichael's famous reply—"The correct position of women in SNCC is prone"—was apparently a joke, but the sentiment was, in fact, shared by many men. Like SNCC, SDS was essentially a "good young boys network" in which men wrote leaflets and women mimeographed them, men made speeches and women made coffee. At a 1966 SDS convention, a group presenting a women's liberation plank was pelted with tomatoes and thrown out of the convention. A year later, a watered down version of the resolution passed. Published in SDS's magazine, *New Left Notes*, it ran next to a cartoon of a miniskirted girl with visible panties holding a placard ("We want our rights and we want them now.")

SDS and SNCC women veterans, meeting first in what came to be called consciousness-raising groups, quickly got down to the job of creating a body of feminist theory. The papers they wrote, among them "The Myth of the Vaginal Orgasm," "The Politics of Housework" and "The Personal is Political," circulated through the movement, bringing more and more women into the fold. At a 1968 anti-war protest in Washington, D.C., more than 5,000 women expressed their disillusionment with women's place in the anti-war movement by symbolically burying "traditional womanhood" at Arlington National Cemetery. Later that year, a group of women picketed the Miss America beauty contest in Atlantic City. (They tossed undergarments into a trash can, but, despite legend, burned no bras.) By the end of 1969, feminist groups were established in more than forty American cities, and feminists were publishing at least a dozen newsletters and periodicals. Yet young, radical men were still heckling and booing "women's libbers" who spoke to anti-war rallies.

Women fought back, wresting power from the men who controlled the powerful underground newspapers of the day. In Berkeley, Chicago, New York and dozens of other cities, women staffers who had been relegated to jobs as proofreaders and office gofers took over as editors. In an all-women issue of the New York *Rat* in 1970, feminist Robin Morgan succinctly expressed the prevailing outrage: "White men are most responsible for the destruction of human life and environment on the planet today. Yet who is controlling the supposed revolution to change that?" She called for a "legitimate revolution" led by those who had been the most oppressed: black, brown and white women. Women, the backbone of the male-dominated New Left/anti-war movement, deserted in droves. With amazing speed, the feminist movement grew as the New Left imploded and the anti-war movement lost steam. By the early to mid-seventies, the women's liberation movement had developed its own sophisticated theoretical base and its own programs, including health and legal collectives, counseling services, national lobbying groups, publishing companies and caucuses within most professions.

The Zeitgeist of the late sixties gave rise to another important social justice crusade—the gay liberation movement. Like the other movements that came of age during that era, it had its roots in earlier times. In the early fifties, living under the fear and repression of homosexual-hunting McCarthyism, gay men and lesbians began to organize secretly. Soon they published their own magazine, *One*, which the post office refused to mail. (The publishing group fought the ban all the way up to the Supreme Court—and won in 1958.) Throughout the decade, homosexual groups quietly established ties with the professions, began publishing brochures and pamphlets and provided help and counseling in their communities. But most homosexuals remained "in the closet." As an early gay activist who was fired from government service in the fifties said twenty years later: "Exposure meant you could instantly lose your job and be barred from others, you could be kicked out of your apartment and not be able to rent another one." Homosexuality was considered a mental disorder; worse yet, it was considered (and in some states still remains) a criminal activity.

Nevertheless, by the early and mid-sixties, gay groups began to initiate lawsuits to press the courts for guarantees against discrimination in hiring and housing. The movement was growing but was still small and relatively clandestine. One night in June 1969 changed all that. Around midnight, four New York City cops descended on Stonewall, a gay bar on Christopher Street. There had been many such raids in Greenwich Village, but this time, the gays inside the bar didn't march quietly into paddy wagons. They threw bottles, jeered the police, set garbage cans on fire. The police were stunned.

Within days, activists formed the militant Gay Liberation Front, and the gay liberation movement emerged as an important sixties crusade. In June of 1970, more than 5,000 gay men and lesbians marched to celebrate the first anniversary of Stonewall. By the early seventies, there were in excess of 300 gay and lesbian organizations in the country, confronting politicians, lobbying legislators, challenging psychiatrists, debating theologians and otherwise championing their cause. In 1973, the American Psychiatric Association removed homosexuality from its list of mental disorders. By the late seventies, some openly gay people were elected to public office and a variety of nondiscriminatory laws were on the books. It looked as if the country was making important strides toward tolerance of diverse sexual preferences. Then came AIDS—and the birth of a new brand of homophobia that is today a major threat to the equal treatment of and peaceful coexistence with America's homosexual population.

What of the legacy of these hard-fought social justice movements? How much different is America at the dawn of the nineties than it was in the early sixties? Certainly racism, sexism and homophobia continue to be strong undercurrents in our society. A person looking for disturbing signs could easily find them: increased poverty among people of color; the outbreak of racial incidents in the late eighties; the eroding of women's reproductive rights by the Supreme Court's *Webster* decision; the creation of a new societal leper—the gay man with AIDS. All this points to serious and deep flaws in the American character and in American institutions. But it is self-defeating—not to mention clearly ahistorical—to imagine that these deeply ingrained prejudices would disappear overnight, or within 25 years. When we look for change this deep down, we need to think in terms of multiple generations.

But there's no denying that important positive changes have taken place. The civil rights movement did force a policy of desegregation that is the norm today. Blacks did regain their voting rights and in fact, today are considered a powerful voting bloc. They have moved into the mainstream of American politics, with 22 serving in the U.S. Congress, others holding important mayoral posts and hundreds in state government. The idea of black pride did lead to a growth of black studies on college campuses and at least the beginning of an appreciation of African cultural heritage. There have been some strides on the state and federal level against discrimination in housing and employment. The record is not good, but it is not all bad, either.

For other people of color, there have also been some victories. Native American groups have forced the federal government to recognize and honor certain treaties and to give official status to some tribes. The Bureau of Indian Affairs has been restructured. There is an appreciation of some aspects of Native American culture and a sensitivity to the degrading stereotypes of the past. Hispanic Americans have achieved considerable political power in the areas of their greatest concentration, California and the Southwest.

In most major universities around the country, battles fought for student power resulted in long-lasting victories. Students now serve on key decision-making committees; their newspapers are for the most part independent of official censorship. They can choose from an invigorated curriculum which includes women's studies, black and ethnic studies and a changing variety of contemporary issues courses. The hallowed "canon" of literature and philosophy—still a hot topic of debate on university campuses—now includes multi-racial, multi-cultural offerings. The university no longer acts a parent in absentia.

For women too the world of 1990 is palpably different from the world of 1965. On the federal level, Title IX, Affirmative Action and *Roe v. Wade* have made real differences in women's lives. Women have entered the workforce at a pace unequaled since World War II. They have entered and are making some small dent in the male-dominated professions and skilled blue collar jobs. Although they continue to earn less than two-thirds of what men earn, equal pay and comparable worth are at least issues on the national agenda. Women may never exert political power as a cohesive voting bloc, but as individuals, some have made it into the mainstream: two in the Senate, 26 in the House. In 1984, a woman was a major party vice presidential candidate for the first time in American history.

The feminist movement has helped focus attention on domestic politics and the denigration of "woman's work"—and with some effect. Women are no longer routinely identified by their relationship to men (Miss, Mrs.). It is now generally understood that women who don't work outside the home for money do indeed work very hard. Some role restructuring is evident as a small but significant minority of men begin to see home responsibilities as an important part of their lives.

Gays and lesbians can now point to state laws prohibiting discrimination in housing and hiring. They have even made some inroads into the ultra-conservative insurance industry, winning concessions in some states that allow same-sex partners to be treated like heterosexual couples in terms of benefits and survivorship. The gay liberation movement has resulted in the construction of a whole area of specialized social services. Politically, gay men and lesbians have also gained some power, especially in California and New York.

But the real legacy of the social justice movements of the sixties may not yet be known. The real legacy may be the result of the life's work of activists like those interviewed in this section: Eva Paterson, the student leader who has been a civil rights litigator for the past fifteen years; Mark Hartford, the Vietnam Veterans Against the War organizer who devotes much of his time to helping solve the problems of the homeless; Eliza Schmidtkunz, the California communard who is now a national officer in 9-to-5; Nelson Johnson, the black student leader who has returned home to work with troubled youth as a Baptist minister; Alice Embree, the former anti-war activist and proto-feminist who now works on women's issues in the Texas attorney general's office; Carlos Calderon, the former Brown Beret and UFW journalist who continues to write exposés on the U.S. military; Martha Honey, a Quaker social activist who, with the backing of the Christic Institute, is attempting to sue the CIA for illegal involvement in Central America; Stew Albert, ex-Yippie sidekick of Jerry Rubin, now active in Jewish peace issues; Terry Karl, the Stanford anti-war leader who is now a Central American expert; Hisani, a former black nationalist who now works as a health policy analyst for the federal government. These people, along with the many other persistent activists they represent, are just now hitting their stride. Their blows for social justice will be felt through the nineties and beyond.

EVA PATERSON, 40
1969: student leader/anti-war activist
1989: civil rights attorney

The daughter of a career Air Force officer who served in Vietnam in the mid-sixties, Eva grew up on bases in England, France and Illinois. In 1967, she enrolled in Northwestern University, just north of Chicago.

"I came to Northwestern very straight, very much following the party line. I remember arguing with people my freshman year who were against the war. They were saying, 'This war's terrible.' And I actually remember saying, 'Well, the president says you have to do this, and you can't contradict the president.' So I came in real straight. I was still in the Girl Scouts in college. I had never even taken a drink of alcohol. And I think I entered in a fortuitous time because all my values were changed. My world was set on its head from a variety of sources.

"Probably the first influence was that of black students from the south side of Chicago. The university had done what I guess would now be called affirm-ative action, recruited and actually admitted a whole bunch of students from the south side. I always considered myself a very middle-class black person—Negro at that time—and these were sort of 'in your face' south side of Chicago folks who had very different views of what it meant to be a black person from the ones I had been raised with. That's when I started getting the seed of doubt. It was both personal exposure to people I respected at Northwestern—people who opened my mind—and also it was the times. You just questioned everything. So I started looking at things real differently. And that seed of doubt has been watered and has bloomed. It's an oak tree right now."

Eva was elected to the student senate her freshman year, and during the next three years she became increasingly active in campus politics, including anti-war, anti-racist and feminist activities. On May 1, 1970, three days before Kent State, she became student body president, a post she used to give anti-war activities a high profile on campus. The class of 1971 chose her as com-mencement speaker.

After being rejected by Yale Law School, she headed for California. There she directed the student rights project for the ACLU of northern California and, in 1972, entered Berkeley Law School. For the past fifteen years she has been a civil rights litigator specializing in employment discrimination. She has sued the U.S. Civil Service Commission, a Naval Air Base and the San Francisco firefighters, representing minorities or women or both. She has also worked on school desegregation and battered women's cases. Currently Eva is chair of a civil rights coalition in San Francisco.

"In 1984 I went to the Aspen Institute, which is kind of this think tank in Aspen, and I met some of my very first Republicans. It was during the middle of the campaign, and Bush was debating against Ferraro. And I had been going through a crisis of confidence, thinking, 'Well the only reason I am on the Left is because this is what I learned in 1968.' If you follow Gail Sheehy's line of thinking about people's growth, that's kind of what you go through in your thirties. You wonder if you're a fraud.

"I've talked to enough friends who've gone through this. I think it's part of one's psychological development. Do I really believe what I believe? Am I really competent? And I had to defend my values in these philosophical discussions against people who were execs with IBM and self-made millionaires. And I came away from that experience realizing that I really do believe these things. It's not just something that I picked up as a fashion in 1968. And that made me feel very good.

"In terms of what I do, the Reagan court is really going to be wreaking havoc with the rights of women. I think they'd like us to just feel so demoralized and despondent that we'll give up. But I will never give up. Generally I'm in the gym working out in the morning when I hear these decisions. And I cry and go, 'Oh, shit.' And then I read the case and figure out how to deal with it. Some of the media want us to go on TV and say, 'Oh, we're defeated, we can't go on.' But, I just say, 'Well, it's another hoop, we'll just jump through it.'

"So I now work in coalitions with people of color, progressive whites, gays and lesbians, disabled people, and I'm chair of a civil rights coalition in San Francisco. We worked very actively to nail Bork. So we're kind of out there doing things. I'm part of the progressive movement, and I'm sure I will be until I die.

"I went to law school in large part because of *Brown v. The Board of Education*. It seemed that the law could be used to strike down injustice in a swift, dramatic way, and it can be. But it also can be used in a bad way. Law is inherently a conservative institution and process, and one of the dilemmas I face as a political person is that law disempowers people. I see my clients assuming that I'm gonna be able to make everything right. And I can't. I can't eliminate racism in the fire department, for example. I can do some things, but they're gonna have to continue the struggle. So to the extent that people feel that lawyers can make everything right, law is not completely helpful. It can only be part of a larger grassroots strategy. But I do think there is utility to the law.

"I have this fantasy that in twenty years we're gonna look back and say, 'Gee, we stayed pure, we hung in there, we could have become Republicans or yuppies, and we didn't do it, and finally things have turned around.' 'Cause I think they will. Although there are days when I feel like we're just rearranging furniture on the deck of the Titanic. But I'm basically still an optimist.

"I think the difference between then and now is I felt so over my head in those days. I was twenty and debating the vice president of the United States. Excuse me. You know what I mean? It was ridiculous. And there was this little voice in me going, 'Fraud, fraud.' I felt like I didn't deserve what was happening to me, and I really had no depth.

"Now I feel like what I have I've earned. If somebody calls me about a Supreme Court decision, I can talk about that because I know it, and I've been litigating it for fourteen years. I no longer feel fraudulent politically. At that time I did, 'cause I was just a kid. And there was probably some notion that this was just a fad. We protest the war. So we're hip and trendy. But it's not hip and trendy now at all; it's anachronistic in a sense. So there's a sense of authenticity, and I don't know if that's just attributable to being forty. But I think I've paid my dues.

"I don't believe there's gonna be a revolution. Some days I wish there were, although if China's any indication of what you get from that, let's keep what we have. Part of it is where I live. I chose an area that supports my values. If I lived in Washington, D.C., I don't know if I'd be like this. But I chose to come to the Bay Area because I knew I'd be nurtured here. Not just the political me but also my spiritual side. I live in an area where people don't look at you as being crazy because you have crystals in your office or you went and lay in the sand during the harmonic convergence.

"A lot of what I believe is embodied in Alice Walker's book, *The Temple of My Familiar*. I feel I'm part of a direct historical continuum with other black people and that I draw on them in a metaphysical way and a historical way for strength. I feel—how can I give up because the Supreme Court came down with a bad decision if my people were slaves? And if my people weren't allowed to read. And despite that, they were able to fight and keep going. And I'm here sitting in this office as a lawyer because of what they did, and I can't stop fighting.

"Plus I'll just be damned if these people are gonna wear me down. I'll be damned if the Meeses and the Reagans and the William Bradford Reynoldses are gonna make me give up. I am, and I say this a lot . . . Eddie Murphy in *48 Hours* walked into the redneck bar and he said, 'I am your worst nightmare.' And that's what I am to these racists. I am bright, I am determined, I have their tools, and I'm gonna stay right in their face."

MARTHA HONEY, 44
1967: draft resistance organizer
1989: freelance foreign correspondent

The daughter of a liberal democrat and a Quaker, Martha grew up in Maryland and Connecticut, living a privileged, upper middle class life, but also learning early that life entailed responsibility to social service. At thirteen, she became involved in a number of Quaker work camps, spending weekends in Harlem doing community projects. In 1964, after her freshman year at Oberlin, she joined hundreds of other white, northern students as they worked on voter registration projects in Mississippi.

"I was working in a town called Mileston, Mississippi, in Holmes County, doing voter registration and teaching in a freedom school. I think we did, rather naively, think change was around the corner. Certainly, that summer in Mississippi we felt, and I think in some ways it's true, that it was a very seminal experience, both for those of us who were part of it, but also for the civil rights movement itself. It was a turning point for the movement; for me, it was an eye-opening experience.

"I remember the first day when I arrived, and I was staying with this fellow, this sharecropper, and he said to me, 'those boys [James Chaney, Andrew Goodman, and Michael Schwerner, the three civil rights workers murdered that summer], they're dead,' and I said, 'no, you're wrong, they're not dead, they've just lost their way or something.' Of course, they were dead. And it was some realization, that violence could be used against us. . . . I had to get over that naivete, that feeling that I was somehow immune to it all. It was seeing firsthand the kind of oppression that the blacks in Mississippi were living under, and being extremely moved by both their poverty and their souls, their spirits . . . and feeling totally alive, totally involved and committed to something.

"The following summer I went back, this time to Alabama, and I worked on a newspaper called *The Southern Courier* that was started by mainly Harvard and Radcliffe students, a number of whom had worked in Mississippi the summer before. I was one of the correspondents based in Tuskegee, and we were basically trying to do a paper that would cut across racial lines and cover the news that wasn't covered in the white press. We had all sorts of harassment, including being intimidated by the Klan. That also was a very important experience, and in some ways, more sobering than the previous summer, because there were much fewer of us from the North down that summer. I was very much on my own, covering stories, and it gave me more of a sense that this was going to be a harder struggle, a longer haul than many of us had felt the summer before."

After graduating from Oberlin in 1967, Martha began working with the American Friends Service Committee in Philadelphia, organizing against the war. But after her summers in the South, she found the work too tame. Soon, she and two friends founded the Philadelphia Resistance, part of a national network of draft resistance groups. From 1967 to 1970, she organized, gave speeches and, she says, "stayed pretty straight." ("My involvement was always more intellectual than cultural.") In 1970, she began graduate work in Afro-American studies at Syracuse, and in 1973, with all of her Ph.D. courses completed, she left to do field work in Tanzania. She and her husband Tony expected to stay a year. They stayed ten.

"We went to Tanzania just when we thought the Vietnam War was over, and we felt we could. We sort of thought that we had a right to travel at that point, that that part of our work was over. Tony came along, and he lined up journalism work with Associated Press, BBC, and I was sitting in the archives day after day, seeing all the great stuff he was doing, and I began to get much more interested in the real lives and events that he was covering than the history I was researching. And so I started working also, and we kind of divvied it up. He took UPI and I took AP, and because there weren't many foreigners in Tanzania, we eventually had a monopoly on the British and the American press, doing all the wire services. We built up almost like a little empire. We covered anything, but largely, we saw our role as trying to explain the problems of the Third World to the First World, to put it in the broadest terms—and in particular, trying to give voice to people who were involved in social change who usually didn't get a voice in the Western press, the liberation leaders and liberation movements. And rather than base ourselves in South Africa and cover the white side, or in Rhodesia or in Mozambique, we made the decision that we were going to cover black Africa, to cover that side of the war.

"We viewed journalism as a form of education. We were seeing historic events take place, and our function was to somehow try to find the language and the tools to explain that to people back home, to educate people. And also we saw investigative journalism as an effort to uncover those issues, those stories, those scandals, that the powers that be do not want uncovered."

In 1983, after finishing a book on Idi Amin and, finally, her Ph.D. dissertation, Martha felt it was time to move on. The family (now including an eight-year-old daughter and three-year-old son, both born in Africa) moved "closer to home"—Costa Rica, where Martha and Tony continued their foreign correspondence work. Tony was almost killed when a bomb exploded at a press conference he was covering. The two set to work, as investigative journalists, to try to determine exactly what had happened. What they found—a tangled web of clandestine CIA involvement—compelled them to mount an unprecedented lawsuit (sponsored by the Christic Institute) against a variety of U.S. officials for interference in Central American affairs.

"One of the things we've struggled with since Tony was almost killed is this notion, particularly in U.S. journalism, of objectivity, a sort of detachment from the story. And our view of journalism is very much different from that. Our view is unconventional, and part of it grows out of our history of social activism in seeing journalism as simply an outgrowth of that, that journalism is a watchdog for the American public and has a very important role in investigation, in uncovering things that powerful people want covered up. It's only with an informed electorate that our democracy will work, so that journalism—good journalism, educative and investigative journalism—is essential to the country's functioning. But that's very different from the prevailing notion that somehow journalists are objective, detached, uninvolved in their stories. I think that really is a myth.

"What we should be striving for as journalists is education and seeing our role as a watchdog and a kind of adversary rather than a cooperative relationship with the powers that be. Not that it has to be hostile, but we have to be willing to put ourselves in a position where we're not seen as part of the team, you know, that our loyalty should be to the American public not to the U.S. officials. This is not something that is accepted by most of the U.S. press. Particularly in Central America we have found that a lot of the journalists there are very careerist, are basically there to make a name, just as a lot of journalists went to Vietnam to make a name. And they're trying to move up the corporate ladder within their news media and are not willing to rock the boat to do really controversial stories.

"When we went on the offensive and brought our own case against the people who had tried to kill Tony and had made our lives miserable through death threats and killing a key witness, and other things in the course of our journalistic investigation, then that was considered somehow stepping over a kind of invisible boundary—moving back into being social activists rather than being objective. We never bought that criterion in the first place. But for many people, that was the watershed, and they said, 'Aha, see these people are just political activists masquerading as journalists.' "

The suit was supposed to go to trial in June 1988, but three days before it was to begin, the judge threw out the case for lack of evidence. Martha's group appealed the ruling. In February 1989, the judge ruled that Martha and Tony had to pay the court costs for the defendants—more than $1 million. That decision is currently on appeal.

"One of the things a lot of us have learned as the euphoria of the sixties wore off and people dug in for the long haul is that social change comes oftentimes slowly and oftentimes it's not permanent. Basically, if you're a social activist, which I think any proper U.S. citizen has to be—that's what democracy means—then you're in it permanently. I mean you can't just look for victory on one issue and think that you're going to retire. It is a lifetime thing, and we make some gains, and we may lose those gains, or the gains may not come as quickly as we expect.

"But I do feel now, coming up to the States, that there's a resurgence of social concern. There's a tremendous disaffection with the government. I mean everybody assumes government is corrupt and doing evil things. And that hasn't always just turned into cynicism and a sense of alienation. People are beginning to organize again, and that feels real good. And actually, the kind of support we've gotten in terms of our case has been extremely heartening, because there was a time when we were really, really isolated in '84 and '85, before any of this became public, when we were being sued for libel and getting death threats and being called traitors to our country by the Ambassador in Costa Rica. But we knew we were onto something very big, and that for a host of reasons—personal, political and professional—this was something we had to keep doing. We don't feel isolated anymore at all, and that is a cause for personal optimism."

ELIZA SCHMIDTKUNZ, 40

1968: socialist/feminist
1989: coordinator of women's health programs/national officer, 9-to-5

> The daughter of transplanted midwesterners, Eliza Schmidtkunz was raised in Redlands, California and grew up with "American Gothic working class" values. "Without the Left," she says, "I probably would have gone to a junior college, been a secretary, married a schoolteacher and done what all my cousins did—lived a sturdy, go-to-church life."
>
> Instead, on a whim, she enrolled in California's most culturally avant-garde public university, University of California/Santa Cruz, and went on to join a West Coast collective involved in underground journalism and anti-war activities. When the commune broke up six years later, she worked at various health-related jobs while raising a child and staying active in social change groups. She had her second child at 38 and now divides her time between working on women's health issues and organizing "pink collar" workers.

"I remember my first day on the campus at Santa Cruz. I had my little Carnaby Street haircut and my little hopsacking suit and I was all ready for college. I had just turned eighteen and, two weeks before, had taught Sunday school at the Presbyterian church. So this guy jumps out of the bushes in front of me. He was wearing a red silk cape and half of his beard was shaved off. And I thought, hey, I ain't in Kansas anymore. The year before, there had apparently been this big college party out in the redwoods where everyone dropped acid and played miniature golf in Renaissance costumes. I heard about that and I really thought I was in fairyland. I mean it was this whole other reality. In an anthropology seminar, we took off our clothes and had a Greek meeting of the minds, or something like that, and danced all night. I just thought it was great. And I felt real lucky because some of my other friends were going to Valley Junior College or going to Vietnam.

"During orientation week at Santa Cruz, this guy I met who was the son of a famous painter said, 'Let's go up to the Last Acid Test.' I didn't know what that was; I didn't know what acid was; I had never been in San Francisco. So we went up there, and—it's hard to describe—you're a kid, you're seventeen or eighteen, and you have all these fantasies, and you don't ever really think they're gonna come true. And this was . . . well, all the fantasies came true. So I came up to this incredible scene south of Market in a garage, met people who were amazing, saw sights I'd never seen. There were women with babies hanging on their breasts, which I'd only seen in paintings. Then we went to some ballroom and heard the Quicksilver Messenger Service and the Grateful Dead. I mean, this really was orientation week for me.

"But by 1968, for a combination of reasons, I had dropped out. I was back home going to Riverside Junior College when I started reading *Soul on Ice* and Che Guevara. Through this history class I was taking, I heard about Herbert Marcuse's seminars in San Diego, so one day I just ran away, just took a bus down to San Diego.

"I got down there and there were all these bizarre people. They had guns in their closets. And I spent all night arguing with them because I was still very Joan Baez peace-y. They turned out to be really sophisticated, fast-talking people—revolutionaries. It was my first taste of hot revolutionaries, and there were black people walking in and out, looking very tough and I thought, hmm, maybe this is the place to be. So I ended up down there with some people who were involved in a radical theatre collective and some people who were involved in starting a radical underground newspaper.

"And we were the rads. We were listening to Eric Severeid every night and spitting on the TV set. The people who were old enough to vote were voting Peace and Freedom for Eldridge Cleaver. I thought we were pretty heavy and pretty tough, but looking back, I can see it was just a bunch of 25-to-30-year-old male graduate students and their 20-year-old girlfriends.

"I was a socialist/feminist. There was always a strong hippie component though—we looked like hippies. We were into back to the land stuff. I mean, us and the Panthers are gonna get some guns and get some land and do it, that kind of thing. I thought that what we needed to do was wrest a free space from the imperialist pig nation and create another reality that people would flock to. I thought that. I knew that would happen. It *was* happening, it seemed to me. This country was rotten to the core and had extended itself militarily, and the Third World would rise. I bought the line that students, black people, Hispanic people and women would rise against the culture that gave them nothing. I thought it would happen soon, like within ten years. We used to joke about what we would really do when we took power. Would we really have time to learn how to take power? Believe it or not, this was a serious discussion."

Eliza trekked up and down the West Coast—from San Diego to Seattle—with members of the commune until the mid-seventies. When the group finally broke up, she moved to San Francisco where she worked for the Medical Committee for Human Rights and later, the San Francisco Women's Health Collective. In 1977, she moved north again, to Eugene, Oregon, where she started working part-time, night shift as a ward clerk for a large hospital.

"It was the feminization of poverty. I mean, we were poor. I really didn't have time or money for anything. I remember that there was this inflammatory poster at the time which showed a black man being electrocuted, and it said something like: This is the result of poverty in America. I was trying to explain the poster to my little kid, saying that's what happens to poor people, poor people are electrocuted, and rich people aren't. And my kid started freaking out, thinking, we're poor, they're gonna kill us. Being poor was a political education."

Just when life was getting a little easier—her job had become full-time, she was working days instead of nights, her child started school—Eliza began trying to organize the nonmedical staff at the hospital. She got fired, filed a grievance with the NLRB—and lost—but got her job back by a fluke. In 1986 she became the coordinator of the hospital's Women's Information Network.

"The revolutionary, youthful me of twenty years ago is not there anymore. It's hard to say whether that's biology or history or philosophy. But I'm a parent, I'm a working person, and I'm forty. I mean, I probably would have been a bureaucrat in the revolution right now. I can't imagine keeping up that pace of life once you have kids and responsibilities or joint pains. Also I think a lot of what's changed my mind is eight years of Ronald Reagan. I mean there is no longer that sense of possibilities. It's not just for people like me on the far left, but for nice little Quaker ladies. They've just been beaten down compared to where they were eight years ago. The part of me that thinks this way, says, okay, I just want to keep disaster at bay. We just have to keep it together in some way; we can't totally give in.

"That's the whimpery, aching joint part. But the wiser part of me says, hey, things take time. The idea of a sudden, violent revolution wasn't real. Revolutionaries in other countries who saw us knew we were white kids with an impossible dream. Even in the context of the time, it was a movement outside of time. I mean, it was a nice flash. But the older leftists had perspective—that's sweet, they said, but let's get real. This takes time. It takes your life.

"If you understand it, that doesn't mean you're cool. It means you are responsible wherever you are to keep working in whatever way you can, as best you can. There were people who were in it for a Sunday picnic. They liked the drugs and the sex and the thrill. But they weren't ever really in it. Once you see how things work, you can't unsee it or ignore it. You can get fashionably cynical; you can cover it up with booze, with drugs, or with illness. But you can't forget it. I couldn't go back to thinking that life was as I learned it in Redlands, California.

"It's like being a good parent or being a good friend. You do it as best you can at every historical moment, and just keep doing it. It's like when you're a little kid, you think you're Cinderella. But when you're big, you realize, hey, you're really a respiratory therapist in Atlanta. When I was twenty I thought I was going to be Provisional Revolutionary Governor of the Western Regional Territory. And now I think I'm a nice, leftist, socialist, feminist lady who's starting a 9-to-5 chapter and who keeps trying to organize where I work."

TERRY KARL, 41
1969: anti-war student leader
1989: professor, Stanford University

Terry grew up on a "very safe, middle class street" in St. Louis. Considered gifted as a child, she was sent to a private school which, unbeknownst to her parents, was run by ultra-conservatives. There she read J. Edgar Hoover and Phyllis Schlafley and learned that John F. Kennedy was a communist. She fought back by writing editorials for the school paper in favor of admitting China to the U.N. In the fall of 1966, she entered Stanford.

"I got to Stanford, and I think that what hit me is probably not a very unique story. It's what hit most people around me. I became aware that the government was lying to me. And that had just never occurred to me as a possibility. I just didn't think that people of authority lied, and it became very clear in Vietnam that that was not so.

"So here I was, a freshman, with my Jackie Kennedy bob and my pleated skirts and my Peter Pan collar with the circle pins and all that stuff. And I see this guy who's president of the student body [David Harris, once Joan Baez's husband, who served time in prison as a conscientious objector wearing blue jeans and a work shirt and the first sandals I'd ever seen on a man. And he's saying, 'War is wrong.'

"I was studying in Italy and France in '68, and when I got to France all the French students I kept meeting asked, 'Why are you in Vietnam?' And I kept saying, 'Who, me?' I didn't know where Vietnam was. And they would go on and on about U.S. imperialism. And of course I later found out that they had already gotten beaten there themselves, which I didn't know at the time. So that made me want to know what it was we were doing. When I returned to Stanford, I began to take part in anti-war demonstrations, and I became extremely active in the student movement. In fact I became, I suppose, a fairly prominent activist. Since the anti-war movement had finally decided that they needed a woman speaker occasionally, I was often it. So I spent a great deal of time—I did a number of jobs to support myself—but my real work was ending the war in Vietnam. I saw it as the single most important thing any of us could do. I come from a family of academic accomplishment, and they were very upset that I didn't go on to graduate school, that I wasn't on track in a sense. And I just felt that those were things that if I ever did them, I would do them when the war was over. That's what I did, and I've never been sorry for a minute.

"I remember coming home from an anti-war demonstration on campus one day, and I was with a guy who was one of the big leaders on campus, and we got into a car and the car was parked in an isolated area. All of a sudden a car pulled up behind us. There was something in front of us, so we couldn't move. These guys jump out of the car—six of them—and they've got ski masks on, and they're carrying baseball bats and they surround our car and start screaming at him to get out. I'm sitting in the car with him, and we've got the doors locked, and it's clear they're gonna beat up at least him, and maybe me, who knows. Very terrifying. And while we were in this situation I saw a whole bunch of students going by. I rolled down the window, and I started yelling for help. So all these students—part of the demonstration—just marched right on over. And one of the guys took off his ski mask, and he was the head of the Palo Alto Red Squad, a policeman, and he flashed his badge and told everybody to go away. And boy, when you have something like that happen, you think: who do you report it to? I'll never forget that because that was a real shocker to me. I think if I ever thought we needed a revolution it was then because the authorities lie, and not only that, they kill. And they're not gonna help you.

"I guess I thought I was a revolutionary, even though I didn't really know what that meant. There was a lot of talk about armed struggle, and there were a lot of slogans going back and forth. And I think I tended to say things that I would not say now. Until it got a little too crazy for me, and I began to look up and say, 'Hey wait a minute. What's going on?' "

Terry graduated in 1970 and left Stanford for San Francisco where she continued her anti-war activities, speaking at rallies, helping to build coalitions and organize demonstrations. When Kissinger signed the peace treaty, she danced in the streets of Berkeley—and wondered what she would do with the rest of her life. She decided to return to Stanford to work on a Ph.D. in political science.

Today she is a professor there, specializing in Central American politics. She has been a consultant on Central American affairs for the Democratic party and, since 1982, has taken various congressional delegations to that part of the world. She organizes conferences and teach-ins, writes for academic and policy journals and is active in political asylum work.

"I think that I'm obviously left of center by any description, at least center in this country. But I think it's important to listen to every constituency and every position, which is something that I didn't always do in the sixties. I thought certain people didn't have the right to speak. Now what I think is that they all have the right to speak, but they don't have the right to speak with all of the power that they have at their disposal. I also probably have a lot more confidence in public opinion than I used to. In the sixties, I thought people really didn't know what to think and that we should tell them—that we knew the truth somehow and that it was our responsibility to tell them.

"Politics is still very much the center of my life. I still hold the same values. I don't believe in intervention. I believe in self-determination. I don't believe in killing people in poor countries for vital interests that are never clear.

"I'm absolutely certain we did a very important thing in the sixties, and I'm very proud of it. I remember key moments. I remember Lyndon Johnson saying he wasn't gonna run again, and me thinking, 'We did it.' I'm not saying we were the most mature movement by any means. There are certainly a million things I would do differently now without question. But the basic beliefs wouldn't be different. It would be the way I'd implement them. I'm not twenty anymore, I have much more respect for other people and their viewpoints than I used to. I understand politics much better than I used to, and I realize that things are pretty complex. But that doesn't mean that I'm afraid to take a stand by any means.

"I don't agree with the people who say, 'The sixties didn't do anything.' We have not invaded Central America in the eighties. And I study that, teach about that, lecture about that. I know very well why we haven't invaded Central America. Ask yourself how it's possible that the most popular president possibly in contemporary American history has as his number one goal getting rid of the Sandinistas, who frankly are not a very potent fighting force—ask yourself, 'Why couldn't he do it?' As much of a wreck as Nicaragua is now, why didn't he do it? Well, he didn't do it because we made something very clear during the Vietnam period. And as much of a rollback as there's been about some of that, I think that the fact is that you cannot commit American troops abroad without a much more serious discussion about the consequences.

"When the Reagan administration started producing these White Papers on Central America, and all this official lying that came out of the Office of Public Diplomacy and the State Department, the fact is that we understood right away what was going on. Many people understood right away, and many of those people were immediately willing to fight, and to say, 'We're not gonna let this happen again.' That's very much a legacy of Vietnam—and a proud one."

MARK HARTFORD, 42
1970: co-coordinator, California Vietnam Veterans Against the War
1989: organizational development consultant

Raised a "good Catholic boy" by "very patriotic" parents, Mark was about to flunk out of his first term at college when he decided to enlist in the army. One month after his eighteenth birthday, in January 1966, he started basic training in Texas. Then it was on to advanced infantry training at Fort Dix, New Jersey, and finally, beginning in June 1966, a thirteen-month tour of duty in the Korean demilitarized zone.

"Here I was, eighteen, and I'd been trained to be an expert killer, literally brainwashed, particularly around the notion of Asians as the enemy and being less than human. 'The only good Asian is a dead Asian' kind of thing. And I was sent to the demilitarized zone in Korea, which is Korea's equivalent of a combat zone, where I did a lot of day patrol, night search and destroy, sat out on guardpost, and engaged in the kind of high stress expectation of a combat situation on an ongoing basis. And the experience was real profound for me in that there was some combat in the area and periodic firefights. I had friends who were either killed in firefights or killed because American patrols ran into each other and thought they were the enemy and fired on each other; or what was called a sapper came in and blew up a compound near us at one point near the end of my tour and killed a number of people that I knew. So it was a significant event, and it made a big impression on me in terms of the impact of war.

"At the same time, as an eighteen-year-old, I was basically thrown into the Wild West. I had a gun, I had an opportunity to use it anytime I wanted to, and I had all the women I wanted, or at least all that I could afford, and anything I wanted to drink. So at nineteen I came back from Korea, as I look at it now, an active, practicing alcoholic with a history of six or eight venereal diseases and a sense of being very old and experienced, and landed back in California, and of course, became a child again to everybody. I don't know how to say it in any other way than that the romanticism got washed out by the reality of the experience. What I came out of it with was an appreciation for the pain and the reality of what war was all about—the fact that you could lose people who were very dear to you in just a blink of the eye. And that it wasn't fun, there was no glory in it, it was hard, it was dirty, it was scary, it was stressful, and it wasn't really well-appreciated by many, anybody, particularly at that time."

Mark married a few months before he was discharged from the army and came home to California with a pregnant wife. For a while he brought home skimpy paychecks as a welder. Then he went back to school on the GI bill. In early 1970, one of Mark's boyhood friends—they had been altar boys together and later enlisted together—introduced him to the VVAW (Vietnam Veterans Against the War). For the next three years, he and his friend traveled throughout California, eventually helping to establish 23 active VVAW chapters in the state.

"As I got more and more involved in it, it became very clear to me that it was a very positive way of somehow working for the future. I had felt that there was no future for my generation, because I felt very tuned into the fact that my generation was getting killed, was getting maimed, was getting mistreated by a government and a political ideology that didn't give a shit about us. It was mainly interested in protecting American business interests around the world by using us as cannon fodder for their war. So I hooked up with Vietnam Vets Against the War and through that experience had what I consider to be a very privileged period of my life.

"The reality is a lot of us were raised to be real good kids, to respect people, to want people to get what they needed, not to question authority, and to protect and defend our country. But we were trained and turned into just exactly the opposite as a result of our military experience. And for a period of our lives we were the opposite of what we were raised to be. And we came back into an environment where we couldn't talk to our parents and the people around us who still saw us in that initial way. We knew what we were, what we had been, and what we had done in some cases. And had to shut it all out. It was so twisting in terms of how we saw ourselves. So a lot of guilt and anger developed as a result of that, and organizing and working against the war as veterans and standing with the anti-war movement and people who had been struggling and who hadn't gone into the military was a very positive thing for us to do."

Through the early seventies, Mark continued to organize around veterans' issues as well as become involved in political defense work. In the spring of 1974, tired of being harassed by the FBI and afraid for the safety of his family, Mark, his wife and two children moved to Ohio. For a while, they lived in a converted chicken coop on a deserted farm.

After some very rough times, Mark secured a job in the Newark, Ohio, public welfare department, investigating the abuse and neglect of older people. A few traumatic years later—during which he gave up his ten-year dependence on alcohol and soon after got divorced—he was recruited by the state welfare agency in nearby Columbus. He worked there until last year. Now he has his own business, consulting and helping other state agencies develop training programs for child welfare workers. He is also a leader in local efforts to help the homeless.

"Progressive values are in fact mainstream values. I don't think they're countercultural at all. I think the right wing in this country, demonstrated by the Reagan administration, has taken away, or attempted to take away from people like myself, values of patriotism and protecting the family, protecting the community, and claim them exclusively for themselves. And what I'm saying is I never lost them, and what I'm trying to do is articulate them in a way that allows me to reclaim them.

"The ideological view that I carry is that a society is set up for the express purpose of helping all of its members maximize their potential for contributing to the society. To me that's the essence of what a society should be all about. And everything we do as a member of society should be to work towards assuring that this is what happens. And that's exactly the opposite of what the Reagan administration's done. It's cut out and shut out huge segments of the population, kept them from having any opportunity at all to maximize their potential. And so the work I've done around homelessness has been driven by the sense that these people are homeless not helpless.

"I mean after all, I come from low-income people. I don't want them living in shelters in the future. These are my people. We're talking about my family, my relatives. I mean none of my people are rich. They're on the edge, they're at risk. They're the people that work at 16,000 dollars a year and less, work full-time, work hard and don't have shit to show for it. I'm fighting for myself in that sense—the collective me: the family, the community, the people that I care about, the people that I came from.

"I think that the nineties are going to see the emergence of a new progressive supertrend like we saw in the sixties that will give birth to a number of new liberation movements, which hopefully will have in its leadership people with the maturity of twenty and twenty-five years worth of organizing. At the same time, we'll have the vigor of the youth that will be emerging at this time, because I'm telling ya, the baby boomers' babies are just now starting to crack high school. I get into high schools now, and I can see it coming. You want to know why I'm so optimistic? 'Cause my kids are growing up. And people my age with my kind of ideas have trained their children to have values that are very positive, caring values, values that say you take care of other people, not just your own issues. It's, not, 'I got mine, I'm gonna get yours.' It's, 'It doesn't matter if I get mine, what do you need and how do we get it?'

"One of the neatest moments of my life was two nights after my daughter was born. We went out to the hospital to visit Linda and to see Kerry—she was just this little tiny thing. We were all excited and happy for ourselves, and we went back, and we sat around the kitchen table and basically got drunk. And we toasted the youngest revolutionary in the world, this little thing called Kerry Hartford. Now I look at her at fifteen, and I see her as a very attractive, articulate, strong woman who in the truest sense of the word—not in the shallow sense I understood it back then—is a revolutionary. When we say we changed the world as a generation, we really did, and it's gonna show up maybe in her children, in the sense that this thing is an ongoing lifelong struggle our children will carry into the next generation, and their children will carry it into the next generation.

"Before we moved to Ohio, one of the last conversations I had with Barry [the boyhood friend with whom Mark organized the California VVAW] was that things were gonna get real hard, that what we were looking at was a period of time where progressive ideology was not gonna have influence. It was not gonna be the leading line in the country. And that what we had to do was to somehow work at keeping the flame alive, keep alive the notion of a progressive view of the world and what that meant in real practical terms. Whatever we did, we had to carry that into the future and pass it on to our children because it was very clear that in the late seventies and the eighties, there weren't gonna be mass movements during this period of time. That it was gonna take place locally. Wherever you were, you had to deal with your local issues. You had to grow up. You had to become a part of your community, and in that process, find a place for yourself that allowed you to continue to articulate your values.

"My life has been one of struggling to survive, poverty, trying to raise children in a world where the dominant view was the antithesis of what I personally believed. And if my children were gonna have a future and if they were gonna have a chance to survive and not be killed in some future war, I had no choice but to struggle. It's not a question for me of even having a choice. I'm a recovering alcoholic. Fifteen years ago I lived in a chicken coop with my family. I know what it's like to be homeless and out of money and in a strange place. I know what it's like to be a veteran who's been abused and neglected and ignored. I know what it's like to be around people who've been treated even worse than that.

"It's not a question of: Do I have the energy? I get tired all the time. I get fed up all the time. My wife and I talk all the time about just saying, 'screw this shit.' You know, I got a nice house. My wife and I have now an income that puts us in the top five percent in the country. My wife's an executive. I'm a well-respected professional in my field. But that's not the point. The point is I've got children, I've got friends, I've got a community, I've got people in my community who need to be helped. I mean you take care of your own. Just 'cause you got yours doesn't mean anything. The question is, does everybody have enough? And the answer's no. So you gotta struggle. That's just it."

ALICE EMBREE, 43
1967: student protest leader
1989: child support enforcement consultant

Known in the movement as "Alice from Dallas," she was actually born and raised in Austin, the daughter of middle class Episcopalians. Her father was a professor at the University of Texas (UT). As a freshman at UT in 1963, she became involved in civil rights issues, at one point picketing the dorm where one of Lyndon Johnson's daughters lived. In 1964, she joined SDS and helped make the UT chapter one of the country's largest. ("I was a local girl gone bad, not an outside agitator, and that always made life interesting.") In 1967, after being put on disciplinary probation for her leadership role in the campus free speech movement, she dropped out and headed for New York. There she and Jeff Shero Nightbyrd (editor of the New York *Rat*) became the ultimate movement couple.

"SDS in Austin was very visible, and it grew to be one of the largest chapters in the country, too. I think it's one of the things about being in the provinces as opposed to the coast. It was different. I mean, we didn't have much of an Old Left bumping around to react to. And I think that the people who were kind of on the fringe, culturally or politically, gravitated together more, and in some ways it became a more outrageous community than, say, the East Coast, where it would have had more intellectual overtones. Here if you didn't fit the Bubba sort of mainstream, you were sort of tossed to the side. You know, Janis Joplin was going to UT then and was part of the whole cultural scene that was going.

"We got gradually more and more involved in anti-war activity and, of course, always had Lyndon Johnson right here in our home town. We sat in at LBJ's ranch in 1965. There were these ways to really get to the top of the power structure because we were an embarrassment to Lyndon Johnson. And we sort of brought the anti-war protest to his front yard.

"In the late sixties, we were just kind of shoved around by events. A lot of the people I knew, including myself, believed the revolution was six months or a year away. I don't know what we really thought—that we would overthrow the entire government. We clearly didn't have a concept of how. We had a concept of upheaval because we were part and parcel of it. But actually changing all of the institutions, all the forms of power, was a little bit beyond us. I mean, we were only what, 22?

"Much later, I can see how we were naive and arrogant in lots of ways, but at the time it seemed like the whole country was coming unglued, and it was. I think it was hard to deal with the seventies. And I think there were years there where it was pretty tough to make that transition into the long haul, in keeping those values and keeping a sense of momentum without having the feel that it was all gonna happen within six months. But it's part of the transition that I think lots of us made."

In New York, Alice worked for the North American Congress on Latin America (NACLA), a radical research group, as well as with Jeff on the *Rat*. During the Columbia University student strike of 1969, Jeff and Alice helped "liberate" documents that linked Columbia to outside corporate interests. Later both the *Rat* and NACLA published articles exposing Columbia's power structure.

In the seventies, Alice worked in a collective vegetarian restaurant, spent a year on an Arkansas commune and returned to Austin to work as a printer for a women's press collective. In 1979, she began a series of mainstream jobs with the University of Texas, where she earned her B.A., and also her M.A. in community and regional planning. Married with two children, living in the home she grew up in, Alice now works for the state attorney general's office in child support enforcement and childcare advocacy.

"At the women's press, we tried really hard to be sort of a righteous political collective and also a small business, and it's just an amazingly difficult row to hoe. And we had constant conflict over how little money we were gonna take in order to further the political agenda. And some of what I feel is it's a blessing to have a job where I can go for forty hours, and I can do work and then I can leave. That wasn't true at the press. You lived and breathed it. I don't think I could be a mom and work at the press. And so it's part of a kind of realistic choice, to opt for a more stable niche and I guess, what the public sector has to offer.

"Sometimes I think our lives are too hectic, and there are things we need to weed out of them to make sure we stay focused on family and things like that. But we have never, either one of us, wanted to abandon our political vision. Sometimes it's a question of stamina, but for the better half of my life now, the feeling that you can make change and that you really need to, has been a part of my life. I'm happier with it being a part of my life than I would be sitting around, 'visualizing,' or whatever New Age people do—as in 'I want to visualize people's victory.' It sort of drives me crazy. I don't think visualizing is any substitute for organizing. And life's a lot more interesting when you're politically active. Sometimes it's too active.

"But I can't imagine life without whatever SDS gave me in 1964, which is a social vision. And I think life would be terribly boring, and I'd be even more morosely introspective. You know, when I went to an SDS reunion, there was this guy, he was an old commie, and he said, 'SDS was my fountain of youth, and it will always be my fountain of youth.' He's about 65. And as I looked around that room, I saw some of the most humorous, passionate, interesting people in the world. I feel very fortunate to have been part of all that and to still be part of it, and I can't imagine just paying attention to the latest fashion trend, or which are the best restaurants to eat at. It just seems like it'd be awfully dull."

HISANI, 35
1969: black nationalist
1989: health policy research analyst

Hisani (her African name) grew up middle class in Houston and Pittsburgh. Active in Houston's black theatre (her mother was the director), she became politically involved with the black nationalist movement early on in junior high and high school. In 1969, she got her first Afro. A year later, when she was considering where to go to college, her first choice was Malcolm X Liberation University. But her mother insisted she take a more traditional route. In the fall of 1971, she entered Howard University.

"All the kinds of outward trappings of political consciousness, I had very early. But it was all on the surface for me then. I didn't understand what it meant to my life, and how long the path moving in that direction really would be. The frustration of seeing yourself move in circles—expending a considerable amount of time and energy, but not really seeing any progress made—made me question whether the route that I was taking was a route that was ultimately going to transform the system into a society that was more humane and actually addressed people's needs, their hopes, dreams and aspirations.

"So there was a transition in my life from involvement in community organizations to something that tried to do more than just patch up the system. I had started studying Marxism by my last year in college, like many people were doing. I was at Howard University, and a lot was happening in Washington then. Washington was a learning environment by itself. I was active in the National Liberation support committee which introduced me to a whole new grouping of people. I met people who were also studying Marxism and who had gone through similar experiences as mine. We were looking for models in other countries and trying to approach the struggle in a more scientific framework. We felt that there were lessons we could learn from other cultures, other societies that had been involved in struggle, particularly African countries, but also China and Cuba and the Soviet Union. So I studied revolutionary movements and became involved in organizations that looked at these countries and tried to see what could be applied to this country.

"After graduating from Howard, I took two years 'off' and worked for a while in a warehouse. It really felt like we needed to develop our ties with working people. I think that time, more than any other, helped me understand the people of the world and their problems. I had come from a middle class family and had what we used to call petit bourgeois values. So coming out of school and working really did help me understand what the working class was all about. It helped me become a little bit more realistic about life and the problems people were facing and how ingrained they were. It was almost as if I had felt we could legislate change and people could suddenly live a better life, and that it was just a matter of changing the people in government. Or, the other side was that there would be a revolution, a violent overthrow as in the other countries we had studied. We were just that naive about the apparatus of the state.

"But I came to realize that the transformation of a people, the transformation of society was much broader than just this balance of power or shift in the balance. Partly, the realization came during those two years I took off after school. But, while I feel like I came to some of this on my own, I also think it came from being involved in the organizations I was and am involved in, forward-looking groups that are really struggling to understand the nature of our society and the political process. I've been involved in essentially the same organization since 1975, the group that's evolved, through different formations, into the New Democratic Movement. And now there's a maturity to our work."

After two years working in a warehouse and another two at more traditional, white collar jobs, Hisani began graduate work at Johns Hopkins University. She earned her doctorate in public health and currently works as a health policy research analyst for the General Accounting Office. The focus of her work is on providing access to health care for all people.

"I've got some friends, people I've come through the movement with, who just seem to have given up. And you wonder if there was some critical time when someone just wasn't there for them, someone who could have helped to guide them or offered their support. That's what I feel has helped me a lot. My husband is politically involved, and we're involved in the same organizations. And I'm with a support network of people. But there were times I felt alone too. I mean there were times when we made it difficult for people to stay in the movement. We ostracized people because they went on to school, or we criticized them because they weren't working class enough or black enough. So some people were just driven away, and they never recovered.

"It's an important question, what keeps people active. For me, it's the association with people. But I know there's something more, because I've tried to be a support for people who just haven't been able to hang in there, who've looked for quick answers. Maybe it had something to do with the quality of the training and preparation I had coming through. I think I came through a generation of some of the best trained activists. The organizations I've worked with, the black youth organizations, have trained what are now some of the most highly respected black leaders. It was something about the experience we went through, the molding and shaping of our personalities, our commitment, and especially the process of study—what happened in China, what happened in African countries—we saw that and were able to internalize it at a much higher level than other people. So we understood that things in this country weren't about change tomorrow.

"The Reagan years were hard, but not as devastating to me personally as to some others because I was involved in surviving in a whole other world, the world of academia. There were so many assaults that we saw on the standard of living, on civil rights gains that you could see slipping before your eyes, women's movement gains, the fight for abortion. It was difficult. But I think, again, that understanding the system helped. I mean, a president can only do so much. We saw the tug and pull with Congress, the balance of forces, and you realized that he could do only so much. I think that if it had gone on much more than eight years, we would have wondered if we could ever recover. Even now, we are looking at the Supreme Court and realizing that Reagan has left a mark there that will be with us for generations to come. But beyond this, I think there is a recognition that change is still possible.

"There were things that happened during that same time period that were cause for optimism. I watched Jackson's campaign grow from being not taken very seriously to, during the second campaign, really becoming a force—an instrument of change in the rules and the platform. So there's a potential for more lasting change. I mean, as long as you have some signs that there's a potential for things to get better, you can fight off demoralization. Once you can see that there's that potential, you can keep the demoralization from overtaking you.

"I think that the sources of power in this country are very entrenched and intertwined with money—that's still my view, and my understanding of that relationship hasn't changed over the years. But it does seem to me now that we have to infiltrate those networks that wield the most influence and authority in society. I don't think it's only working from within the system, because the system in many cases is corrupt in how it's structured. You've also got to mobilize from outside. The linkages of people I've maintained that are outside all the official structures I operate within are extremely important to me.

"But for me, having children has definitely made a difference. When you become responsible for someone other than yourself, you think twice about the choices that you make in life. My husband and myself, by ourselves, could just pick up and leave because we disagreed with something at work. But when someone else's life is dependent on yours, it forces you to be more responsible in a way that you may not have been. I almost think it makes you a lot more conservative in your thinking, more cautious. We've begun to think, to wonder and question: Are we more conservative now than we were or is it just aging, maturity that leads to cautiousness? I don't know.

"My attitudes toward different institutions, like the church and the police, certainly have changed since college years. Part of it, I think, is that those institutions have changed, at least a little, for the better. And this reflects our successes. These are struggles that we waged and that we've seen, in some sense, come to fruition. It's nice to reflect on that. It gives you another sense that things can change, that people can make a difference. So there's something about that idealism of youth that you hold on to. I enjoyed college and the years after that. I enjoyed the opportunity to think about the world and envision what it could be like. That's a luxury that I don't really have any more. Now I have to think about all the interests and concerns of my family.

"The vision is still with me, but I'm much more pragmatic in terms of how I see myself or us achieving it. When you transform a society, real people are affected, and those people can't just be bulldozed over; they've got to be won over. That's the way our society works. And as long as we're here, we have to play the game by the rules that most people have grown to expect.

"So you see signs, and you take heart from them. But you can't say that it's going to happen in your own lifetime. For example, in my own work, I've been involved in health care, developing a health care system that guarantees everyone access to care regardless of their financial situation. Now, I don't think that's so far off. I think the struggle today is being fought and won in separate arenas—the struggle around health, around housing, around education—there are people in each of those arenas who are working for a better system. But because the problems are so complex and deeply ingrained, the process of getting there is taking longer than maybe I would like. But I see the forward motion. I don't envision an overthrow of one government and the installation of a new one, to solve all our problems. That idealism is no longer with me. But I definitely see the forward motion."

CARLOS CALDERON, 42
1969: Brown Beret/alternative journalist
1989: freelance writer

With his tangle of black, curly hair, Zapata moustache and dark-rimmed glasses, Carlos Calderon looks just like he did twenty years ago—only a bit fleshier. But his life today bears little resemblance to his life two decades ago. Then he was in the thick of it: a leader of the San Diego Brown Berets, a writer for the radical San Diego *Street Journal* and a committed SDSer. Today he lives quietly, operating a small news service from his Oregon home.

As an undergraduate at the University of Texas in El Paso, Carlos was more interested in sports than politics. But his experience as a delegate to the 1968 Democratic National Convention quickly changed that. "It was an incredible shock and had a radicalizing influence on my life," he says. "I was absolutely positive that fascism was around the corner, and I knew I had to become politically active."

He did. In addition to joining SDS, the Brown Berets and the *Street Journal* collective, he traveled to Cuba with the Venceremos Brigade. Back in San Diego that winter, as one of the most visible members of the local Brown Berets, he was indicted on counts of criminal syndicalism, attempted murder and

manufacture of firearms by a local grand jury. (Two counts were almost immediately dropped; the third was later ruled unconstitutional.)

"I had just returned from Cuba. I had been back in the country about five
days when Kent State and the invasion of Cambodia took place, and I
thought, oh shit, this is the real thing. I was absolutely convinced at this point
that the revolution was right around the corner. In the Brown Berets I had
some title like minister of education. It was patterned after the Black Panthers
and everybody had some sort of silly title. We had uniforms too: brown berets
and African bush jackets. There was this guy, a police agitator who had infiltrated the group, he was in charge of military training. He made it a re-
quirement that everyone get a shotgun, and we were supposed to go out every
week or so and go target shooting.

"Later I was one of three Brown Berets indicted by the San Diego County
grand jury, and I was in jail for about a month. The bail was enormous. What
had happened was that that summer, right before the Chicano Moratorium,
San Diego magazine had done a story on the Chicano movement. And most
of the people in the Chicano movement were rather boring . . . kind of
like the Chicano version of Ralph Abernathy, just business people, nothing
colorful about them. So the fellow who did the story, he had interviewed all
these guys and then he got to me and his eyes just lit up. Because, wow, here
was a live one. He got a picture of me in my brown beret, and I had a Lenin
pin on it. It was taken in my room in front of this poster of Mao Tse-tung.
I gave him a couple of pictures, one of which was of me on top of a captured
American tank at the Bay of Pigs when I had been to Cuba. The police and
the FBI were absolutely convinced that I was a protegé of Che Guevara and
Fidel Castro and that I was one of the most dangerous men in America.
I wasn't."

In 1972, Carlos changed his political allegiance to the October League, a
Maoist splinter group of the SDS, and edited the group's newspaper for a year
and a half. Later he edited the United Farm Workers' newspaper during the
union's most intense and violent years.

"All the experiences I had had in the movement up to this point could
not have prepared me for the Farm Workers. That was just fear, just
absolute unbridled fear where your asshole just puckered up because
you were so damned scared out there. It was probably the same kind of fear
that blacks experienced in the deep South during the civil rights movement.

"I remember covering one strike, and there was this kid, this sixteen-year-
old kid, who went into the field to take a pee, and he never came out. You
know, it was like, where is Ramon? They went in to look for him, and they
found him, and he was just a bloody mess. The teamsters had gotten a hold

of him. I remember at a rally in Davis, some sniper started shooting at Cesar Chavez and I was right next to him. The fear one experienced in the Farm Workers when one went out into the fields or any strike or demonstration situation was just incredible.

"The UFW was like a bottomless pit. There were never enough bodies, enough time, and whew, I finally just got burned out. After a while, I just crashed and burned."

Carlos left the movement to pursue a career in mainstream journalism, which took him to a small southern California daily and later to a national boating newspaper. Today his one-person news service specializes in covering aviation and boating news. He also writes on military issues and national politics for the *Democratic Communique*, a radical newsletter he and his long-time companion edit.

"So I went from the Farm Workers to covering yachting at the Los Angeles Yacht Club. And at times it was pretty strange. I was hanging out at Marina Del Rey, hobnobbing with really wealthy people. I remember it really got to me at this awards ceremony at the L.A. Yacht Club. It was quite a shindig. I felt like I was right in the midst of *The Great Gatsby*, a surrealistic *Great Gatsby*. But after a while, I just got used to it. There's this phenomenon in journalism that you begin to act and look like who you're covering. So a little bit of it did rub off on me, like I bought a pair of topsiders. That's as far as I went.

"I'm not a fanatical Marxist-Leninist anymore. As a matter of fact, I'm not a fanatical anything anymore. But I still have a lot of the same ideas I had when I was in the movement. I still believe that the U.S. is a militaristic bully, and that we live in a militaristic state.

"I have a wise old man that I talk to once or twice a month, a retired trade unionist. We were talking about the affairs of the country the other day, and he said listen, this is the only country we have. It's like, you have a house, but you don't like it, but it's the only one you've got, and you can't get another one. So what do you do? You don't tear it down, you change it. It's that way with the country. It's the only one we've got."

STEW ALBERT, 49
1968: Yippie
1989: Jewish activist

There's an irreverence, a kind of Woody-Allen-on-acid humor, that gives away his past. He may be nearing 50, he may be married, he may wear sports coats when he gives speeches, but there's no doubt Stew Albert was, and in some ways still is, a yippie. He spent years in the trenches as a writer for the Berkeley

Barb and *Tribe*, a staffer for the National Mobilization Committee, an unindicted co-conspirator during Chicago '68, a founder of People's Park and a Jerry Rubin sidekick. Now he's an outspoken local leader in the progressive, peace-oriented New Jewish Agenda. Through it all, he hasn't lost the sense that life—and social change—should be fun.

Born and raised in Brooklyn, he came from a politically liberal, culturally conservative first generation American family. His flirtation with the Left began in James Madison High School in the 1950s.

"For some reason—and if I was in therapy I could probably tell you why—I got interested in socialism during my senior year in high school, which was totally ridiculous for that time. I'm talking about the late fifties. I think it was while I was studying for the English Regents. I had to read novels. So somehow I got a book by Upton Sinclair, and I read it and it seemed so persuasive that I just took over some of his ideas. But I didn't do anything. I still ran with the same gang. We were into weight lifting and hanging out. It wasn't like I went to demonstrations or thought of going to demonstrations or had any thought that my political ideas would change my life.

"I began reading in college. For some reason, I became somewhat of an intellectual. I wasn't at all that way in high school. In fact, I did rather poorly in high school. But in college I got intellectually turned on. I don't even know if this happens to people nowadays—getting passionately interested in various ideas, going to libraries to read everything, finding people at school to talk to. The civil rights movement started, and I was totally sympathetic to it, totally sympathetic. And I was reading books by C. Wright Mills and people like that. I remember going to a Ban the Bomb rally in Madison Square Garden where Eleanor Roosevelt and Norman Thomas and Walter Reuther spoke. I was going out with a girl who was a red diaper baby, and this was actually my first exposure to progressive culture. She did get me into going to rallies and demonstrations.

"The thing that had the biggest effect on me in those days was that in 1960, with a friend from college, I went to Cuba. That was very daring. It was still legal to travel there, but given the coverage of Cuba in the American press, which was really at a fever pitch, it was kind of daring to go. I was looking for adventure. I was definitely trying to break with my cautious, conservative, frightened, boring childhood. I was sympathetic to the Castro government. He seemed like a very exciting figure, you know, like a real life Errol Flynn with politics. So I went down there and lived on a collective farm for a few weeks, and traveled around. It was extremely exciting. And that had a big effect on me. When I got back, I found out that the FBI had come to my school to look at my records. And that was the beginning of a long relationship with the Bureau."

After earning a B.A. in history from Pace, Stew signed on as a welfare department caseworker in the Bedford-Stuyvesant section of Brooklyn. In 1965, depressed over a relationship gone bad, he hopped on a Greyhound bus—"99 days for $99"—and eventually landed in Berkeley. For the next seven years, he was deeply involved in the anti-war movement. Arrested more than a dozen times, he was always in the thick of it: the Pentagon Demonstration, People's Park, Chicago '68, Washington May Day. He developed close ties with the Black Panthers and went on national speaking tours with Jerry Rubin.

In 1972, after the Democratic National Convention in Miami, he and Judy Clavir, a *Barb-Tribe* colleague, moved to a cabin in the Catskills. (They later married and now have an eleven-year-old daughter.) For the next seven years Stew freelanced for a variety of magazines including *Crawdaddy* and *University Review*, and Judy wrote her Ph.D. dissertation and began teaching. In 1979, they returned to the Bay Area where Stew took a job as a private eye and, with Judy, edited *The Sixties Papers*, an anthology of movement documents. Five years later, escaping the craziness and expense of Berkeley, they moved to Portland, Oregon.

"The second part of my life started after the summer of '72. My life changed and started taking on more the form that it has today. That's when you start saying, well, your life's changing, but are you holding on to your values?

"What are sixties values? I think there are many. Informality—the sixties challenged formality as a cultural style; a dedication to peace, sort of rejecting the cold war; a kind of international sympathy for the underdog, whoever was getting kicked around; a concern about process, the idea of participatory democracy; the idea of treating people in an equal fashion, anti-hierarchy, which later the women's movement picked up on but it really went back to the early days of SNCC and SDS; a dislike and mistrust for the Establishment, especially militarists, the wealthy, politicians; the idea of treating people as ends, not means; and the idea of fighting, not being passive, fighting for your ideas.

"Sometimes I feel haunted by these values, like they're a burden, and other times they are a solace and a way of living in the world in a way with which I can really feel strong and good. But they are definitely still a part of me.

"The values have remained fairly consistent. But when you go beyond that, in terms of what the world is going to be like, what are the chances of these values being realized, and how to go about realizing them, political tactics, that's really a whole other issue. Certainly in the sixties I had this view that either there was going to be a real change in America and the West or there was going to be some kind of barbarous fascism taking hold. So I had a kind of apocalyptic vision, even though it wasn't as extreme as some people. I didn't think that revolution or fascism was around the corner, but I had a sense that what was going on in the sixties would continue and grow—the underground press, the various organizations, the communes, the whole alternative culture would continue to grow and expand and become more powerful. Basically I thought that two Americas would develop: the America that began to take shape in the sixties and the America that took its form from the fifties. One America would hold power, the America of the fifties, and one would challenge it. At some point, probably through some sort of collapse of the economy, I thought things would get very extreme, and then one side or the other would win. If the fifties people won, they would destroy us, and there would be barbarism. And if we won, we would elminate them, and there would be an advance in civilization. But neither happened. So there you go. That was my vision.

"Today the conservative culture is dominant, and it's a real act of will—you have to show a certain amount of strength—to hold on to some of these old values. Because everything around you is saying you're a sap for holding on to these values; you know, just get it for yourself, get it for your family, protect your own—and that's it. And that's really what the eighties have been about. And to say, 'No, we want to have a broader vision, a broader sense of community,' can make you sound like a real schmuck sometimes. People look at you, and a lot of them don't even know what these words mean. Literally, you might as well be speaking in Middle English.

"But I am not totally controlled by the time I live in; I'm an independent individual. There's something in me that's larger than convenience and conformity. And that makes you feel more alive and gives you a certain strength to feel that you can in some way shape the period in which you live, to make it better."

NELSON JOHNSON, 46
1969: black student leader
1989: Baptist minister

A native of North Carolina, Nelson served in the Air Force for four years after high school. There he became involved in "a lot of racial discussion and small racial incidents" as he struggled to figure out what he believed. Originally attracted to the philosophy of Martin Luther King, Jr., he was beginning to move in the direction of Malcolm X by the time he enrolled in North Carolina Agricultural and Technical College in the fall of 1965.

"My initial involvement at college was in the tutorial service out in the community—nothing radical about that. But one of the things that led to was a very clear understanding on my part that those programs that were designed to merely nurture the wounds were simply not sufficient and that we had to take a clearer look at what caused and continues to cause the need for kids to be tutored.

"I started to demonstrate against the war in Vietnam, and I was so severely criticized by the military people, the colonel in charge of the ROTC there, that I was really shocked. I mean all we were doing was standing around holding signs. All of these things just provoked me to greater and greater involvement and analysis, where ultimately I set out to organize poor people in the city of Greensboro, forming the Greensboro Association of Poor People. We did rent strikes, cafeteria strikes with food service workers. We staged sit-ins to try to integrate various places, that kind of activity. We had nonviolent marches and demonstrations in support of these kinds of things. That was generally what I was involved in during the mid-sixties.

"In the late sixties, our whole movement took a more radical turn with the formation of a national black student organization. During the founding convention for the group in Greensboro, the whole thing erupted into a full-scale rebellion for three days with one person killed and a few people wounded. It was one of those kind of landmark events for all of us involved. I really got projected into a leadership role, not so much for what I did, but for what I refused to do, which was apologize for anything or to say that the students were wrong. So I was seen as the leader of it, and I ended up getting tried and sentenced to two years in jail. [He served three months. The rest of the time was commuted after the governor responded to political pressure.]

"It's hard to give the flavor of all of this now. It was a very tense time. What was going on in the late sixties was broad-based involvement of the black community. We had moved from just discussion, voting and kind of reformist activities to a fairly radical stance, an openly revolutionary stance in the sense that we were advocating that there had to be fundamental alterations of the social structure in order for black people to realize any justice in this country.

"I never disliked or fully rejected King. I always admired his courage and his commitment. But I think I reached a conclusion in my own mind that as a practical matter, the world didn't work like that. And I was pretty sincere and pretty loyal to what I believed. As you engaged the issues, people really confronted you and forced you to take a stand one way or the other, and I increasingly moved toward the position that you had to meet this kind of violence and arrogance with appropriate measures. Oftentimes these measures were not nonviolent. You had the right to defend yourself. You had the right to organize for fundamental change and to push for it, up to and including violent methods. I had come to that conclusion by '67, '68."

In the early seventies, Nelson spent much of his time organizing black student groups on campuses around the country. Back in Greensboro, he started seriously studying Marxism as he organized local black workers. In 1979 he was instrumental in organizing a demonstration in Greensboro against the rise of the Ku Klux Klan. A Klan and a Nazi group organized a counter-demonstration, and during the melee that ensued, someone shot into the crowd. Five people were killed and nine, including Nelson, were wounded. He was arrested and charged with, among other things, inciting to riot. For the next seven years, Nelson's role in the famous Greensboro case consumed his life.

"Initially, what happened hardened me in my views that the country was in a fairly imminent economic crisis, that it was headed toward economic collapse, that it was very important to press very hard to organize people to take advantage of that—otherwise we would be the victims of a kind of fascist development. And I became more convinced of that because that's exactly what it looked like to me. I mean we were pretty blatantly attacked, and the entire legal system of the state and the national government seemed to blame us for what happened. It became a kind of public denouncement of communism in general with more references to Moscow and Beijing than to Greensboro almost.

"It was that kind of mood. It was a very oppressive atmosphere. I think I may have over-generalized that in terms of the rest of the country, but I'm absolutely sure of how it felt in Greensboro. People were afraid. Very few people would come out to support you. But we had to press on. And it looked like we were going against all odds. We kept demonstrating and saying what we were saying, and going to jail. I was under 100,000 dollars bond while the Klan's highest bond, for the person charged with murder, was only 50,000 dollars. So the whole thing just hardened my view that we were headed for a period of severe economic decline and depression.

"But it wasn't as imminent as it appeared to me then. I think the basic tenets of that position were true and remain true, but the flexibility within the social structure was much greater than I had realized. It's all much more sophisticated than I appreciated at the time. I don't think that whatever is done to delay or absorb it can negate the movement, but it might not take the form that I originally thought it would: vast polarization between one group and another and an explosion and revolution. I no longer see it that way. I don't rule it out, but I see other possibilities for how the struggle might unfold.

"My view of the economy is essentially the same today as it was then in terms of its exploitive character and the kind of destruction it does to the environment and the long-term interests of the people. I think the most significant thing that has changed is that my tendency used to be to see people as all bad or all good, and I no longer really see people that way. I see that there's some good in all of us, that all of us are prone to do things wrong as individuals and as a class. That has humbled me a great deal.

"I think there is a possibility that we can avoid a mass, violent occurrence in the struggle for social change. That's different from what I originally thought. I thought we had to prepare for it and not entertain any illusions that we could avoid it. I thought you had to build into the consciousness of the people the inevitability of massive, armed conflict. I'm no longer of that persuasion.

"Some of the shift might have to do with growing older. But I wasn't a kid in 1979, remember. I was 36. I think some of it has to do with my faith. I've since become a minister. I've made a considerable effort not to reject all of what I believed before even though that's what people automatically assume. I want people to understand that what I do reject is the kind of categorical condemnation of people as a group or as a class. That has really changed. And once that changes, it necessarily shifts some of your tactical thinking. In other words, if it's possible for a significant number of people to be changed themselves without dying then that will have some influence on what you think about the social process."

In the early and mid-eighties most of Nelson's time was devoted to fighting the charges brought against him as a result of the 1979 anti-Klan demonstration. He was also involved in a counter–civil suit against Greensboro, the Klan and the federal government. In 1986 his life took a new direction when he enrolled in divinity school in Virginia. Today he is an assistant pastor in charge of outreach programs at his home church in Greensboro.

"I think it's great that we have black elected officials. That's fine. I think it's great that we have black lawyers. That's fine. But I think very little progress is going to be made in the legal process. Generally, those things are a reflection of something that's going on in society. And electoral politics in this country I think compromises you. Most people are totally compromised by the time they get into a position where they could do some good. So what I actually think is that we have to organize something more basic, more radical than anything you could ever do approaching it from the electoral or legal perspectives or even from the perspective I was involved in when I was younger.

"I want to spent all of my time at the very bottom of the black community among the underclass, the most oppressed—and when I say that people have the capacity to change their views, those are the views I want to change, because right now there's a vast portion of our population that really exists in a kind of hopeless state. I believe—and I think this is more of a moral, religious question than a legal one—that we were not made to be that way. I think that people like myself, people who have some experience working politically, need to go back to the base of our communities to engage people at a more grassroots level, and to organize there. That's what I want to do. And I think that's more fundamental to social change than the legal process or the electoral process.

"Now I don't mean to come off as a Jesus freak, but Jesus is a model in the sense that he concentrated on the lost, the lepers, the lame—objectively the underclass of his day—and thoroughly condemned the institution of the religious structure of that day. And all of that seems to be confused and lost in today's world.

"It's very refreshing to bring this perspective to a people who need to hear that that's what the symbol of their faith has been. This has nothing to do with the kind of ceremony and compromise that people have associated religion with. I think the church itself has to be redeemed.

"I think it's very important that we reclaim what it means to believe in the essential worth and value of a person, and if we can affirm that for the least among us, then we can affirm it for all of us. That's where Jesus went, to the disenfranchised people, to affirm that they were somebody—because they *were* somebody, not because of what they had, or what they had accumulated throughout the years, but because they were human beings. So if people could claim that understanding of themselves, then we would be in the process of challenging everything that would deny our self-worth and our selfhood, and this would be absorbed into many of our institutions and social structures.

"But in fighting against these institutions, I think we absorb many of the values we're fighting against and gradually change into the thing we're fighting against. My faith perspective is not a guarantee against that, but it's a much better aid in preventing that from happening than anything else I've ever found."

POLITICAL ACTIVISM
II

Tom Hayden seemed to be everywhere in the sixties: the founding of SDS, voter registration drives in the South, urban grassroots organizing in the North, the 1968 Chicago convention, Berkeley's People's Park, the Columbia student strike. By plan or serendipity, Hayden was part not only of many of the major events of the era but also of the prevailing philosophies, from the optimism and moral certitude of the early civil rights movement to the frustration and violence of the late sixties. To a great extent, his own political career paralleled the development and evolution of New Left politics in this country.

The only child of Irish Catholic parents, Hayden was born and raised in a quiet, cloistered middle-class suburb of Detroit, Michigan. His accountant father was an Eisenhower Republican who headed the local American Legion post. His mother, a librarian, was devoted to Adlai Stevenson. Although he says in his autobiography, *Reunion*, that his parents' Catholicism was "more formal than fervent," they nevertheless sent him to the local parish grade school run by Father Charles E. Coughlin, the controversial right-wing "radio priest" of the 1930s. Hayden says he doesn't remember any political sermons. What he does remember, even at that early age, was feeling constricted and alienated but at the same time, feeling helpless to rebel.

At the local public high school, he quickly became part of a tight-knit clique of students who, he says, "shared a sense of being different." A classmate later put it more bluntly, describing Hayden as a "hell-raiser." He edited the school newspaper and, on the side, produced an underground paper, *The Daily Smirker*, a cross between the *Daily Worker* and *Mad* magazine. As for political consciousness, he was, he says, "still a blank slate."

In the fall of 1957, he arrived at the University of Michigan in Ann Arbor, only fifty miles but another world from his provincial suburban home. There he was introduced to left-wing politics through talks with Al Haber, a campus hanger-on who founded Students for a Democratic Society (SDS) in 1959. Hayden, absorbed with his work on the *Michigan Daily*—where he rose in the ranks to be editor during his senior year—declined to be recruited into the group. But his own political awareness grew as he reported on the burgeoning civil rights movement in the South.

In the summer of 1960 he hitchhiked west, where he planned to cover the Democratic National Convention for the *Daily* and learn firsthand about growing student activism by visiting the Berkeley campus. In California, he got what he was looking for: a powerful, albeit condensed, political education. He met with Berkeley student activists, watched anti-HUAC protests on Sproul Plaza, interviewed H-bomb enthusiast Dr. Edward Teller (after whom Dr. Strangelove was modeled) and visited farmworker organizers in Delano. Outside the convention hall in Los Angeles, he saw marching civil rights demonstrators, including Dr. Martin Luther King, Jr., whom he interviewed on the picket line. "Ultimately, you have to take a stand with your life," King told him.

Back in Ann Arbor, Hayden used his editorial position to urge support for the civil rights movement, among other progressive causes, and traveled south to report on the activities of SNCC. Approaching graduation, he was offered a job with the Detroit *News*, but he turned it down. "I did not want to report on the world," he writes in his autobiography, "I wanted to change it."

In the fall of 1961 he set out to do just that with Sandra Cason ("Casey"), an SNCC worker he had married after graduation. Their home base was Atlanta. For the next two years, Hayden was SDS's field secretary in the South, participating in voter registration drives and desegregation attempts. He was arrested while trying to desegregate public transportation facilities in Albany, Georgia, and beaten during a voter registration drive in McComb, Mississippi. These experiences were, he later wrote, "both a necessary moral act and a rite of passage into serious commitment."

From the Albany jail, he composed a letter to his friends at SDS who were soon to meet to decide the fate of the tiny group. As he wrote, he envisioned SDS as a national organization that would be at the core of a new student movement. Two weeks later, Hayden was drafting what the group thought of as "a manifesto of hope" and "an agenda for a generation"—the Port Huron Statement. The document, with its calls for participatory democracy and social justice, was the first national statement of the New Left. For the next year, Hayden served as the president of SDS, setting up offices in his Ann Arbor apartment while he studied the work of C. Wright Mills in graduate school.

But he soon realized, as did others in SDS, that participatory democracy needed doing, not merely talking about. In 1964, Hayden co-founded the Economic Research and Action Project (ERAP), designed to aid the urban poor by setting up grassroots community organizations in northern cities. Hayden took charge of the ERAP effort in Newark, New Jersey, where he helped organize the community to pressure city government to respond to its grievances. The Newark project, which outlasted all the other ERAP ventures, ended after the summer of 1967 race riots. Hayden described the frustrations that gave rise to the riots in *Rebellion in Newark*, published by Random House later that year, which a reviewer in *The Nation* called "a brilliant little book."

After Newark, Hayden turned his attention to the anti-war movement. He had traveled to Southeast Asia in 1965 for the purpose of establishing contact between the American peace movement and North Vietnam, and in 1967, he went again. At a meeting in Czechoslovakia, American anti-war leaders suggested that the North Vietnamese release some captured American soldiers as a gesture of solidarity with the peace movement. Hayden flew to Cambodia where three POWs were released into his custody. He continued working for the release of other POWs throughout the war.

Back in the United States, his involvement with the anti-war movement, like the war itself, escalated. Along with Rennie Davis, he was project director of the National Mobilization Committee to End the War, the group that helped organize the demonstrations during the Democratic National Convention in Chicago. Designed to be an alternate "people's" convention, the original plan called for nonviolent, legal picketing on the sidewalks outside the delegates' downtown hotels, rallies, marches and concerts, topped off with a Yippie Festival at the Coliseum. The city, then ruled by Mayor Richard J. Daley, refused to issue the necessary permits. Instead, 11,000 Chicago police were put on full alert, and 6,000 National Guardsmen and 7,500 U.S. Army troops were called in. One thousand agents from the CIA, FBI and Army and Navy intelligence services descended on the city. What ensued was later described as a "police riot." Hayden, Davis and six others were arrested and indicted for their leadership role in what authorities were trying to paint as a "conspiracy." The much-publicized Chicago Seven trial (Black Panther leader Bobby Seale, the eighth defendant, was removed to stand trial on other charges in New Jersey) resulted in contempt-of-court citations for both the defendants and their lawyers. In addition, five of those on trial, including Hayden, were found guilty of crossing state lines to incite riot. But on appeal, Judge Julius Hoffman's sentences were overturned when it was determined that he had antagonized the defense and displayed improper behavior.

After the trial, Hayden went to Berkeley where he became a founding member of the Red Family, a commune once described as a "great bastion of radicalism and experimental living." In between the interminable debates over male chauvinism and women's liberation (which ultimately split the commune), Hayden wrote articles on the war for *Ramparts* and *Rolling Stone* and traveled around the country speaking at rallies. Back in Berkeley in May 1971, he spoke—and was arrested—at a demonstration to celebrate the second anniversary of People's Park, a state-owned vacant lot that students and others had transformed into a park. Later in 1971, he met Jane Fonda at an anti-war rally in Ann Arbor, and the two spent the next several years speaking out against the war, campaigning for Senator George McGovern and organizing the Indochina Peace Campaign in an effort to stop U.S. clandestine involvement in and indirect aid to the Thieu regime. Fonda and Hayden married in 1973.

In 1976, Hayden ran what he now calls a "symbolic campaign" for the U.S. Senate, using the slogan: "The radicalism of the sixties is the common sense of the seventies." Running against the heavily favored incumbent John Tunney, he gathered important endorsements and financial support and made a surprisingly strong showing, proving to himself and others that he had a good chance to succeed in electoral politics. Capitalizing on the momentum of the campaign, Hayden organized the Campaign for Economic Democracy (CED) which called for control of corporations, full employment, a restructuring of the tax system and support for rent control. He and Fonda took to the road, delivering their message of egalitarianism to a wide range of audiences. By 1980, *Esquire* was calling CED the "largest single organized force on the California Left."

In the early eighties, Hayden made a serious—and successful—bid for the California state assembly, and since 1982 he has served there, representing Santa Monica. Known as an activist and reformer, he has worked concertedly on environmental and workplace issues. "It took a long time for me to accept that far from becoming a police state, the system had worked," he confesses in his autobiography. Now, as the nineties begin, Hayden is very much a part of the system he once tried to topple, yet, as he says, "I remain an optimist and an enthusiast for my original ideals."

"In 1960, eighteen- to twenty-one-year-olds, that is, college students, could not vote nor could blacks in the South. So, that's 25 million citizens who were excluded, and that's important to remember when you ask why people chose not to work within the system. The answer in the early sixties was that you couldn't. The second thing is that the Democratic party, which was then the natural beacon for liberals or even radicals with an interest in politics, made a fundamentally wrong turn with regard to Vietnam and became the party that escalated the war. And that, particularly in '65, meant that on two counts, voting rights and Vietnam, electoral politics was a closed avenue except to those who were already there or those who were wildly romantic about it or people who were already maybe plugged in and had no options.

"But for most young Americans coming of age between '60 and '68—whether they started with SDS, or they were in SNCC, or they were in the Eugene McCarthy campaign—it was hard to imagine a viable role in electoral politics for one of those two reasons. And then all that changed. Because of the momentum of the civil rights issue and the Vietnam issue, the Democratic party moved towards reform rather than closer to the Republicans. And that was the unexpected event. By 1968, I had come to assume the worst and to think that anything other than the worst was a rosy illusion. The Democratic party, in fact, was significantly reformed—not revolutionized, but significantly reformed—between 1968 and 1972, against my expectations, against my predictions, at least. And I guess I've just learned from that.

"I would say that the point for me that was quite a moving moment was the period of 1972 after McGovern's nomination. Jane and I and a number of others were campaigning on the road to end the Vietnam war and to have people participate in the presidential elections. And there was a moment where we were at the state fair in Ohio, which was a real high point, a real moving experience, because it was a reconnection with the mainstream in a very real way. It was either gonna work or it wasn't gonna work. And I remember we got into a half-joking, half-serious, very emotional thing because one of the people who was part of this organizing drive and had set up state fairs visits took to wearing this American flag pin on her jacket. And then we all started wearing American flag pins. And it just became a triumphal moment. Even though McGovern by then was clearly wounded, fatally so, by the Eagleton disaster, there had been throughout the whole year a change in the Democratic party. There was an inclusionary spirit that had taken over and ended the rule of the previous bosses.

"I viewed the world in the sixties through a left perspective. It was not associated with any particular doctrine or group on the Left. I mean it was independent, but it was still a point of view that required a kind of left critique and left confirmation. And I'm still a creature of that tradition and feel all the more informed by it. But what remains of the Left? I don't know the answer to that.

"Part of the problem is the way the world has changed and continues to change so rapidly. Anybody who knows what side they're on is most fortunate, or perhaps an idiot. I mean, I find myself working with the Chinese students who survived the massacre in Beijing and fighting against the Chinese embassy here in California, which is trying to encourage corporate investment in their country. So you have the pro-capitalist, free enterprise people in collusion with the Chinese communist government. You've got myself and the Chinese students who are trying to at least have a moratorium on any further economic relations between the two countries. And I would not have expected this twenty years ago. That was not in the cards.

"I think the politics of trying to fashion a third party are quite frustrating and probably won't go anywhere, although I'm willing to be surprised. The efforts to create a labor-based Democratic party are pretty unlikely because of the occupational dynamics and the growth of the middle class. And I think the skepticism, the valid skepticism, about public bureaucracies as well as private corporations robs the Left, the democratic socialist Left, of a lot of its self-confidence and potential base.

"There's, I think, a tremendous need—and I know it's going on—for a lot of intellectual questioning and reformulation of what is central to those of us who came out of the sixties, out of the New Left. The only thing I come back to is a participatory democracy as a vision of how a society should work, and populism as far as how to change society. But on the doctrinal issues about what's the proper balance between the public sector and the private sector and the international issues of what's our proper role in terms of a world economy, I think a lot of work needs to be done, intellectually.

"I think we have more participatory democracy today than we did in 1960. The political process has been changed from backroom deals to primaries where voters choose the presidential candidates. There's far more recognition of a need for participation of employees in the process of making economic decisions. There's far more enfranchisement of neighborhood groups and community activists against developers. The principle of participation I think has become more strongly embedded than it ever has been before.

"Participatory democracy also meant, however, a more utopian experience—something like the Paris commune or the events of 1968, in which people rise out of their personal lives into some kind of common struggle for radical change. And I just think that that ebbs and flows, and that that's not a permanent fact of life. It shouldn't be and can't be. So it can appear that we're in an apathetic time, far from a participatory ideal, but when you think about it, people have demanded more control over their lives. You or I may not always like the results, but it's definitely been a trend in that direction.

"The reason that it remains a conservative direction in terms of public policy, I think, has to do with the electorate. For whatever reason, voting is a minority habit in this country, and so politics tends to pay most attention to special interest groups and middle class voters. And so unless you have a very angry or radicalized middle class, politics will tend to have a very conservative drift. The only thing that could break that, as I say, is a radicalized, angry middle class, or some unknown scenario that brought millions more people into the voting process.

"I think that political power is very fragile, and it can be won even if the country's going in another direction or the country's divided. Reagan won the presidency because of the disillusionment in the country and the confusion in the country and the skepticism about Carter. And Reagan was a strong leader, and he had some beneficial breaks: the removal of the hostage issue the first few months of his presidency and his ability to survive the recession and bring down inflation, which the Democrats hadn't been able to do. So he was able to solidify a government whose driving ideology was somewhat to the right of where the American people were, and I think that the Mondale campaign had nothing dramatically new to offer, and the country was relatively stable.

"In '88 there was a real opportunity again for reform on issues of education, child care, health care, tax reform, going from Star Wars to some more productive investments, and the campaign was essentially lost by the Democrats, by the Dukakis people. And so we have Bush. But that's not necessarily a reflection of what the possibilities of politics are. It just means that the Republican party was more able to exploit opportunities in a confused decade than the Democrats were. And the result is a government that is a little more forcefully and certainly far more ideologically conservative than the country. What I'm saying is that we've lost political opportunities.

"I'm not good at predictions. I would have thought a ten-year space after the sixties would have led to the revival of some kind of movement.

"But it seems to me that there are all kinds of issues today that might inspire a mass movement even beyond our borders, whether it's homelessness and hunger or the environment, there are issues. It could be that the people have a sense that leadership is meeting, negotiating, talking about these issues, and this brings a lull where otherwise people would be out in the streets. That's among the people who do vote. And then it could be that the political underclass—I don't mean the racial underclass, but there's a political underclass—has just given up. So if you have a tacit belief in leadership, you know, that Bush and Gorbachev are going to work something out, then those millions of people are going to tend to stay within the system instead of going in the streets. And if the more alienated constituency has given up, then you have a very low likelihood of either an impetus to reform or to militance. That's what we have now.

"Given the alternative, people will always prefer evolution to revolution. I think [Richard] Flacks [the New Left sociologist] is right about that. I'd go further: People will always prefer apathy. It's actually the American way. If you look at the country's history, the entitlement to life, liberty and the pursuit of happiness is a private entitlement to a good private life. And the democratic calling, as I read our country's history, is reserved for when it is necessary. It's a responsibility, it's a burden that has to be taken up when government fails. But it's not been seen except by liberals and idealists as a high human calling. It's been seen as dirty work that somebody has to do. The less government the better. And that's the American cultural balance: Democracy as a system that can be utilized when all else fails in terms of private attempts to build a good life for yourself or your family. So, apathy is the most common political response called for by the way the system is set up.

"Evolutionary reform is the second response that is expected, and revolutionary consciousness is predictable only at certain moments of almost complete breakdown, where you have to get involved, you can't be apathetic, and where the system of reform doesn't seem to work effectively enough. And you've had that throughout American history. As Flacks I think points out, there have been periods of extreme militance—the abolitionists, the Civil War, labor violence, the sixties, generally at points when the system had failed. But even in those periods, the outcome so far, in our history, is that under radical pressure, the system tends to accommodation and flexibility.

"After much sacrifice, a lot of blood is spilled, people's hearts are broken, the reform comes. Often the reformers and the radicals and the revolutionaries are very unhappy and get no satisfaction, but for the mass of people, the reform comes, whether it's the eighteen-year-old vote or the Voting Rights Act for southern blacks.

"I'd like nothing better than to live a private life and contemplate my existence and life's meaning and be a writer and be a good parent and enjoy living in southern California and playing baseball and going fishing and skiing and reading. I love life. But I don't think I've ever been comfortable with that being my whole life. I have a desire also to translate my ideals and my ideas into action, and so I've always been a political animal as well. And I enjoy the rough and tumble of politics and movements and trying to accomplish change. And if the need arises, I'm ready for the barricades too. But I think it's unhealthy to live solely for the barricades because it leads to frustration and burnout. But there is something important to it because private life and merely participating in civic reform doesn't touch the soul.

"There's, I think, a desire for greatness and transcendence in the soul that is met only by revolutionary moments when everything is at stake. And this may be merely a man's view of the world, but it's certainly true of young men. It's why they are fascinated with war. It's why mass movements are typically powered by young people, even if they're led by older people. The jails are filled typically by younger people, and the battlefields are covered with the bodies of young people. And I don't know what that is—the desire to test yourself, the desire to encounter death and see what you're made of? I wish it was more noble than that. I mean it is also, I think, the desire to live your ideals. But it's very existential. And it does meet a certain need, I think, that humans have.

"First and foremost, we all have to decide on what we consider to be a useful and right livelihood. And I think being in elective office is one such livelihood. That's on the level of organizing your life in a useful way, which I think is the most important thing. As far as a strategy, obviously there's a range of ways that social change is achieved, and in a parliamentary, democratic system, politics is one of them. I don't place a weight on what is the most important. I don't think that there's a necessarily more moral or more practical approach for all times and all places.

"Also, I happen to like the work. There's all kinds of speculation about why one would continue to do this. And I don't mean to oversimplify, but it comes down to liking the work. If you like it too much, you become an addict to it and too much of a political animal. But if you view it not as an occupation that you're enslaved to for purposes of fame and ego gratification, but if you view it as a craft, then it becomes something that's your work. You work at it. And every day, if you're looking for it, every day's got some new challenge or something new to learn about, something new to get better at, or some fault to try to correct. So it gives a certain texture and meaning to life that I find, on balance, very satisfying. Stimulating.

"I enjoyed the first two elections, which was very much a referendum for the voters on whether they were comfortable with somebody with the image of Tom Hayden being in office. That was a truly emotional experience, and it was reaffirming. In terms of legislation, not just in terms of campaigns, I have some special interests: the conditions of working women—issues like video display terminal safety, pay equity. I have committed a lot of time to working women's issues, and I do see some small changes. Also the reform of California's system of higher education, which again is a major legislative commitment. And there have been some small changes in terms of under-graduate education and the empowerment of students as a whole new generation of activists on the campuses that I'm trying to work with. And I guess I'm probably known most for environmental issues, the cleanup of Santa Monica Bay and the passage of an anti-toxics measure in 1986.

"I don't know where the energy comes from to keep on doing this. I think it's ultimately unknowable. People will speculate on it and try to individualize it, or psychologize it. But my answer is, I think you have to generate a sense of interest in politics as a craft. What makes writers want to write all their lives? They get a joy out of writing. Or they get meaning in their lives out of writing. If you're a political organizer, you've got to get joy out of the process of organizing and meaning out of it. You can't measure it in terms of what the results are always going to be. People who tie dry flies to catch rainbow trout do it their whole lives. And nobody thinks they're odd. It's a craft.

"I mean you have to really enjoy the process, and I think that means that you get some ego satisfaction about having an effect, and you get some window into yourself, so that through the process you're seeing things about yourself that enable you to enjoy your life, or change your life, as you wish to. And if it's not there, you can't go on. You become a zombie. I mean there are zombies in office who are there for the pension, or there 'cause they don't have any other place to be. I don't know any other answer.

"Beyond that, you have to ask whether you have a messianic complex or a martyr's complex. And even if I do, it's not much of an answer for anybody else. You've gotta be looking for a common answer that ties you to other people, otherwise you have to view yourself as a purely isolated individual.

"Being a parent definitely has an effect on what I do. I think I would be involved in politics as craft with or without kids. But in many ways, the pull of parenting is away from politics. I know I've made choices based on being a parent not to pursue certain career options. So, I see personal life and political life as being at odds with each other on some basic level, as well as creatively intersecting. But I've never found them to be mutually reinforcing or a perfect balance.

"It's more than just the time you spend away from home. I think that political work is somewhat desensitizing. That's why so many people need time off. They go home after work, and they need to cool out for two hours. It's because nobody has found a way to make work a matter of ecstasy. There's a lot of boredom to it that you have to go through and a lot of pressure and stress and competition and viciousness and backbiting and power plays, and it's inherent. And the love of power and the power of love are two very different things. Very different.

"Twenty-five years ago I was more innocently optimistic, and today I have more of a sense of tragedy that scars my idealism. But I know that you have to be idealistic as a necessity. I mean the world's not gonna get better through pessimism, although some have made that argument. Conservatives make that argument. But I don't think there's any choice. I just finished Michael Harrington's book, which he wrote just before he died. And he seems to me to come to many of the same conclusions. I mean there's a lot of statements of doubt in there when it comes to predicting the future, but what's the choice?

"He says the choice is to be involved in what he calls visionary gradualism. And I think that's right. You have to have vision because good things flow from good instinct and good desires. You have to be gradualist because no matter how hard you try, change in social structures, not to mention human behavior, is slow—for the most part. Occasionally, there's a revolutionary moment, but for the most part, evolutionary politics is not a choice, as if there's an alternative. It's inevitable."

Tom Hayden was the Renaissance man of sixties politics, emerging from student activism and the early civil rights movement to draft the New Left's first national manifesto, organize the urban poor and help direct some of the era's major anti-war protests. Few individuals have been at the forefront of so many significant political events—but hundreds were there in the ranks, running mimeograph machines, making phone calls, painting placards and collecting donations. And millions more answered the call for the demonstrations and marches Hayden and others organized. Throughout the sixties, political activity of all kinds, from lunch counter sit-ins to mass rallies, cumulatively attracted close to ten million people, many of whom believed they had a personal responsibility to contribute to the process of social change. Sincere political activists—both the leaders and the rank and file—felt a moral obligation to act on behalf of the social vision they shared. They saw politics not only as a means of creating a humane social system but also as a way of finding meaning in personal life.

Of course, not all political activists of the era were sincere. In fact, as documents procured under the Freedom of Information Act later revealed, an astounding number were FBI and CIA "plants" who not only successfully infiltrated most major left-wing groups but often acted as *agents provocateurs*, spurring the groups to dangerous, usually self-defeating action. To others, political activism may have been an ego-drenched romantic fantasy. But to a large number, the commitment was real.

The fact that many of these activists were college-educated kids from comfortable middle class homes was, then and now, used against them to disparage the movements they were a part of and call into question the depth of their political commitment. But history shows that middle class malcontents have been the backbone of many of this country's radical and reform movements. Merchants from the just-emerging middle class played a significant role in the American Revolution. Middle class men and women were vital to the social movements for abolition, urban reform and temperance. Middle-class women mounted and sustained the fight for women's right to vote. Journalists and political reformers raked the muck and busted the trusts in the early part of this century. There is no denying that populism, unionism and some strains of socialism had their roots in the working class, nor that many of the most dedicated early civil rights workers and black, brown and red power advocates were themselves poor. But in America, much political action has come from the bourgeoisie, and the sixties were no exception.

Nor were the sixties an exception to the rule that political activity in this country seems to come in great concerted bursts with many different movements emerging almost simultaneously from the same spirit of reform and rebellion. In the decades before the Civil War, abolition, women's suffrage and temperance coexisted, with many of the same people working for all three causes. At the turn of the century, socialism, progressivism and feminism vied for public attention. In the sixties, the civil rights movement segued into the anti-war movement; the black, brown and red power movements emerged within months of each other; feminism and gay liberation surfaced soon thereafter. As Buffalo Springfield sang portentously in 1967: "Something's happening here / What it is ain't exactly clear."

And it wasn't clear, not to those inside the movements nor those outside. For all the media attention given to the radical leaders and the big demonstrations of the sixties, the movements of the era were essentially leaderless and fairly disorganized. The notion that seven or eight leaders orchestrated (or conspired to orchestrate) everything that happened in Chicago in 1968 was, in movement circles, laughable. While a certain amount of planning was part of any event, people who went to demonstrations knew that spontaneity, individuality and inspired anarchism were as much or more a part of the day as were scheduled speakers.

Ideology didn't unite the movements either. True, the many groups making up the student, anti-war, feminist and various power movements shared a basic opinion: "The system" no longer worked. But the radicals among them believed that America's problems stemmed from monopoly capitalism and that the fundamental structure of society must be changed, while the reformers wanted substantive changes within the system to make it more equitable and inclusive. Within the radical camp, there were significant divisions not only among various left-wing sects, but also between those who believed in the inevitability of a working class revolution and those who believed that they personally should act as the source of revolutionary violence. For some, race divided the society into "us" and "them;" for others, the divider was class; still others focused on gender.

But most of the millions of people who took part in the political activities of the sixties were not impelled by ideology. Various "grouplets" might indulge in heated debates over the relative merits of Maoism or Marxism—and certainly some groups self-destructed over these ideological battles—but what most demonstration- and rally-goers cared about were issues: making integration a reality, stopping the war, ending unequal treatment of women and minorities. Lacking leaders, organization and common ideology, the political movements of the sixties existed on energy born equally of anger and optimism, and on commitment to the issues as they unfolded.

The height of sixties' political activism may have been in the last few years of the decade, but the seeds were sown generations earlier for what would become the New Left. In fact, the old American Left had enjoyed its heyday a half a century before. In 1912, the country had a socialist congressman, 79 socialist mayors in 24 cities, and numerous state legislators and elected officials in more than 300 municipalities. More than 1,000 socialists held elected office in 1912, the year a million Americans voted for Socialist party leader Eugene V. Debs for president.

But deep disagreements about America's involvement in World War I, coupled with ideological differences made apparent by the Bolshevik revolution, caused the bitter infighting that began a decades-long decline of the Left. For a brief moment in the 1930s, the radical Left appeared united under the Popular Front banner, which attracted distinguished artists, writers and intellectuals to the Communist party. But intense factionalism continued to erode the movement from inside, while McCarthyism battered it from the outside. By the late fifties, when Tom Hayden and other New Left pioneers were in college, the Old Left was old in the very worst senses of the word: weak, ailing and cantankerous.

The student movement that began in the late 1950s was born of—but almost immediately moved to disinherit itself from—the Old Left. While some of its founders were literally children of the Old Left—the sons and daughters of Communist party and ex-Communist party members, known as "red diaper babies"—others were less self-conscious heirs to the traditions of the American radicalism. The issues that compelled this new generation were far-flung: the suffocating conformity of the mass culture, the segregation and racial violence in the South, the growth of the military-industrial complex and, perhaps above all, the threat of nuclear annihilation. These pre-Vietnam New Lefties, as Todd Gitlin says, "aspired to become the voice, conscience, and goad of [their] generation."

In the late fifties and early sixties, the student movement began to develop at different college campuses throughout the country, the same places that, ten years later, would still be political hot spots. In Berkeley, students formed SLATE, a reform-minded campus political party. At Harvard, the Committee for a Sane Nuclear Policy sponsored rallies and Tocsin, a left-wing reformist student group, attracted some of the best and the brightest (including Gitlin). Meanwhile in Ann Arbor, Al Haber, a campus hanger-on and son of a university professor, quietly moved in to take over an almost defunct New York–based student organization called the Student League for Industrial Democracy (SLID). A 1905 offshoot of the League for Industrial Democracy (LID), itself an offshoot of once-powerful trade unions like the International Ladies' Garment Workers' Union, SLID was little more than a mailing list and a dusty desk when Haber recruited a few University of Michigan students (including Hayden) to the organization. He soon renamed it Students for a Democratic Society (SDS).

By the late sixties, SDS would be the largest organization of the New Left, with 100,000 members and hundreds of campus chapters. It would, in fact, become the largest American organization anywhere on the Left in fifty years. But in 1960 it consisted of Haber working a mimeograph machine in New York, Hayden reporting in from the civil rights battles in Mississippi and Georgia and a few dozen activists at Oberlin and Swathmore. What SDS was really about was not articulated until June of 1962 when, at the organization's summer convention, Hayden presented the New Left's first manifesto, the Port Huron Statement. "We are the people of this generation, bred in at least modest comfort, housed in universities, looking uncomfortably to the world we inherit," it began. "We would replace power rooted in possession, privilege, or circumstance by power and uniqueness rooted in love, reflectiveness, reason and creativity. As a social system, we seek the establishment of a democracy of individual participation. . . . If we appear to seek the unattainable . . . then let it be known that we do so to avoid the unimaginable." From its inception, SDS thought of itself as "the vanguard for a swelling social force," according to Gitlin, who succeeded Tom Hayden as the organization's president in 1963. There was a strong feeling that "SDS stood for students-as-a-whole, and students-as-a-whole stood for the young."

Although neither SDS nor any other single organized group dominated New Left politics in the years that followed, the intuition proved correct: There was, indeed, a swelling social force. The civil rights movement had ignited a flame; America's growing involvement in Vietnam fanned it. In April 1965, 25,000 students—as many protestors as there were at the time U.S. troops in Vietnam—marched against the war in Washington, D.C. By the end of the year, President Johnson had committed 184,000 troops. At the close of 1966, 385,000 military personnel were in Vietnam. For the next five years, the war would be become the focal point of leftist political activity.

In the spring of 1967, with troop strength edging above 400,000, a throng of somewhere between 125,000 (police estimates) and 400,000 (organizer estimates) listened to Martin Luther King, Jr. call on blacks and "all white people of good will" to boycott the Vietnam War by becoming conscientious objectors. In July of that year, General William Westmoreland, the man in charge of running U.S. operations in Vietnam, asked the president for more money and more troops, stating publicly: "We are winning, slowly but steadily." As the body count climbed, Johnson complied, ordering 50,000 more men and women to Vietnam. Meanwhile, the Air Force was running 2,000 missions a week, and the U.S. had already defoliated almost two million acres in South Vietnam. The October March Against the Pentagon brought more than 100,000 protestors to Washington, but, even as anti-war sentiment spread, the Left was feeling increasingly helpless to affect government policy.

By 1968, the protest against the war was moving into the mainstream. Wisconsin senator Eugene McCarthy surfaced as an anti-war candidate for the presidency. Baby doctor Benjamin Spock, Yale chaplain William Sloan Coffin and Catholic priest Daniel Berrigan were all convicted of anti-war activities. The Quakers, Unitarians and Methodists publicly condemned U.S. bombing policy. But U.S. involvement continued to escalate, with 530,000 American troops in Vietnam, 50,000 dead and 100 billion dollars already spent. The American military was in the process of dropping what would be, by the end of the war, four times as much bombing tonnage as was dropped during the entire second World War, including Hiroshima and Nagasaki.

In a time of such violence and aggression abroad, the two assassinations that rocked America in 1968 seemed horribly consistent. On April 4, Martin

Luther King, Jr. was murdered in Memphis. On June 5, presidential hopeful Robert Kennedy was shot just minutes after claiming victory in the California primary. To the Left, which had been momentarily buoyed by Johnson's decision to take himself out of the 1968 presidential race, the back-to-back assassinations along with the unrelenting escalation of the war ushered in the beginning of a short-lived era of confrontational politics.

Still, peaceful demonstrations and protests continued through 1968 and 1969, with 200,000 New York high school and college students participating in an anti-war strike, and 85,000 marching down Fifth Avenue. Later, a national student strike involved almost a million college and high school students. But the changing tenor of the times was evident that spring at places like Columbia University. In mid-March 3,500 students and 100 faculty members refused to attend classes as a (quiet) protest against the war. The next month, after several weeks of relatively polite protest concerning the on-campus presence of a cold war think-tank and the university's expansion into the surrounding black community, SDS and local black activists led close to 1,000 Columbia students in a week-long occupation of five campus buildings. It was a watershed for SDS, whose membership soared in the wake of the much-publicized Columbia "victory." More important, it signaled the growing legitimacy of militant protest within the movement. Nowhere was this more evident than that summer when 10,000 assorted radicals gathered in Chicago to hold an alternative presidential convention (a pig was their candidate) and to protest the war. In what a special commission report later termed a "police riot," more than 100 protestors, reporters and photographers were injured, and 350 people were arrested. To some on the Left, notably many of the older, pre-Vietnam era organizers, Chicago was a sign that something very wrong was happening to the movement. Careful study, informed debate, grassroots organizing and peaceful protest, the hallmarks of early sixties political activity, were being replaced by what some considered the self-defeating romantic fantasy of "revolutionary violence." But to others, the Columbia occupation and the Chicago demonstrations were reason for great rejoicing: The Left was willing to fight for what it believed.

At college campuses around the country, students were turning to direct action. From 1968 to 1969, there were more than 100 politically inspired campus bombings, attempted bombings and incidents of arson. In the spring of 1969 alone, 300 of the country's largest colleges and universities, holding a third of American students, saw sizable demonstrations. At one-quarter of them, students led strikes or building take-overs; at one-fifth, there were bombings or property destruction. In April 1969, all eyes turned to Harvard, the bastion of elite education that had supplied so many of the New Frontiersmen for the Kennedy administration, where several hundred students seized the main administration building, ejected nine deans and locked themselves in. In October, the spotlight was on Chicago, where a few hundred people answered the call of the Weathermen, an SDS splinter group, to participate in four "Days of Rage." When the window-smashing, car-trashing melee was over, almost 300 people were under arrest, and 75 police and fifty demonstrators were injured. But, as it turned out, the Weathermen were not the bellwether of the sixties protest movement they claimed to be. They were, instead, the most visible indication that the Left's most powerful organization, SDS, was disintegrating.

There is a saying that if you arm the Left, they'll stand in a circle and shoot each other. Ideologically, that's what happened in 1969 when, at SDS's last national convention, the group split between three warring factions. The Progressive Labor faction (PL), which controlled about a third of the delegates to the convention, had been gaining power within SDS. With their short hair and aversion to rock 'n' roll and other accoutrements of hippiedom that might offend "the workers," PL wanted to "Marxize" SDS and forge a student-worker alliance. Competing with them for the hearts and minds of the membership were two factions stressing Third World connections: the Revolutionary Youth Movement I (RYM I), otherwise known as the Weathermen, and their rivals but short-term allies, RYM II. In the midst of this intense sectarianism sat dazed SDS rank-and-filers who watched as the organization imploded.

Throughout the sixties, SDS leadership had tried to create an umbrella organization of the Left that would lead the fight for social justice. And, although they began by severing ties to the Old Left, they had tried to be reasonably inclusive and to avoid the bitter in-fighting that was the unhappy legacy of the Left. But in the end, the organization fell prey to the same extreme factionalism that had blown apart the once-powerful Socialist party fifty years earlier. When SDS fell apart in 1969, it left in its wake a ragged collection of small, fractious collectives, many of which went underground in the seventies: the Weathermen (soon to be renamed the Weather Underground), the Revolutionary Union, the October League, the New World Liberation Front, the Red Guerilla Family, the August 29 Movement and the Communist Labor party, to name a few.

The internecine ideological skirmishes of the late sixties were extremely important—but only to a very small group of people. The majority of those on the Left were either unaware of or uninterested in these battles. But few could miss other ominous signs that the movement was in trouble. Charles Manson, arrested a day after the Days of Rage for a series of grisly murders he and his "family" had committed that summer, looked and lived like a hippie. He and his long-haired followers made music, took LSD, lived communally and used the jargon of the Left. The Weathermen praised him for "offing those rich pigs," as leader Bernardine Dohrn put it, but others were increasingly queasy. Was Manson a natural byproduct of the movement as it was evolving? The gruesome violence at the Rolling Stones' Altamont concert two months later again called attention to the dark side of sixties culture.

Just a few months earlier, more than 300,000 people had peacefully coexisted in the mud at Woodstock. But at the racetrack southeast of San Francisco, with security provided by the Hell's Angels, a black man was stabbed, beaten and kicked to death while dozens of concert-goers looked on. Violence seemed endemic. In Chicago, police fired nearly 100 shots into the apartment of two sleeping Black Panther leaders, killing Fred Hampton and Mark Clark. In a Greenwich Village townhouse, three members of the Weather Underground died when a bomb they were assembling went off. At the courthouse in San Rafael, California, seventeen-year-old Jonathan Jackson ("Soledad Brother" George Jackson's brother) led a kamikaze raid that left him, two prisoners and a judge dead. In Madison, Wisconsin, a graduate student working late into the night at the Army Mathematics Research Center became the first casualty of a movement bombing. To some, it seemed as if the youth culture was becoming, in Gitlin's words, a "death culture."

But the mass movement, compelled by the one overwhelming issue of the day—the war—continued on. A week after the Days of Rage, hundreds of thousands gathered in Boston, New York, Detroit, Chicago, New Haven and Washington, D.C., to protest the war. In mid-November, three quarters of a million people—the largest single protest in American history—took part in the Vietnam Moratorium. The next spring, when Nixon announced that U.S. troops had invaded Cambodia, college campuses erupted. At Kent State, after a demonstration and some rock-throwing, Ohio National Guardsmen opened fire on unarmed students, killing four and wounding nine. Within a week, student strikes closed more than 100 colleges across the nation. At Jackson State in Mississippi, two black students were killed and eleven injured.

At the time, it felt as if the anti-war movement was being reinvigorated, but in retrospect, the post-Cambodia uprisings were the last hurrah of the student movement. Campus protest continued, but there were fewer demonstrations in 1970–71 than in the year before, and fewer still in 1971–72. But in the wake of the Cambodia invasion and, a year later, the Pentagon Papers revelations, liberals were finally flooding the anti-war movement. The war, meanwhile, was very slowly winding down. In September of 1970, troop strength in Vietnam fell below 400,000 for the first time since early 1967. The now-old New Left—weakened by factionalism, split over the issue of "revolutionary violence" and disillusioned by its own lack of power—was disbanding. Tiny underground cadres (one of which claimed 25 bombings in the Bay Area in 1975) remained, as did a few small, above ground organizations. The New American Movement, a group of local coalitions trying to evolve a socialist model suited to the American experience, claimed 1,000 members and forty chapters in the mid-seventies. The Midwest Academy in Chicago trained radical organizers. Members of the Washington, D.C.–based Fifth Estate Lecture Bureau toured 27 states in 1975, lecturing on how to thwart the government's domestic intelligence-gathering.

Most of those who continued their political activism through the seventies continued to be driven by particular issues. Feminism, environmentalism (especially the anti-nuclear movement) and gay liberation emerged as important mass movements, although certainly not on the scale of the anti-war movement. Many former sixties activists, although continuing to "think globally," were now, in the absence of an overarching movement for social justice, "acting locally." They banded together to shut down nuclear power plants, clean up rivers, organize community centers and elect local officials who would reflect their values and priorities. To society at large, selectively informed by the mass media, it looked as if political activism died when the Paris peace pacts were signed, in January 1973, and the last U.S. troops left Vietnam, two months later. But for many sixties veterans, strong political commitment continued.

To understand the persistence of this commitment, MIT psychologist Kenneth Keniston suggests forgetting the widely held "radical rebel hypothesis," the view that radicalism is merely the neurotic, adolescent rebellion of kids against their parents and, by extension, adult society. Keniston, who has spent years studying the New Left, says no, that for most radicals, politics comes not from youthful rebellion but from principle—and principle stays with you for the rest of your life. The studies of other psychologists and sociologists bolster this theory. University of Arizona researcher Doug McAdam tracked down hundreds of mostly white northern Freedom Summer volunteers and found that those who made the trip to Mississippi in 1964 were still living the effects of that radicalization more than twenty years later. In another survey of civil rights activists, Florida State University sociologist James Fendrich found that more than half called themselves "radicals" ten years after their participation in the movement. Berkeley Free Speech Movement activists questioned fifteen years after their involvement were far more likely to hold radical political beliefs than their nonactivist contemporaries. "They have grown up," concludes the psychologist Alberta Nassi, "but they do not appear to have grown out of the political philosophy that galvanized their activist youth." In a study comparing activist and nonactivist University of Michigan undergraduates, sociologists Dean Hoge and Teresa Ankney found that ten years after their involvement, activists were more interested in political affairs, more suspicious of free enterprise ideology, more opposed to fears of communism and more alienated from the military than their nonactivist contemporaries. A very recent investigation of a group of former radical commune members found that thirteen of the sixteen people, all of whom are now in their forties, continue to identify themselves as "socialists" or "progressives."

These and other surveys clearly show that many sixties activists maintain their leftist political philosphy as they grow older. But what of their activism? Here the results are less dramatic. The former Free Speech Movement activists, for example, were only slightly more likely than their nonactivist contemporaries to be members of sociopolitical organizations. Of the sixteen radical commune members, who twenty years ago were involved in anti-war protests, military resistance, the Chicano and Native American movements and various countercultural activities, today only four consider themselves politically active. Of eighteen radicals involved in the burning of the Bank of America branch in Isla Vista, California, seven remained politically active in the intervening fifteen years.

Why are some sixties veterans strongly committed to leftist philosophy yet less active than they used to be? There's no easy answer. Studies indicate that former sixties activists are less likely to suffer from the "careerism" of their nonactivist contemporaries (see "Right Livelihood") that would make outside commitments difficult. On the other hand, many choose socially-conscious jobs that often require long hours for relatively low pay. Those who have decided to have children—especially those who have waited until their thirties—want to spend not just "quality time" (the yuppie euphemism for sandwiching your child between career obligations) but quantity time. It is not simply that "career and family"—the growing responsibilities of middle adulthood—have caught up with sixties activists. It is the *types* of careers they've chosen and the *quality* of family life they are striving for.

But the changes in their personal lives account for only some of the slackening in their political involvement. As the seventies progressed, it became increasingly difficult to sustain political activism, even for those who had the time and energy. With the Left fragmented, localized and often isolated, there seemed to be fewer and fewer opportunities for effective action. And in some ways, the need for intense activism seemed to diminish. As sociologists Jack Whalen and Richard Flacks theorize in *Beyond the Barricades*, flagging activism may be the result of sixties activists seeing that the apocalypse they predicted did not come to pass. "Instead of intensifying polarization and hardening repression, the early to mid-seventies was a time of accommodation and reform," they write. "It did not seem far-fetched by the mid-seventies to imagine that a revival of the New Deal coalition, invigorated by increasingly politicized minority communities, by a burgeoning of left-leaning educated workers, and by the women's movement, could win majority support for a new era of progressive reform."

Some of those reforms did materialize—from tougher pollution standards to *Roe v. Wade*—but the new era of the eighties was hardly progressive. Running for office in California in 1976, Tom Hayden proclaimed that "the radicalism of the sixties is the common sense of the seventies." But with the move to the right during the eighties, this "common sense" began to look very much like radicalism once again, and veteran activists have found themselves and their concerns, if marginalized, still as "relevant" as ever.

This section of the book includes interviews with a wide range of political activists, from those who participate in mainstream politics to those working for change outside traditional structures. Most of these people have been active, to one degree or another, throughout their adult lives. Charlie Dee, a serious socialist who became a committed citizen activist in Milwaukee, Wisconsin, came close to representing that city in Congress. Richard Schoeninger, an itinerant hippie in the sixties, was elected mayor of Eureka Springs, Arkansas. Former underground journalist Geoff Rips is now the policy coordinator for Jim Hightower, Texas's fighting populist Secretary of Agriculture. Outside the mainstream politics, ex-University of Wisconsin student leader Max Elbaum is now a leader in Line of March, a Marxist-Leninist organization. Mindy Lorenz, an anti-war veteran, is coordinator of the Greens national clearinghouse. Former SDS national secretary Greg Calvert is "acting locally" as president of a grassroots neighborhood organization.

Several sixties veterans are involved in labor issues. Ellen David Friedman, a high school activist whose commitment deepened with age, is an organizer for Vermont's largest union. Fred Miller, founder of the Long Beach *Free Press* and now a waiter in San Francisco, is active with the Culinary Workers, that city's largest and most racially diverse union. Ellen Bravo, who began marching against the war in 1965, helps organize office workers as the head of 9-to-5's largest chapter, in Milwaukee.

New Left historian Kirkpatrick Sale estimates that the protest movements of the sixties left behind two to three million men and women who will call themselves radical for life. Many have learned the two big lessons of the sixties: "everything is political" and "the issues are interrelated." Like the people in this section, they will continue to work for change. They will, in the words of a sociologist who studies former activists, "continue to exert a force in American politics consistent with their long-held beliefs."

With his close-cropped, neatly styled blond hair and guileless good looks, Charlie Dee looks like a small-town midwestern businessman. You could imagine him organizing a Jaycee benefit or speaking at a Toastmasters' banquet. But Charlie has spent most the past twenty years in the trenches, fighting for social and political change.

The product of an upper middle class St. Louis upbringing, he lettered in five sports in high school and went to a private liberal arts college that, even at the height of the sixties, had more radicals on the faculty than in the student body. Charlie played basketball—but he also joined the anti-war movement. After graduating in 1969 and spending a year "hanging out and being a hippie" in Boston, he began a Ph.D. program in American Studies at the University of Iowa. There he became increasingly politically active and met a mentor who taught him Marxism over late night beers.

"It was that class analysis that fueled my emotional desire to get the hell off of safe university campuses where talk was cheap and it was easy to be a radical. Right around that time, I heard one of the most powerful speeches I've ever heard in my life, a speech by Stokely Carmichael. He said this incredible thing: This movement, the anti-Vietnam War movement, has been comprised of the privileged, white, upper middle class. He was describing me. And he said that those people have been brought up to expect that when they want a new bike, they can get a new bike. When they want a college education, they could get a college education. So why are we surprised that when they decide that a war is wrong and a socio-economic system is wrong, they could expect that they could change it in the next year because they are used to getting what they want.

"He said, it is important to recognize that this is an historical point of view, and that the energy you spend today trying to change the world is no less important if those changes do not occur until after you're dead than if they occur within the next year. And what upper middle class kids—and he was saying this to an audience filled with them—have to understand is that the struggle for change is an extremely long struggle, and there are many heroes who have gone before us. Everyone has a role to play. But it ain't gonna change overnight. And you have to judge your own role and the tactics you choose based on the long historical view rather than that of the spoiled child who gets whatever he wants.

"I mean, holy shit. He was talking right to my soul. And I recognized instantly that he was right. I'm not saying that instantly I internalized all of this and understood precisely what it meant. But I knew that I was part of the problem he was describing. I began to think of my role for the long haul, not just how are we going to get people to the next meeting or the next demonstration.

"So at that point, I felt that the major decisions in my life were going to be made based on what was best, what would most push ahead the movement for social change. I didn't know specifically what that meant in terms of what organizations I would be part of or how I would make my living, but I knew I wanted to be where there were more experienced radicals that I could learn from."

Charlie left school without his Ph.D., spent two years in San Francisco as part of a socialist collective—"my apprenticeship on the Left," he calls it—and then moved back to the midwest to join the Wisconsin Alliance. The statewide activist-socialist group was attempting workplace organization by gaining control of local shops and unions. For the next six years, Charlie hid his educational background and took jobs based on the priorities of the organization, from working the graveyard shift at a Briggs and Stratten factory to serving as an emergency room orderly.

In 1979, disaffected with the Alliance and now the father of an infant son he hardly saw, Charlie began to build a teaching career. As an instructor at Milwaukee Area Technical College, he immediately became involved in curriculum reform and joined the teachers' union. In addition to the remedial English classes he was hired to teach, he started teaching a course on foreign policy issues and initiated the first course in the Wisconsin higher education system on the history of the Vietnam War period. He made himself an expert on Central American issues and, in the summer of 1982, he was one of 22 people selected statewide to visit Nicaragua.

"The trip really represented a transformation in my thinking because up to that time I had stayed out of electoral politics. My seventeen or eighteen years of experience to that time was always around issues. I looked down my nose at electoral politics as sleazy, based on personality, filled with superficial people I had no respect for—and I wasn't going to waste my time. But because of the trip to Nicaragua—seeing, eating and drinking with people whose lives depended on sometimes one-vote margins in the Senate and the House on aid to terrorists, that convinced me that for someone like myself to remain out of electoral politics was not only stupid and pretentious, but was a real disservice to the movement for change in the United States. So I came back from Nicaragua and started lobbying. I participated in a congressional campaign, and our congressman was elected. But more important, I became active in lobbying for Central American issues. I started hanging around more in Democratic party circles, becoming more active.

"Then I heard this speech by Ed Garvey—organizer and former leader of the Football Players Association, the first person to organize professional athletes into a union, and get them into the AFL-CIO. Ed had come to Wisconsin to become assistant attorney general and then was running for U.S. Senate against an incumbent Republican in 1986. I heard the guy give a speech in Christmas of 1984, and I thought, Jesus Christ, this guy sounds like *me*. He has the same analysis of the world as I do—and he has the chance to be a U.S. senator. So I wrote him a letter and I said I had two goals: one was to defeat the incumbent Republican senator, the other was to transform the thinking of the Democratic party on foreign policy issues. And I said we ought to get together because I was willing to work my ass off for him. So we got together. We instantly liked each other, and I gave a year-and-a-half of my life to his campaign. I became his issues and research director. I took a partial leave of absence, and a corresponding 8,000 dollar cut in pay.

"My activities with him gave me a new kind of credibility and acceptance by labor honchos. And one of the things I decided from that was that all of my previous stereotypes of people involved in electoral politics—although there were exceptions—were accurate. It is a dirty business filled with sleazy, superficial people. But I also realized that I could do what it took to be elect-ed, and that my skills were at a higher level than some of the people who were out there running for office. So I sort of got the notion during the Garvey campaign that if the right opening came up, I might run for office."

In 1988, Charlie ran for the U.S. House of Representatives from Milwaukee as "part of Milwaukee's new generation of leaders . . . the citizens' voice for Congress," according to his campaign literature. He mounted a professional campaign, and was considered one of the top candidates when the incumbent congressman, who had previously announced that he would be running for a vacant Senate seat, changed his mind. Charlie dropped out of the race and endorsed him. Since then, Charlie has continued to teach and remain active in community affairs.

"I don't think my vision of the world is substantially different now from what it was in 1970. The shortest version of that vision is that the history of the world as well as the present reality of the world are characterized primari-ly by a struggle between the wealthy and powerful, who want to maintain their wealth and power, and the majority of the people, who are neither rich nor powerful, and want to achieve more of each. I think that is the best tool for analyzing history and the best tool for analyzing present reality. I stand clearly with the powerless and poor in their struggle. And I don't think that's changed.

"What I do think has changed is the role I play in that struggle and the tactics that are appropriate at this historical moment to achieve a change in the world. I think those things have gone through major, major changes for me. Part of these changes are due to changes in the world, in objective reality, and part are due to what, for lack of a better term, I'd call my maturity. I am much more selective in who I brand as enemies now. I have a much clearer vision of where my talents and energies can be used most effectively. And I think I have a lot clearer vision of the allies one can have in trying to effect social change.

"Right now I'm working with a group of people who are taking two targeted neighborhoods in the city of Milwaukee and offering income to everyone who is below poverty level in those neighborhoods if they will be part of our demonstration experimental program instead of county, state and federal welfare programs. We want to show through job training, wage subsidies, and providing health care and day care, that the same amount of dollars that are now being spent on welfare programs which are breeding a culture of dependency, can be spent in a more productive way.

"In this program I am working with presidents of banks, executive directors, a group of CEOs and presidents of insurance companies. I am working with people that it would have been very easy to identify as enemies twenty years ago. But I am working with them very effectively because there is a common interest.

"I've got certain skills. And one of the things I can do is sit down with rich and powerful people and try to identify what kind of shared interest we have and how we can accomplish things without being intimidated. In some ways that's a result of my background. I grew up and went to school with the sons and daughters of rich and powerful people who intended to become rich and powerful themselves, and I was able to beat their brains out on the basketball and football fields—so now I'm not intimidated when I sit down in a meeting room with them.

"People sometimes say I'm cynical because I'm so critical of things, but my response is, cynicism is a world view, it's not a particular critique of anything. There are still things that just outrage me, but I think I still believe in the capacity of people to change, the capacity of conditions to change, and of institutions to play a more positive role."

ELLEN DAVID FRIEDMAN, 37
1970: student activist
1989: union organizer

Ellen became an activist early in life. At fifteen, she was picketing Long Island grocery stores in support of the United Farm Workers' grape boycott and attending a class in Marxism taught by Michael Harrington. While still in high school she did door-to-door fundraising for ghetto education projects. The daughter of liberals—her father was the director of the New York City Commission on Human Rights, her mother was involved in Women's Strike for Peace—she enrolled at Radcliffe in 1970. There she quickly became involved in the anti-war movement, emerging Central American issues, community organizing and the formal study of political economy and Marxism.

"As soon as I began reading critiques of capitalism, I was completely captivated intellectually with the analysis of historical materialism, dialectical materialism, and that became a tremendous intellectual structure for me. I studied anthropology and read structural anthropologists, and I studied psychology, and at that time there was such a trend of intellectual ferment to rethink all of these disciplines from a materialist point of view. So, my consciousness was changing, and these changes became and still are part of my world view. But even though I loved intellectual examination and discourse, what I really always loved more was organizing, particularly organizing not within the Left per se, but both class and labor organizing.

"It must have been that second day of school, there was a demonstration in Harvard Yard and Cheyney Ryan [Harvard anti-war leader expelled the previous year] came to speak. If I remember it all correctly, Harvard security police swooped down and yanked him off the stage and tried to pull him out of the yard. The result was that he was arrested, and a bunch of us were arrested and brought to Middlesex courthouse. They brought us in but they never actually pressed charges, except against him. So he had charges brought against him, and the next week there was a hearing on these charges, and the same group of us went back to the courthouse and disrupted the proceedings and were all sort of rounded up again. Once again we were sort of restrained, but didn't have any charges pressed, and then had to come back the next week for the next hearing, and the same thing happened again. For me, this was a very important indication of what was what.

At Harvard, Ellen moved through SDS, the Progressive Labor (PL) faction and the New American Movement (NAM), becoming increasingly fed up with the sectarianism of the Left. In 1974, she graduated and moved to Vermont, where she almost immediately became involved in creating alternative structures like food coops and health clinics. She also became a grassroots community organizer who attempted to forge ties between radical youth and working class people.

"I was living in collectives with lots of people and growing a lot of food and cutting our own wood and heating with wood and cooking with wood— the whole nine yards. It's very interesting in Vermont. While it's true that there were many years of mutual suspicion and isolation from local folks, it's also the case that Vermont has this native tolerance. So we also made some wonderful friendships with local people who had never seen anything like what we were doing, but it was fine, because they were interested.

"I became the director of the Vermont Alliance, and we decided to raise money and hire a lot of organizers to work in local communities around the state. And I was successful in raising the money. But after a number of years of doing this, I was quite disheartened. I was just not interested in spending my time talking to rich people, to raise money to do this work. It was not my cup of tea. So I left and looked around for a regular working person's job, and I went to work at the grocery store in the town where I was living. I worked there for two years, and it was wonderful, wonderful. I got to know everybody in town, and it was a great place to do organizing. I did a lot of counseling and talking to young people going to school, and that was the time when the nuclear freeze was on, and we were voting in all our town meetings. There was a lot of organizing to be done on that. There was also a real acceleration around organizing, particularly around El Salvador.

"In Chelsea, which is the town where my husband and I have lived for ten years, there was a group of people who we were very close to—we were not all living together, but we had a study group, a traditional Marxist study group that sustained over a period of ten years, met every other week, and we did a lot of projects together."

Ellen has continued working and organizing on the Left through the eighties. In 1981, after returning from a trip to Cuba, she organized the Vermont Solidarity Conference to unite various progressive groups throughout the state. (After the last session was finished, she went into labor and gave birth to her son.) When the effect of that gathering began to wane, she organized the Jobs, Peace and Justice Conference and, just as that was beginning to lose steam, she became involved in building a statewide Rainbow Coalition, which she later chaired.

"What happened with the Rainbow Coalition is that we went to the state nominating convention, the state Democratic convention to nominate delegates in '84, and we knew nothing. I had never been involved in the Democratic party and had no interest in it, really. We had decided there were these seats open for national Democratic committeeman and committee-woman, and had no idea what they were but people thought I could give a good speech, so they said, 'we'll nominate you, and you can just give your speech, and that'll be that.'

"So I gave a speech—and then got elected by these 1,200 delegates. That was really amazing. I was elected to a four-year term as Democratic national committeeperson, which for me was almost unmitigated pain. I've never really had any illusions about taking the Democratic party over or moving it leftward or anything, although in Vermont I think the effect of having such a well-organized Left has been in fact to move the Democratic party a lot to the left. So I did that, and I used it as an opportunity to raise issues and provoke confrontations, particularly within the party here."

Since 1986, Ellen has been an organizer with the Vermont National Education Association, the state's largest and one of its most progressive unions.

"For me, it is the most integrated thing I can do, working with a labor union, because I believe that the class struggle is the engine of change. I think that to be with working class people and to help them organize provides the basis for really helping people see and learn more about the world and about collective self-interest and about the nature of change. And just as a personal matter, it moves me deeply to see people take charge of their lives.

"A major change for me has been in my thinking—and I think this probably has to be true for the Left throughout the world, and certainly in this country—my thinking about socialist construction, particularly at the present moment. I was never starry-eyed about the Soviet Union and Eastern Europe, perhaps a little more starry-eyed about China but I think I have more of a sense of the role and importance of democratic rights, which certainly in my younger years I criticized a little more freely as being bourgeois illusions. But I think that's something that has changed my sense of what the popular struggles are that are going on in Eastern Europe and in China particularly right now, and what that means about how socialism can be built. But I think my basic values are unchanged.

"I'm finally in a job where I'm making an income, and that's a big change for me. I really was essentially supported for many years, either living in a manner that didn't take much, or supported by my husband. And that needed to change for my self-respect. I needed to be able to know that this work was valued enough by someone that they could pay me for it. And that has been wonderful. I think there's probably only one or two jobs in the state that could do that, but this has been a perfect match. And having money to spend and not worrying about paying the bills is a change. It has allowed me to travel a little bit. We've been to Cuba again, and we went to Eastern Europe last year. I value that, but mostly I give a lot of money away, particularly to the Rainbow Coalition.

"I've become a parent, which was another life change. At a certain point I had to realize that I was not taking seriously enough my obligations to either Stuart [her husband] or my son in terms of time. Somehow I felt it was okay to work all day and come home and be on the phone all night or go out to meetings, and go out to meetings every weekend. I would say about three or four years ago, it occurred to me that that was not a good long-term strategy, so I have had to change that. Rather than going home and making a lot of phone calls, I'll stay a little later at work and get them done, so I don't confuse my son, particularly, about what the home is for. That it isn't just an extension of my work life. That was very hard at first; it gets easier as I go along.

"My ideology makes me concerned all the time with the distribution of the world's resources. There's probably not a day that passes when I don't have a conversation about this with my son, to make sure that he understands that the way we live is not the way the world lives. In part, when we went to Eastern Europe, it was with that in mind. It is an area of the world with a great deal of austerity, and that was important for us for him to see. And for us too.''

FRED MILLER, 48
1968: founder, Long Beach (CA) Free Press
1989: waiter/union activist

The son of working class Republicans, Fred was raised in an industrial suburb of Chicago. After graduating from high school in 1958, he drove out to California to visit an older sister and look for work. When he couldn't find a job, he enlisted in the Navy instead, spending the next three and a half years stationed in Long Beach. After he got out, he attended first Long Beach Community College, then Long Beach State College, where he switched his major from electrical engineering to philosophy and joined SNCC.

"I was a working class kid. I was a very superficial thinker. And all of a sudden I was confronted with 'what is good?' I had never thought about anything like that before. It was really the beginning of critical thinking for me. I mean I was never taught to think. It really pisses me off. I think a lot of working class kids were never taught to think. I was never taught to go to the root of things. When I started studying Marxism, that really helped my thinking immensely.''

In the mid-sixties, Fred was an "underground paper boy," traveling up and down the California coast delivering different alternative papers to little stores along the way. Later, he and a small group of friends started a head shop, selling hippie paraphenalia, and using their income to support their political work. In the late sixties, he joined the People's Commune in San Diego, a group involved in anti-war activities, military resistance and publishing the San Diego *Street Journal.*

When the commune fell apart in the early seventies, Fred and some members trekked north to Oregon where they lived in a country commune and started a tree planting cooperative that still exists today. But as he planted saplings sprayed with deer repellent, he noticed some of his co-workers taking sick. Concerned with herbicide use in the forest, Fred and a few others founded the Northwest Coalition for Alternatives to Pesticides (NCAP), which exists today as a powerful lobbying group. For seven years, he was director of NCAP and editor of the group's newsletter. In 1983, he moved to San Francisco.

"I decided to move because I felt I came to a dead end in what I was doing. I wanted the stimulation of a large city with ethnic diversity. So, as a fallback position, I got a job as a waiter. I got a job fast, and I got it at a union restaurant. Once I got my feet underneath me in the job, I started promoting the union. I got myself elected shop steward. At that point, in my restaurant, even mention of the union got people fired. Now there are people who support the union openly.

"So much of the union activity is just getting decent contracts signed, just cost of living stuff, an increase in benefits just to keep up with the cost of medical services. Simply to sign a new contract, without any of the sexy stuff you read about like child care or parental leaves, but just to get a decent wage, is a major issue. The other big issue for me is rejuvenating the union.

"It's been one of the best unions in the country in terms of rejuvenating its membership. But by my estimation, they've really reached only about 2,000 of us out of 13,000. That's a problem, when people don't identify their own interests as one with the larger group of people they work with. It's very difficult to get people motivated, and employers are aware of that.

"Capitalism, racism and patriarchy are so intertwined in the ideology of American life that it's hard to separate them and hard to defeat them. But I think in the workplace, you find that those three things come together more than in any other common facet of life—so it's up to labor to struggle against them.

"I do things differently now than I did before. I'm 48 years old, and I don't have the kind of energy I once had. I have a better perspective. I have a better feeling for what's important. I don't drive myself. I'm an atheist, and I believe there's only one life; this is it. I'm a working class person, and I'm not working solely so I can give my money to poor immigrants or homeless people. I'm working to get a roof over my head, food on the table, and to enjoy the fruits of my labor. Certainly a portion of my money goes to things I just talked about. But a portion of my money goes to—well, I like going out to eat. I like to sample what life has. Life is not only a struggle. That has been a major realization for me.

"I didn't have any problems with turning forty. I've never had any problems with age or aging. What I did have was an insight that I had to stop working seven days a week, ten and twelve hours a day, begin to kind of take a look around me, and, well, smell the roses. And to take the time to do the things that I do with a little more style, a little bit of flair. So the energy for doing things in the political sphere comes from the energy I get from being in the world and enjoying some of the nice things in the world, like friendships and leisurely dinners and going to the race track and traveling and having plants in my house. That has given me the energy and sustenance for the long haul. If I had to live like I lived at one point with twelve of us in a five room house with no hot water, no showers—and a baby. . . . If I had to live my life like that, no thanks. I wouldn't have the energy to do anything else. But since I've experienced all that, it's helped me to understand as I've gotten older that you must pace yourself.

"Still I have this internal battle that surfaces almost on a monthly basis, as regular as periods just about, that, Jesus, Fred, you're just not doing very much. I've tried to analyze this. I mean, am I guilt-tripping myself for not doing stuff or am I actually not doing stuff? And I think what I've found is that my life has a kind of pulsating rhythm. I will be extremely active for some time and then lay back for a while. That's really been my rhythm all my life but I've only just realized it.

"Part of it is figuring out where I fit in. One time when I was kind of depressed, I went to a demonstration, and I looked around me and thought: Jeez, I'm this old, gray-haired guy. I didn't like it. But that was just because I had the blues. But sometimes, in the demonstrations I go to or the meetings I attend, well, I've heard it all before; I've heard it for the past 25 years. And some meetings are poorly run, and I've been there for three hours, and I think 'what the fuck?' It's that I've gone through all that stuff and progressed, and lot of people haven't."

These days, Fred edits a newsletter for workers at his restaurant and has dreams of starting a tri-lingual union newspaper. He helped remodel the union hall and has been organizing cultural activities for members. Fred and his new woman friend recently moved in together. It's the first time in 25 years that he is not living communally or in a group house.

"Back in the seventies, I was involved in a really good political/work/cultural scene, a very integrated life with tree planting and Marxist study groups and great potlucks and knowing this whole range of people and having a small measure of power in the larger world, being able to affect things. I felt in the fabric of things, part of a community, sometimes a leader of a community.

"Now there are no organizations around that I'd like to join, that would provide the political talk as well as the cultural community that I want. So I talk to my friends, of course, but really my politics develop in my own head and from reading. I hunger for the kind of community I used to be part of. Those days were good in a variety of ways. You got a sense of what a community could be."

ELLEN BRAVO, 45
1966: anti-war activist
1989: organizer, 9-to-5

Ellen grew up "on the wrong side of the rapid transit tracks" in otherwise posh Shaker Heights, Ohio. A scholarship got her to Cornell in the fall of 1962 where she studied classics, did support work on Freedom Summer and marched in her first anti-war demonstration. (The thirty marchers were pelted with eggs.) In 1966, she went to Cambridge on a Fulbright fellowship.

"So I had this incredible contradiction between this very elitist thing I was studying and this place I was studying it in, and what else was happening in my life, which was two things: One was that I was in the anti-war movement in England. There was a large group of Americans in London who were doing anti-war activity, and I helped organize what turned into a sit-down protest of the American ambassador speaking at Cambridge. But also I was engaged to and then married to a man who was Greek. And we were involved in the Greek democracy movement, the anti-dictatorship movement, in which I was the only woman and the only American in the group that we worked with. It wasn't so much that they would have kicked you out for being a woman, it was that the other women knew that wasn't what they did, it wasn't their place. They sold raffle tickets and made the food. But I didn't, I went to meetings."

She and her husband moved to Montreal in 1968 and then back to the States in 1970, where Ellen got a job teaching women's studies at a college in Maryland. "There wasn't much to draw on," she remembers. "I was making it up as I went along." She taught in San Diego for a year too, but when she moved back to Baltimore—and got divorced—she found there were no teaching jobs.

"Suddenly I was on my own, and I had to get a job. And I was also doing organizing that I liked in the community, writing for some community newspapers and working with this women's group, the Baltimore Women's Union. So I just got an office job because that's what I'd done in college. I type a hundred words a minute, I have good skills. I knew guys who took jobs, like doing painting or construction work when they needed money, and they were able to continue their organizing work. They would get a job for a while or work part-time. But I couldn't work part-time because office work paid so little money. Then I started thinking, *this* is what I should be organizing around.

"So as early as '74, although I did not know the language for comparable worth, that was the issue. I realized if women don't have economic equality, all the other social issues that we fight for won't be enough. And also, I realized that if we couldn't involve women like the women I worked with, if the women's movement wasn't a movement among these women, it would never succeed. So that really marked a change in focus for me.

"I think the thing that started to change for me was the headiness of the anti-war movement, of thinking we're gonna stop the war, we're gonna change the world, we're gonna win overnight. And realizing of course that it's long-term, much slower change. And that it has to involve the people whose lives are most affected by oppression and exploitation. And that we have to be able to speak in a language that makes sense, instead of the rhetoric that was so prevalent in the student movement. But I didn't change my analysis of what was wrong in the power structure, that the majority of the people weren't really running the country, that it was pockets and not people that determine priorities. That analysis didn't change.

"There were two things from my past that kind of fed into what I was thinking back then. The first was about my mother. She went back to work when—I have a twin sister—when we were fourteen. And she went to work specifically so that she could earn money so that we could go to college. All the years before that my dad had been the only provider. We didn't have a lot of money, but we were okay. We just didn't have money to save for college, we didn't have luxuries or extras. My father had an accident shortly after my mom started working, and it turned out the reason he had the car accident was that he had cataracts. In those days, of course, cataracts were a big deal, so he was out of work sixteen, eighteen months. So suddenly, my mother's income was the only income. And unlike when my father provided the only income, we couldn't make it. We really were having hard times. My mother was a social worker, and she had a college education. And yet she made so little money. And I realized, at the time I just assumed, if your mother was the only person working, then you were in trouble. You know, I didn't ask why that was true, I just knew it was true.

"The other thing that happened to me was when I was nineteen and at Cornell, and I just went through this big freakout about what career will I choose? What will I do? I knew I wanted to get married and have a family, but I also wanted to have—who knows what I would have called it then, be an intellectual is probably the word I would have used—have some kind of intellectual life. And I just couldn't decide how to choose. And I really just felt like I had to go one way or the other. And this professor came up that was a good friend of mine, and he asked me what was the matter. I must have been sitting on these stairs. And I told him. And he said, 'I know three women who've done both,' and he named them for me, and I said, 'Fine, I will too.' And that's how I thought of myself as an exception. If three other people had done it, then I could.

"Of course, what changed for me as I got more political was that I realized that people shouldn't have to make those choices and that it shouldn't be a question of whether you could or couldn't be exceptional. Men didn't have to choose between having a family and having a job or a career, and far from calling that 'wanting it all,' I just call it wanting a life. Just a life. We should have exactly the same expectations for ourselves as for men. So these were all things that were haunting me, and I started to look for some sort of organizational form for this."

In the mid-seventies, Ellen found herself back in the midwest, first in Chicago, then in Milwaukee. She married again, had two sons, continued to do office work and continued to look for an organizational base for her concerns about working women. In the summer of 1982, she found it when she attended 9-to-5 summer school. She returned to organize a Milwaukee chapter, which is now the organization's strongest. Today she is a full-time paid organizer for Milwaukee 9-to-5 and serves on the national committee.

"Someone I knew, knew someone who was going to this 9-to-5 summer school, and I got a ride. I remember calling and telling them, 'I'll sleep on the floor, I'll stand in the back of the room,' because I'd missed the deadline, 'please let me come.' And of course they were delighted to have people come. And when I got there it was like, okay this is the group I've been looking for. One of those things where you suddenly feel at home. What really impressed me, first of all, was that it was a multiracial group, which is so unusual in the women's movement. These were really grassroots leaders, I mean they were people who were giving speeches and doing workshops who you knew were new at it but were good at it. And you could tell that leadership development was real important in this group. And that it wasn't just a group of superstars. There was a tremendous range of age and experience.

"And the goal of this group wasn't to help women get out of being clericals, although obviously that was okay if people were looking to advance, that was a legitimate concern, but the main thing was to upgrade the category. This organization recognized that the majority of women aren't going to become lawyers or accountants, and while it was important to get into nontraditional jobs, and it was important to get into male-dominated jobs, we also had to do something about the undervaluation of female-dominated jobs. So rather than saying, 'I'm just a secretary, I should do something else,' we had to say, 'I'm not *just* a secretary, a secretary is an important thing to be.'

"I think there's nothing more energizing than watching women coming into their own. From the initial phone call where someone's practically in tears and really in a mess, to seeing that person get support and speak up and realize that change is possible if you're not all by yourself. And then to see people start to win things and see them get respected for that instead of getting punished for it. And to see them become leaders. That's really incredibly energizing and exciting. For me, the thing about the sixties that was really important, or the thing about being part of a social movement that was important, was learning that change is possible. And then of course the hard lesson is, that doesn't mean it's possible without long and hard work. It doesn't come as fast as some of us thought.

"I get so angry when people say things like, 'You can't organize women, you can't organize low-income working women.' I think the crucial thing is that people feel powerless, and they don't see that it's possible to make change. They either perceive there to be too many risks or that it will be futile. And what organizing is really about is to help them get in touch with the power that they really can have by acknowledging the skills they already have and teaching them new ones and by putting them in touch with other people like themselves.

"I think that one of the problems of the sixties was that there were some people who were going through a personal rebellion who'd always gotten what they wanted, and when massive social change didn't come right away, they just gave up and said, 'Well, this isn't possible' or 'This isn't desirable anymore.' But I think there were a lot of people who, even though they had their disappointments and their youthful excesses, also really learned the value of collective work and of setting goals and analyzing tactics and figuring out allies, who learned a lot of those lessons and went on to apply them. I think there are still a lot of us out there who are trying to make a contribution to people's daily lives."

GEOFFREY RIPS, 38

1969: anti-war activist
1989: policy coordinator for Jim Hightower

A soft-spoken Texan who ventured north for many of his formative experiences, Geoff Rips spent almost fifteen years as an alternative journalist. At a small, liberal arts college in Connecticut he joined SDS, demonstrated against the war, worked on the alternative newspaper and, one week before graduation, was arrested for blocking the entrance to a nuclear submarine base. Back home in Texas in the early 1970s, he ran a natural foods grocery store while writing for underground papers like *Space City News, River City Times* and *Eagle Bone Whistle*.

"In the late sixties and early seventies, I was certain there was going to be a major upheaval in the system. I don't think I knew much about Marxism, but I guess I subscribed to a kind of Marxist approach, some kind of blending of the Marxist and hippie approaches. I believed in collective enterprise in living and schooling and working. And that's what I wanted to see happen, and that's what I thought was going to happen. I had a pretty apocalyptic view of the world. You know, when you're nineteen or twenty, you think everything is going to change, and you're going to survive it, and it's going to be great to turn everything on its head. Now with two kids and a mortgage and parents who are getting older, I'm not so willing to see everything turned on its head, though I think it should change.

"In broad outline, my critique of the system is no different today from what it was twenty years ago. But in specifics . . . I think I have a deeper respect in terms of what people go through, your average working person, why that person is not politically conscious at all times, what that person is up against. I'm more tolerant. In my current job, I find I have to work with all kinds of elements—like good ole boy Texas legislators—whose humanity I can now appreciate which I couldn't have fifteen years ago. At the same time, I don't think that philosophically I'm any closer to them than I was fifteen years ago. I guess I'm resigned to the fact that things will change incrementally, and to get that change you have to work things out with what you're presented with."

In 1976, Geoff left Texas for New York where, during the next six years, he edited a newsletter for the Committee for Latin American Political Prisoners, worked on a book about government sabotage of the underground press (*Unamerican Activities*), ran PEN's Freedom to Write Office, freelanced for the *Nation* and wrote fiction and poetry. In 1982 he headed back to Texas once again to assume the editorship of Austin's *Texas Observer*. Since late 1986 he has worked as policy coordinator for Jim Hightower, a nationally known progressive leader and head of the Texas Department of Agriculture.

"What I really am is his Office of Ideology. Most of the projects in the department are run through me to make sure they're serving the right interests, make sure they're really geared to helping the kind of people who do not usually benefit from government programs.

"Hightower is trying to foment a populist revolution of sorts through the Department of Agriculture, trying to put financing in the hands of people who do the work, getting money to farmworkers to start their own vegetable co-ops. We're trying to put together right now a Populist Alliance much like what happened in the late 1800s. In politics, we're working on everything from trying to get same-day voter registration to bringing more people into the political process. It generally involves electoral politics, which is something I have never much believed in—though I worked for McCarthy, McGovern and Bobby Kennedy. Now I think it's the only game we've got.

"Since 1982 when Hightower and others were elected, there has been a change in politics in this state. Also the state has had economic hard times for seven years now. There are possibilities now that there weren't before. We've managed to bridge gaps between destitute farmers and people living in the inner city of Houston that I know has never happened in this state before. So there is some reason for hope.

"But I still don't believe in electoral politics, how it functions today, how I've seen it function from the inside. I mean it's a big lie that this is a democracy. It could be, but it isn't. But I think that the dirty little secret is, if allowed to function the way it was conceived, it could work. We could bring real democratic ideals to life."

MAX ELBAUM, 41
1968: student anti-war leader
1989: Marxist-Leninist organizer and editor

Raised in a liberal democratic household in Milwaukee, Wisconsin, Max graduated from high school in 1964 and says he spent the next three years as "an alienated youth." The nature of his rebellion was "pretty primitive," he says, "just a lot of thumbing your nose at society." From 1967 to 1970, he attended the University of Wisconsin, one of the nation's radical hotspots, where he assumed leadership roles in SDS and anti-war activities. In 1969 he bet his father 20 dollars—"not an insignificant sum at the time"—that there would be a revolution in five years. In 1974, he reluctantly paid off.

He continues to this day to work for fundamental social change. At first, he supported his political activism by working as a physical therapist. For the past twelve years, however, he has been on the paid staff of Line of March, a Marxist-Leninist organization. For the past seven years he has been one of the editors of *Frontline*, the organization's biweekly newspaper.

"Some people became activist without ever taking a very philosophical point of view; some people developed an ideology without ever necessarily being involved. I began to consider myself a Marxist before I was actively involved in protest. I had been to a march or two and spoken out against the war at rallies, but I was not an activist per se. I was just running around being rebellious. But I'd spent a few years working in Milwaukee in an industrial truck place, and I had some experience with large-scale mass production, and even though I didn't come from a working class background, I saw certain things about what seemed to make this society go—and Marxism made a lot of intellectual sense to me.

"I think I decided in June 1968, a day in June in 1968 in an apartment on Spring Street in Madison, and I remember saying to myself, 'Well, I think what I'll do with my life is to become a political activist.' I didn't have any particular career ambitions at the time. It was a combination of ideology, the spirit of the times, probably some alienation, a whole range of things. And I remember deciding, 'Okay, I'll put this ideology together with activism, and that's what I'll do with myself.' I remember making that decision and I've never regretted it. I still feel the same way, frankly, and that was 21 years ago

"Some of our assessments about what's possible in a time frame are wildly, tremendously shaped by the immediate period, and that, I think, is the biggest mistake—that we didn't have a sense of proportion and enough of a sense of history or where we fit into a broader process.

"I think a lot of the people who didn't have that sense of proportion had a hard time. In my opinion, it is easier for people to remain activists and be committed to a progressive social cause, whether it's Marxism or some kind of point of view that allows you to link humanitarian values to a perspective that sees some material development and allows you to put your own historical time and your own life in some kind of proportion. And then I think you're in a much better position to deal with all the surprises and disappointments that history's gonna throw your way.

"I pretty much do believe that while there are a lot of backs and forths, the general trend of history is toward greater and greater potential for human beings to develop their talents and energy, and greater and greater conditions for people to make a better society. I think that's rooted in the development of science and technology. I'm also tremendously impressed with all the different ways in which people take up the fight for social justice. It keeps happening despite all kinds of terrible odds. You can point to hundreds or thousands of people who take that up. And I think it's really encouraging.

"The Reagan years were a tremendous reactionary disaster. We suffered a lot of setbacks, but I think in the end progress will prevail. The danger of the human race blowing itself up is real, and I think that could happen. And the need to take activity to prevent that from happening is urgent. But short of that, it seems to me that looking at tens of years and hundreds of years, that the trend is toward more progress and more potential. While I have an understanding about why people get disillusioned, I've never been very compelled by that. There's always just a lot of things to point to about some of the progress and some of the marvelous qualities of human beings.

"One of the things about the period in the sixties—even though the movement had many flaws and a lot of problems—was there was a real mass activism that sowed the seeds of developing the kind of institutions and organizations and collectivity that gave a glimpse of what it would mean to build some kind of durable thing. You don't really have that in the U.S. today. And I think that puts activists at a tremendous disadvantage. And so you see all these folks who are progressive and oriented towards social justice out there on their own, trying to figure out what the hell to do.

"There are not that many countries where a whole generation of people are activated then ten years later are not part of some political party or current. Now everyone's out there on his own."

MINDY LORENZ, 43
1969: anti-war sympathizer
1989: coordinator, Greens national clearinghouse

The daughter of a staunch Goldwater supporter, Mindy learned early how to stand up for her political beliefs. As a graduate student at the University of Maryland in the late sixties, she became an anti-war activist and a mediator between angry grad students and conservative faculty members.

"I was living in Washington, D.C., at the time that Martin Luther King was killed, and those events had just an incredible impact on me. I went downtown the day after the shooting to bring living supplies into churches and saw armed soldiers on the corner. The day before I had been into D.C. and it looked like it always did, and then the next day it looked like an armed camp. Those events just tremendously influenced me. I was very idealistic—I still am—and the fact that people were being killed for their beliefs, especially

Martin Luther King, Jr., I guess helped make the point that has been growing in my awareness all these years, that there's a lot at stake when people are very serious about wanting things to change."

> After receiving her master's in art history, she married, had a child and then divorced. Through the seventies, she says her activism was at "a low ebb" as she earned her Ph.D. and struggled with single parenthood. In the late seventies, she started what she thought was to be her career as an academic at the Claremont College near Los Angeles.

"Then in 1980 I saw a show on television about the church women, the American church women who were murdered in El Salvador. And it was like a bomb going off in my head, and I thought, 'Oh my god, we're into it again.' And I could just see all the issues coalescing in terms of what had been going on during the Vietnam War, and so I just sought out information on what kind of organized activities there were in anti-intervention circles, and quickly became active in CISPES [Committee in Solidarity with the People of El Salvador] in Los Angeles, and started organizing a campus chapter. The situation personally grabbed me because it just seemed like some of the lessons that I had learned about what our government should and shouldn't be doing in the world were just coming to a kind of crisis point once again. And so, I got involved in the sanctuary movement.

"For me this was a real life-affecting set of activities because during the Vietnam War I wasn't meeting people from Vietnam. I wasn't meeting the people that we were directly involved in the bombing and experiencing the impact that things were having in their lives. But here with the Central American refugees, I was meeting the people who were directly affected by what we were doing and, boy, that was really intense for me. Very, very painful. But very important in consolidating my personal awareness that I couldn't just do this part-time, I couldn't do it on weekends, I couldn't just do it sometimes and then forget about it. Personal experience with the people deepened my commitment, and sort of led to my making a decision to leave academic life full-time. It was interfering with my ability to spend the number of hours that it took to do my job well, and also it was interfering with me feeling like I had the freedom of action to do what I needed to do with my political work and not worry about the ramifications with my job.

"I knew very well the implications of what I was doing. But I realized that I did not want to be an academic, although I love to teach, so my decision was really to try to find a better balance between part-time teaching and my political work. And that's what I've been trying to do ever since. Again, knowing full well that I was condemning myself to not making nearly as much money, having no job security, and having tenuous benefits.

"It was an intense kind of family dynamic. My daughter was nine or ten years old in the early eighties. It was difficult for a young kid to have to face her mother getting arrested and possibly spending time in jail. And meeting these people from Central America who were very strange to her and very threatening in many ways, having a lot of people around the house, and hearing about our house being under surveillance—it was very difficult.

"My daughter's sixteen now, and she has a very different perspective on things from that of most people her age, and I think she feels very proud of that. But it's also hard for her because it separates her a lot from her peers.

"It was in the midst of doing the Central America work that I realized that single issue politics seemed somewhat limited to me. I mean, they were important, and it needed to be done, but I guess my personal frame of reference was to try to develop a really comprehensive way of seeing the way the change needed to happen, knowing that some of it was definitely short-term emergency kinds of urgent issues.

"At one point I read about the German Greens and just had a very superficial understanding of what their program was about. So I wrote for their program, their platform. Reading that, it was like another kind of light bulb going off, I read the program and I thought, 'Oh, my god, here it is. This is it.' It was saying everything that I had been thinking about, and they were already organized and already out there in a visible way, already running people for office on the basis of a platform that just seemed to address all this comprehensive relationship between nature and women and domination and the environment. It was all laid out. And almost immediately at an antinuclear rally I saw a banner saying 'Greens,' and it was like a miracle. I thought, 'God, I can't believe it.' I went to a meeting, and that was it. That was about five years ago.

"I think the time that it takes for fundamental changes to happen is sometimes very discouraging. But I do feel that just on this very broad scale, I think the history of human cultures has been a slow progression toward, I guess we'd just have to call it the establishment of ever more democratic institutions.

"I think that globally we're beginning to understand what it takes to have truly democratic institutions in a way that I don't think has been understood before. And I think the Greens model of understanding what it takes to have truly democratic institutions is the best I see in the world. It takes massive citizen participation, otherwise it's going to be a form of oligarchy or a form of fascism, or closer to the models in the past where you basically had a benevolent, centralized leadership and a rather passive and uninformed mass of people. And I think that has to change in order for a democracy to function. And I think more and more people are realizing that.

"Electoral politics is undeniably an important aspect of the Greens movement everywhere in the world. It's not the only part of it, but I think that to be able to work both within the existing power systems and to work outside those power systems, to develop strategies so that both happen simultaneously and remain linked with each other is an important set of experiments that we have to carry out. And it's not an either/or, it can't be, because it's rather difficult to work outside of the system. Change has to come simultaneously in many areas, and I think the Greens are developing an analysis that really recognizes that complexity. It's not a matter of just dropping out and trying to ignore the power system, it just cannot be done.

"For me, the core issue has always been domination, trying to recognize domination wherever it occurs, whether it's in family dynamics or interpersonal or a broader kind of social level. I don't know why I have felt that so staunchly over the years, but that's the struggle I had with my mother, it's the struggle I've had in my personal life in relationships with men, and I just see it as the basis of a tremendous amount of suffering in the world. And until we can individually and collectively organize ourselves to create institutions and structures that are based on core values of not dominating, not needing to competitively dominate, we're just going to keep doing the same stuff over and over again.

"I talk to people all the time who say, 'Oh well, you know, nothing ever came of the sixties.' And they've been holding a kind of pessimism for twenty years because of that. But the sixties did lead to something. It wasn't just this intense period and then everything died. It was part of an evolutionary process. It's hard to talk to people about a long period of history. People just see the kind of devastation around us and say, 'Well, you know, if you guys can't do something in the next five years, forget it. We're not gonna join.' But I think what Greens end up realizing is how deep these things go, and unless you're in for the long haul and unless you're willing to really study the history of these issues, we will only continue to repeat the same failures.

"Having that broader picture, for me, is what keeps me going on a day-to-day basis and helps to give me the courage. It is really the seat of my optimism, and I think if I were to lose that broader picture and understanding of things, I would feel very swallowed up in the immediacy of the suffering. The Greens have a spiritual and historical and theoretical understanding that I have not found in any other political group I have ever worked with. Being part of the organization has allowed me to live in a way that feels very integrated and just feels terrific."

RICHARD SCHOENINGER, 41
1969: itinerant hippie
1989: mayor, Eureka Springs, Arkansas

A self-proclaimed "counterculture-artist-bum," Richard grew up in rural Illinois. After a brief stint at the local college, he took to the road, living out of his pickup truck while he did odd jobs from Denver to Los Angeles. For twenty years, Richard worked construction, planted trees and detasseled corn, living a nomadic life with his only responsibilities his truck and his dog. In 1987, his

travels took him to Eureka Springs, Arkansas, a little Ozarks town that had
been a fashionable spa in the late nineteenth century.

"I never did a job in my life any longer than one year. So I was pretty rest-
less. I was a dropout. And I came to Arkansas to drop the rest of the way
out, because Arkansas had one percent of the population. The people down
here were real individualistic and independent, and they judged you for who
you were. I got along real well, and I thought I could be on my own here and
not be connected to anything or anybody. So I figured I'd live in Arkansas
with everybody else that doesn't want to have anything to do with anybody
else. Okay, fine.
"When I got to Eureka Springs, I just didn't want to leave. See, I don't
know how to describe myself except as eccentric and unique and individualistic, and there were a lot of those people here. I'd always been a one per-
center somewhere else. And in Eureka Springs my eccentricity was just the
same as anybody else's. I didn't stick out. So when I got out here all the rest-
lessness of two decades just left."

After decades of living on the fringes of society, Richard decided he liked the
town so much he not only wanted to join it, but also help run it. He declared
his candidacy for mayor of Eureka Springs after getting a haircut and a shave,
having a suit custom tailored, buying wingtips—and inheriting enough money
to fund a vigorous campaign.

"I found out who was going to run—there were a couple of other people
that were gonna run—and I made the comment to a friend, 'Golly, I can do
as good as that.' And he said, 'Well, why don't ya?' I'd inherited some money, first in my life. So from being a drifter, I now had an opportunity. I had
no material focus at all. A used pickup truck that did okay was about all I
really had. So I had the opportunity to afford a campaign fund and to do it.
"I had a check for 50,000 dollars one day, had no idea it was coming,
and had nothing in my life at that time. Just scraping by, odd-jobbing and
hanging out. And a past track record that was sketchy. I'd never done anything longer than a year. And I'd done a lot of things a day or two or a month
or two and gone on. I really was looking for something to apply myself to,
and so I had the opportunity to spend 3,000 dollars, 5,000 dollars on a campaign for mayor of a town of 2,000 that paid 24 dollars a year, and I could
do it my way and I was independent.
"There's three ways you can run a campaign that I know of. You can talk
about issues, or you can say you're the best fellow for the job, or you can say
the other fellow is the worst fellow for the job. My opponent chose to say that
there were no issues, and that his opponent was the worst fellow for the job
because of not knowing anything about his past and being a hippie and just
getting a haircut and a shave and putting on a suit is not enough. He said

that there were no real problems, and that everything was fine, and that everything would be taken care of. And that it was no big deal.

"I was a dynamic speaker compared to him. I had issues and enthusiasm and my personal energy. I was so wound up in this thing, I had never thought I would come out from being dropped out and campaign and do something like that. And I just kept getting more and more into it and not wanting to win on a charisma basis but to win on issues. And I won by a substantial margin, which means other people cared about the issues too.

"I want to get the quality of experience here protected through the planning commission, the ordinances about types of business and zoning. I want it to always be a place where residents can live. I don't want it to become a shopping center or just a mall, or to be inundated with development so that it's no longer a home.

"There's a chance here to cultivate the community into a place that can get better, with things like wildflower roadside plantings, recycling, expanding the parks commission, and walking paths and trails. Civic things. I would like to be known for a cultural renaissance here, having music festivals and music and artists in the park and things like that.

"I used to think I had to exist outside the bureaucracy in order to keep my values. But now I think that's a cop-out. Oftentimes our criticism of government is negative because we see it as something that ruins our way of life. But I found that by becoming part of the system, by becoming the system, the focus of leadership for the system, that one can implement the qualities in a community like the attitude of the police department, the relationship of the different elements and interests in the community, to have balance.

"Small town government is a constant encounter session with people who forget you're human too because you represent a symbol of something they don't have to be nice to. You know how relatives are so horrible to each other with their honesty? Well, your constituency, they're gonna let you have it, unabashedly, directly. I've had threatening phone calls and I've also had very wonderful experiences. Like reading the mail today, there was a lady that said that I should be struck down by God, and there was another who said, 'wonderful, I think you're doing a marvelous job, great and inspiring.'

"The mayor's job doesn't pay. I do it for free. And I work overtime. I ran to be a full-time representative mayor. I had to learn how to be effective, to keep my ego and territorial maleness out of things, which provides results in how to be effective, and if you keep that in mind, then you do a lot of humbling things. You talk to people you don't want to be nice to. You deal with people that you think can't be dealt with. And you learn skills about power and position and truth and justice that amaze you sometimes or appall you too.

"I used to be much more ethereal and romantic, and I'm much more practical now. I think I was escaping from responsibility and commitment and reality, all of which I have in megadoses right now in my life.

"I bought a slum house here, and I did a little to fix it up. I work sixty hours a week or more, and I'm looking for a relationship. I used to braid my hair, had about a foot-long braid, and I didn't shave for ten years at least. Now my hair's above my collar and I shave every day. I even wear underwear. When people ask me what was the most difficult thing about being mayor, I say, 'Two things. Rules and wearing underwear. And I've gotten used to the underwear.'

"I got involved in political activism because I wanted to help. And it's been rewarding. If you are involved, you can learn how to get things done. If you're not involved, you can't get anything done.

"In the sixties, we identified problems and attacked the problems without really knowing what could be. It's really different to identify problems than to identify solutions. And too many of us identify problems and then walk away. Well, that's easy. The evening news identifies problems every day, but they don't identify answers. And so getting in the business of problem-solving is what we need to do. And you can do that by being involved. You can't do it by being uninvolved.

"But I find that the structure of government we have is flexible, and it's as good as the people that are involved in it want to make it. And there is nothing about our system or government that keeps us from doing the things that we want to do. Because it allows for change."

GREG CALVERT, 52
1966: national secretary, SDS
1989: community and gay activist

A battle-scarred veteran of the New Left, Greg was raised by his grandparents on a small Finnish farm in southwest Washington. He strongly identifies with the "decentralist, anarcho-syndicalist tradition" of his ancestors. Greg was never really a liberal, he says, but radicalized early on, talking up civil rights in his all-white high school and engaging in sit-ins with a traveling mixed-race church group in 1955.

In the late fifties, he studied history at the University of Oregon. Then it was on to Cornell on a Woodrow Wilson scholarship. In the early sixties, he studied in France, was exposed to French left-wing politics, and came out as a gay person. Back in the States, he took a teaching job at Iowa State University.

"I loved teaching. The response from the students was overwhelming. In the two-and-a-half years I was there, from January 1964 to June 1966, I became the young radical professor, like many others around the country at provincial universities, who became the center of radical activity, the organizer by default. I certainly never sought that position because as a gay person in Ames, Iowa, in 1964, '65 and '66, it was indeed a painful situation. I was open about being gay with friends whom I became close to. But at that time in Ames, Iowa, it would have been extremely difficult, if not impossible, to declare myself publicly as a gay person.

"The next year, one of my students was elected student body president as an avowed anarchist. It made the *New York Times* magazine section. He said in the interview for that article: 'Well, I come from this Catholic background in this working class community, and I went to Iowa State and there was this young, radical history professor named Greg Calvert . . .' And that was truly what happened. A lot of students were radicalized in their thinking by taking my classes.

"In the spring of '66 I was very conflicted about my life. I did not feel I should stay at Iowa State anymore because I felt I was becoming too much the focus of the new student movement, and that in a teaching position there were conflicts built into this kind of situation, some of them moral. I was encouraging draft resistance on the part of my students. But I felt it was unfair of me to be suggesting that they take a position that might send them to jail when I myself, because I was past the age of 26, was not in jeopardy. So in my head, I was trying to manage this. I had pretty much decided that I wanted to work at least part-time in the movement, but I wanted to make more of a commitment, to take the risks I was asking other people to take."

In June 1966, he attended the SDS convention in Ann Arbor and in August became the national secretary. In SDS, he became identified wtih the draft resistance position and in the fall of 1966 he worked as that organization's liaison to the National Mobilization Committee.

"I regard the first Pentagon demonstration in October '67 as one of the great successes of the anti-war movement. We turned what the Marxist-Leninists wanted to be a confrontation with police into a teach-in around the slogan 'join us.' It was one of the most brilliant, most beautiful moments in the anti-war movement. Actually, some of the troops, a small number, tried to join us. Many were exposed to the anti-war movement through dialogue on the terrace, right in front of the Pentagon's front doors, and it scared the generals to death. They kept changing the guard every hour or so until they finally ordered the crack troops in to beat the demonstrators. And I made what I regard as one of my best contributions to the movement. I got up and gave a speech saying that we had won and that we should retreat and go out and organize.

"That became my strategy—not to engage in confrontation with the police, which was becoming the tactic that was overwhelming any strategic sense in the movement. It started the week before the Pentagon demonstration, the development of the so-called mobile tactics—playing hit and run games with the police in the streets. Those mobile tactics which were, in part, a result of frustration with the perceived passive stance of civil disobedience, were a disaster for the New Left. I saw the Pentagon demonstration as part of an alternative for active nonviolence. Instead of just sitting down like the pacifists wanted to do, I said, let's turn this around into an active situation and make this a teach-in to the troops. Then when we've done our thing, we leave. I thought that made good sense, and I still do. I thought that if that had been the lesson that people had gotten from the Pentagon demonstration, the movement might not have torn itself apart.

"Unfortunately, people like Tom Hayden and Rennie Davis got control of the Mobe [National Mobilization Committee] and were joined by people like Abbie Hoffman and Jerry Rubin, who wanted to take the notion of mobile tactics and apply it to the Democratic National Convention in 1968. Jerry Rubin, in a meeting in early 1968 in Chicago, when asked what his program was said, 'Radicalization means smoking dope in the parks and fighting with the pigs in the Loop.' That simplistic, brutal and rather idiotic sense of political awareness unfortunately became the accepted position in Chicago, which I think was an outright disaster. It was exactly the wrong step after the Pentagon. We should have decentralized and focused on organizing larger and larger constituencies and not engaged with state power at the level of the police. That was just silliness. It fed people's most romantic, bizarre, adventurist fantasies. That is where I regard the movement as hopelessly derailed."

Run out of SDS national office by what he calls the "Stalinist faction," in 1967, Greg moved to Austin, Texas, where be became involved in GI organizing at Fort Hood and worked on a book later published by Random House (*A Disruptive History: The New Left and the New Capitalism*). During the seventies he worked as a paraprofessional psychotherapist in Illinois, Massachusetts and Texas, specializing first in treating drug and alcohol abuse and later in the problems of returning Vietnam veterans. It was during this time that he met his long-time partner, Ken Carpenter, a draft resister who spent a year-and-a-half in federal prison. Together they moved first to Santa Cruz, California, where Greg went back to finish his long-dormant Ph.D., and then Eugene, Oregon.

"I wanted to settle some place where we could become part of the community and do the kind of work that we're still dedicated to doing, including grassroots, democratic community organizing. And in this community, we have found a place for ourselves. We're both active in the South University neighborhood association. [Greg was recently elected president.] We participate in monthly meetings with other neighborhood leaders, and we're very active now in trying to stimulate involvement in the neighborhood associations as a way to do democratic decentralist grassroots organizing in the area."

In an articulate position paper recently presented to a group of neighborhood leaders, Greg wrote: "The truly important political question of our day, or so it seems to me, is whether democratic community can be saved, built, or restored on sound ecological-economic bases around good values that are not repressive and promote human diversity and freedom to grow." Greg and Ken have set up a nonprofit educational association called Communitas to sponsor seminars, conferences and political education forums that promote, in Greg's words, "democratic, decentralist, ecologically involved politics that have a strong emphasis on spiritual values." They are both involved in the Greens movement and in gay issues.

"I consider myself a nonideological radical. My political, philosophical, spiritual viewpoint endures because I have moral stamina. It's *sisu*. *Sisu* is a very special Finnish word which means something like determination, moral determination. Sometimes it's translated 'guts,' but that English colloquialism doesn't really capture the sense of the Finnish word. *Sisu* is what the Finns had when the Russians invaded in 1939 and they became the only small nation to have stopped a superpower. *Sisu* is also what the Finns had when Hitler demanded the Jews from Finland and the Finns said no. *Sisu* is stopping the Russian tanks in the snow with what were apparently the first Molotov cocktails. When they ran out of bullets, they poured gasoline in their vodka bottles. *Sisu* is how the Finns managed to make it all the way from Mongolia to Finland across Russia.

"I'm attributing this to these remarkable people who I am related to on my mother's side and who raised me as a little kid. I grew up in extraordinarily difficult circumstances. My parents lived in a Hooverville when I was conceived, a set of shacks the workers had built out of discarded lumber up in the mountains when they couldn't get jobs. So I grew up knowing poverty. We were so poor on the Finnish farm that my grandfather used to sell the butter and buy margarine instead and use the extra money to buy oatmeal to put on the table. I worked extraordinarily hard as a boy. I had my first forty-hour-a-week job when I was nine years old, working in the fields in berry patches. I was let off every morning at the day labor hall and got on a truck with migrant Chicano workers and worked in the fields picking berries and beans. I did stoop labor when I was eleven, weeding mint fields, and practically broke my back. I raised hogs. I had a paper route and a job after school and cooked and washed for my father and brothers when my mother was committed to a mental hospital when I was thirteen. *Sisu*. That's how I keep going."

RIGHT LIVELIHOOD
III

Gloria Steinem has been a symbol of feminism for two generations of women. One of the most visible leaders of the mass women's liberation movement, she was a founding editor of the movement's journalistic linchpin *Ms.* magazine, and a tireless writer and public speaker. In the mid-sixties, she was dubbed "the pin-up girl of the intelligentsia"—a remark doubly insulting for its denigration of her own intellect and its sexist reference to her beauty. Through the years, like other attractive women with brains, she has had to fight an uphill battle.

But uphill battles were not new to her. Born in Toledo to a free-spirited father who could never quite earn a living and a talented mother who was crippled by bouts of depression and anxiety, Steinem learned early how to fend for herself. Her parents divorced when she was eleven or twelve, and she and her mother lived in a rat-infested basement apartment in an East Toledo slum. Although her mother was an Oberlin graduate who had had a career in journalism before she married, Ruth Steinem was virtually incapacitated by a series of nervous breakdowns and could not work. Her preteen daughter became her sole caretaker, bringing her mother, as she later wrote, "an endless stream of toast and coffee, bologna sandwiches and dime pies, in a child's version of what meals should be." She imagined that she was adopted and that her real parents ("just your stock central casting parents" she once told an interviewer) would someday rescue her. She dreamed of tap-dancing her way out of Toledo, and in fact, entered amateur night competitions and won a local TV talent contest.

In 1952, after spending her senior year with her older sister in New York, she enrolled in Smith College. There she excelled academically, won scholarships, was elected to Phi Beta Kappa and, four years later, graduated *magna cum laude* with a major in government. Following graduation, she went to study at the Universities of Delhi and Calcutta on a Chester Bowles Asian scholarship. She found the classes "pointless" but gained an important political education when she traveled with a group of radical humanists through southern India, then in the throes of extreme social unrest. It was here also that her career in journalism began, when she wrote freelance articles for several Indian newspapers as well as a guide book, *A Thousand Indias.*

Returning to the States in 1958, Steinem was unable to find a reporting job in New York City and so took a position with the Independent Research Service, an offshoot of the left-leaning National Student Association (NSA), in Cambridge, Massachusetts. Later it was revealed that the NSA was substantially funded by the CIA but Steinem had no awareness of the connection at the time. In 1960, still determined to become a journalist, she moved back to New York, where at last she landed a job writing captions at *Help!*, a magazine of political satire. Her first break came two years later when she freelanced "The Moral Disarmament of Betty Coed," a before-its-time piece on the sexual revolution, to *Esquire.* In 1963, she published an article that came back to haunt her for years, "I Was a Playboy Bunny." An insightful expose about a seeminglyly fluffy subject, it gained her, she now thinks, just the wrong kind of notoriety. Although the article contained the seeds of feminist thought, Steinem was mostly remembered for dressing up in a scanty costume. Through the mid-sixties, she made her living profiling celebrities like Michael Caine, Margot Fonteyn, Lee Radziwill and Paul Newman for major women's magazines. During the 1964–65 television season, she wrote scripts for "That Was the Week that Was," a critically acclaimed series specializing in biting political satire.

In 1968, at age 34, Steinem began to come into her own. Clay Felker, publisher of the newly launched *New York* magazine, hired her to write a regular column on politics, and it was there that she found both her political and journalistic voice as she wrote about the progressive and radical events of the time. She covered Cesar Chavez's Poor People's March in California, became involved in Angela Davis's trial and supported Robert Kennedy's bid for president in 1968. Later that year, Steinem was catapulted into feminism when she covered a meeting of radical feminists who talked openly about their illegal abortions. "It was the first time I heard women speak the truth in public," she later said. From then on, her life revolved around women's issues.

In the late sixties and early seventies, she was a regular on the TV talk show circuit and traveled throughout the country on lecture tours. Hoping to widen the image of women's liberation, Steinem always spoke as half of a lecture team with a black feminist partner, first childcare pioneer Dorothy Pittman Hughes, then lawyer Florynce Kennedy, and finally activist Margaret Sloan. She later wrote that her travels taught her one important lesson: Despite the mainstream media's trivialization of feminism, "daily rebellions and dreams of equality" were sprouting up everywhere.

In 1971, she joined with Betty Freidan and Shirley Chisholm to establish the National Women's Political Caucus, which encouraged women to run for political office. She also helped establish Women's Action Alliance, a non-profit organization aimed at mobilizing working class people of color to fight discrimination. Also in 1971, she began plans for a new kind of magazine for women.

Ms. hit the newsstands in January 1972 and sold out its complete run of 300,000 copies in eight days. Since that time, Steinem has been deeply involved with the magazine, first as its editor, then as a regular contributor and, most recently, as a consultant and member of the *Ms.* Foundation for Education and Communication. At the height of early seventies feminism, the magazine was reviled by more radical women for its "bourgeois feminism" and Steinem was attacked as a lightweight—and worse. But both the magazine and its co-founder survived.

Through the seventies, Steinem remained both politically and journalistically active, editing and writing for *Ms.*, helping to organize International Women's Year (1977) and participating in such groups as the Coalition of Labor Union Women, Voters for Choice and Women Against Pornography. "It's one of the ironies of being a writer and an activist at the same time that, just when you feel you have the most to say, you have the least time to say it," Steinem wrote in the introduction to *Outrageous Acts and Everyday Rebellions*, a collection of her essays and magazine articles, published in 1983. She did find time in the eighties to collaborate with photographer George Barris on a biography of Marilyn Monroe. "The things that happened to her were the things the women's movement has tried to prevent," Steinem said at the time.

Today Steinem divides her time between the *Ms.* foundation, working on women's issues—particularly reproductive freedom—and her own writing. Her latest project is a thoughtfully inspirational volume called *The Bedside Book of Self-Esteem*. "I used to have a recurring dream," she wrote in *Outrageous Acts*. "I was fighting with one person or many people, struggling and kicking and hitting as hard as I could. . . . But no matter what I did, I couldn't hurt any of them. No matter how hard I fought, they just smiled." Sometime in the eighties, she says she stopped having the dream. "I realized that women were offering each other a new and compassionate kind of power."

"I suppose that from childhood I always identified with, not victims because I think that's not a very good term exactly, but people who were suffering unjustly, and I don't know what that comes from. My mother, maybe—she was always very empathetic. I don't know, I think maybe it's just in people unless it's beaten out of you. But for years and years I didn't understand that the reason I felt that empathy was that I also was from a group that was being treated unfairly, a group called 'women.'

"Nobody'd ever told me that women were a serious group. So that empathy always attached itself to other groups. I mean I was always working for the farmworkers or civil rights. Before the women's movement I didn't understand that I was also part of a serious group. But I guess the sense of injustice when you see people who are suffering, people who enjoy inflicting punishment on others, is what makes me the most crazy. I think it includes, as it does for a lot of women, animals and the earth as well.

"My radicalism certainly didn't begin at Smith. I mean, there was absolutely not a moment of light in the fifties. I liked college while I was there, because I liked my friends, and they were all very nice people, and they gave you three meals a day and books to read. I mean, what more could you want? But they were all books about everybody else doing something. And indeed, the first 30,000 years of history in which women were the gods was cheerfully consigned to prehistory. We started out with Plato, who wasn't shit as far as women were concerned, and there was no relief from the denigration of women, from Plato to Freud and Marx and so on.

"I'm sure there were individual feminists at Smith at that point, I hope there were, but I didn't know them, and the feminist books were locked up in the rare books cage in the library, and I never saw them. All I knew was that if we worked very hard we could get to be the wives of executives and do charity work in the suburbs. That's what we were supposed to do. I certainly didn't question any of it. So I think for me part of the awakening was living in India for two years. Certainly, much more than being at Smith.

"I would say that it took me about twenty years to get over my college education. For the book that I'm doing now, I found a study that shows that women's self-esteem diminishes with every additional year of education. And that was certainly true for me. That is, I knew a lot, but I came to believe more and more and more that I couldn't do anything. I could learn about what men did, I could regurgitate facts and theories skillfully, but I couldn't do it myself. Hopefully, it's much better now. Nonetheless, the higher up in education you get, the more likely you are to learn about male accomplishments in textbooks, and the less likely you are to see any women honored in authority, in administration or as professors. So I think you become smarter and smarter, but it's more and more derivative.

"I once spoke at a feminist conference in Appalachia, which was the first big, big women's conference that drew women from all over the Appalachian area, all the three states, and women came out of the hills and hollers in their pickup trucks and hitchhiking and bringing their quilts. It was a wonderful meeting. And I never forgot it because these women went from real life experience to radical feminism in ten minutes because they didn't have to detour through Marx and Freud and all this intellectualization of our inferiority. They just said, 'It's not fair. Why won't my husband let me drive the pickup truck? Why can't I get a driver's license? Why can't I work in the coal mines? It's the only good job in this area. Why do they say women are bad luck in the mines and they won't let us within a hundred yards? It's the only good job.' They had a much clearer look at real life.

"You know how when you first discover injustices, not that they haven't always been there but you thought they were natural, you thought they were inevitable—especially women, I think, thought that our role was inevitable and so on. And when you discover that it's not and the depth of the injustice, you think, 'Well, surely if you just point this out to people they will want to change.'

"I mean I always think of one example. When I was in college in the fifties, an extraordinarily daring thing to do was to . . . well, there's always been student housing around Columbia, and it was segregated, a lot of it, so what we would do was that someone white would go to this landlord and say, 'I need a room or an apartment.' Someone black would go first, and they would be turned down, and then someone white would go, and they would be accepted, and then this would be reported to Columbia. That was the fifties. In the sixties we discovered Columbia owned the housing.

"So this was just a symbol of the many ways in which you realize that injustice is a much deeper part of the structure. I mean consciousness-raising means realizing that it can be different, it can be better, and that's the first huge step, and some people do change. But there is, of course, huge institutional injustice, and profit, both in the sense of money profit and 'having-your-dinner-cooked-and-your-socks-picked-up-off-the-floor' profit. And especially for women and men, a whole sense that you're not a real man unless a woman is somehow subordinate to you. So, the depth of it certainly I didn't realize fully when I first got involved in the women's movement.

"You know how the light bulb goes off over your head? When I was writing for *New York* magazine—this was about '69 I believe—I went to cover an abortion hearing that an early feminist group was holding in a church downtown in the Village in New York. They were objecting to a hearing held by the New York State legislature on the question of liberalizing New York State's abortion laws. Of course there was no *Roe v. Wade* then. And the legislature had invited fourteen men and one nun to testify.

"So these women said, 'Wait a minute. Let's hear from the women who've had this experience.' So they held this hearing in the church basement, and some very courageous women had agreed to get up and talk about their abortions and what had happened to them, step-by-step, just exactly what had happened to them. And it was a time I never forgot. I'd never heard women tell the truth in public before. Never. And women in the audience started to get up, with tears streaming down their faces, to tell what had happened to them. I had had an abortion too and never told anyone. This had been when I was 22 and newly out of college. And suddenly because of that hearing I realized, if one in three or four of us have had this experience, why is it illegal? So it was the beginning of the unraveling process for me, and I think for many women, because reproductive freedom is so basic to our lives and health. I mean if we can't control our bodies from the skin in, we're never going to control our lives from the skin out. So whether it's women in Africa who are challenging genital mutilation or women in Ireland who are sneaking in contraceptives or women in the Soviet Union who are objecting to the use of abortion as the main means of birth control and trying to get contraceptives . . . I mean, you know, whatever form it takes, it's all about reproductive freedom.

"The 1989 *Webster* decision would depress me if it were a setback with the majority of people—but it isn't. Because the support for safe and legal abortion has steadily grown, and it still is growing. The problem is that we haven't translated these issues into the presidential elections. So we have had two presidents who were elected by thirty percent of the populace, and both of them were pledged to appoint anti-abortion judges, and they did. So it's angering but not depressing.

"You have to take the long view. After a while, from reading and talking and just experiencing, I got a more historical view, so that I realized that there had been many revolts against patriarchy, and that patriarchy and racism had been around for 5,000 years, and the first wave of feminism was just one wave of a much, much longer revolution. You know, the first wave of feminism, the one that achieved a legal identity as human beings for women of all races, that took one hundred and fifty years. In this wave we're trying to achieve legal and social equality, and that will probably take a century too. And there'll probably be waves after that before we have societies in which your gender or your race is not a controlling factor, but only one of a thousand or a million factors in each unique person. I believe that day is coming. Not in our lifetime, of course, but I'm optimistic that it's achievable.

"But I also understand that we could go backward. Nothing is automatic. Change is not automatic. I think society is trying to make us grateful for industrialization, which theoretically lessens the need for physical strength and helps women. You know, that's all bullshit. You can have just as much, if not more, inequality in an industrial society. It depends who controls it. In fact, if the secrets of technology are not taught to everyone equally, it makes the society more polarized than it was before. I mean agricultural societies are in many cases more equal. I'm not saying they're equal but they're more equal than industrial ones and technological ones, because the women's economic role of growing food and so on is not distant from men's roles. But if only men know the technology of industrialization, computers, space travel and so on, it polarizes us much more. Anyway, progress is not automatic ever—but it is also always possible. It depends on what we do.

"I guess in a way, at least one of the things that's changed for me during the past twenty years is a sense of time, because now I do understand that this is a lifetime process, not just something that one does for a few years. It's an organic part of life. That realization helps you pace yourself better. I mean burnout is a function of naivete, I think. Burnout is a function of thinking that if you are just flat out, totally active for five years or ten years or twenty years, that'll do it. So now I have a better a sense of time.

"And I have a much greater faith in women. Because I realize very well that if I don't do it someone else will do it. I no longer feel I have to respond to every request for speaking or writing, that I can make choices and indeed, that I should make choices. Each of us should do what we can uniquely do. The point of the women's movement is that each woman is her own leader and so the movement has to make clear that there's not some new imperative, some new role model, some new stereotype—me or anybody else.

"Supermom and superwoman have been anti-feminist stereotypes for a long time. It's part of society's response. First society says, 'No, you can't be an engineer or a jockey or whatever it is you want to be because that's unconventional.' Then, of course, when you do it anyway, they say, 'Okay, you can do that but only if you do everything else you did before and therefore don't disturb society. Only if you cook three gourmet meals and dress for success and have two perfect children.' You know, it's impossible of course. It puts all the burden on women. Superwoman . . . I don't know how many cover stories we devoted to trying to kill off superwoman.

"I have a friend who's sixteen years old, and she was saying to me that she recognized that whenever it was in the late sixties that we stood up and

said, 'Wait a minute. Women are not biologically inferior; we can do everything that men can do'—that was a huge step. But that in retrospect it
seemed enviably simple. Things seem more complicated now. And I said,
'Yes, but the next big simple leap forward is that men can and must do everything women do. It will be when the boys in your class, as often as the girls,
are asking: How can I combine career and family?'

"That's not breaking down roles to me—it's expanding. It's that each of
us is a full human being who's been discouraged from developing a part of
our humanity. There's a circle that's one hundred percent. Women have only
been allowed, say, thirty percent of it. Men have been allowed maybe seventy
percent. But each of us has been deprived. I mean we already know from
thousands of studies that the most creative men and women are the men with
the most 'feminine' abilities and the women with the most 'masculine.' In
other words, the people who are the most complete.

"So for each of us progress lies in the direction we haven't been, so to
speak. I think *The Mermaid and the Minotaur* was really the best, the deepest
analysis in this regard because it shows the importance of men both raising
children and being socialized to raise children. That's what develops flexibility, patience, compassion, empathy, all the things that men need if they're not
gonna blow us up and them too.

"I think, in general, women get more radical with age while men get more
conservative. Young women are the most conservative they will ever be because they haven't yet experienced being in the labor force, having children
and discovering who takes care of them and who doesn't, aging, and all the
things that radicalize women. I'm not saying that young women aren't
activists—they are. Let me put it this way: A woman of eighteen has more
power in society, as a sex object and a worker and so on, than she will when
she's fifty. A man of eighteen has less power at eighteen than he will when
he's fifty. So it's always been true, in the last wave of feminism, this wave,
always, that women get more activist with age, whereas men tend to get more
conservative. Not all men and not all women, but in general.

"For me, that has meant that I'm more willing to be myself instead of what
other people expect me to be and therefore to flout convention. In my younger years I kept saying, 'Oh, yes, I'm definitely going to get married and have
children, just not right now.' But I assumed I would do it sometime, because
people treated you as crazy if you didn't. Now it wouldn't occur to me to
justify it in any way.

"I think I'm more radical today, using radical in a sort of classic sense of
'going to the root.' Of course, in the sixties it was defined as not voting and
so on. I think the idea that there was a choice of being within the system and
outside the system was a false choice. I don't know anybody who's outside
the system, really. And I think we all have to be in both places, or all places.
In other words, the whole idea of inside/outside, yin/yang, masculine/femi-
nine is bullshit. I mean there's not two ways of doing something, there are

a thousand ways or one or four hundred. We need to surround goals from all sides. The linear approach doesn't work. To the eyes of a sixties radical, when I tell people to vote, I would seem not radical. But in my eyes, part of covering all the bases is part of being radical. That means using electoral politics as far as it can be used—understanding its limits but using it.

"I think my strength comes from other women. I think that's where my strength comes from. None of us could last by ourselves. I mean, by myself I would have gone on thinking that biology was destiny. We are each other's textbooks. It was listening to other women tell the truth that made me understand myself. So I think first it's other women and some other men. And second, it's a kind of defiance. I am not going to argue with somebody about whether or not I'm a human being. And I'm not going to obey unjust laws. If abortion is illegal, I'm going to do everything I can to publicly flout the law. I'm just not gonna accept it. I will not be made invisible, and I will not let other people be made invisible if I can help it. I think we're all born with an attitude of defiance. It just gets beaten out of us sometimes. Maybe I was lucky because I didn't go to school until I was about twelve.

"I think both from a movement and a personal point of view, the idea of the length of the process is one of the most important lessons we've learned in the last two decades. But there are many other lessons. For instance, that the end doesn't justify the means—the end is the means. That was another problem of college; that's what they taught you. Things like Machiavelli and Marx, and the end justifies the means. Of course, the end is dictated by the means you use. You can't, for instance, give people freedom. They're too weak to take it. You can't make a revolution from the top. You can only make it from the bottom, like a house. There are all these things that turn out to be the opposite of what we were taught. Because that definition of revolution was very limited. It was just sort of who's going take over the army and the radio stations or something. That's very small potatoes. So I think the length of the process and the integrity of the process are two big lessons for me.

"We've always known that the personal is political. That was certainly a watchword of the movement from the beginning, but we keep realizing it over and over again in bigger and bigger ways. I hope that more young women will be saying, as they are now saying somewhat, 'I hope I can have as interesting a life as my mother,' as opposed to 'I don't want to be anything like my mother.' I hope that men will be raising children as much as women are. I hope that we will have established reproductive freedom as a basic right like freedom of speech.

"To put the raising children point more generally, I would say that women have moved into the world of men, but men haven't moved into the world of women. So it's not just raising children, it's also everything that has to do with the domestic sphere and also the emotional sphere. I think because we had more motivation to do so we've moved farther towards becoming whole people. But we can't go on having two jobs while they have one. And they can't go on missing the parts of themselves that they're missing. That's the next big leap forward, I think. If men consider that they might have four or five years of extra life to gain, that's a pretty big reward. The life expectancy difference is what, eight years? So we could even it out. That's not a bad offer."

Professionals with a Social Conscience

Socially conscious professionals integrate their work with their values. Gloria Steinem is not a journalist *and* a feminist, but a *feminist journalist*: a writer who covers, comments on, analyzes and attempts to further the feminist agenda. Her profession doesn't merely reflect her political beliefs, it is the primary way she expresses them.

In the sixties, so integrated a life seemed impossible. To work within the system, especially within elitist, white collar professions, and to maintain one's political integrity was thought impossible. Sixties orthodoxy, powerfully and unconditionally stated, was: You're either part of the solution or part of the problem. Clearly, being a member of a mainstream occupation—which, almost by definition, placed you, in sixties parlance, in the belly of the beast—was being part of the problem.

The professions, after all, were home to the bourgeoisie. They afforded the comfortable life to those they allowed entry. They paid well enough to support more than modest materialism. They promised security and thus tended to breed complacency and ultimately, resistance to and fear of change. The professions were criticized, and rightly so, for being bastions of white, male upper-middle-class conservatism. Even now, more than twenty years and a full generation of feminism, black and brown power later, they continue to be elitist strongholds. Only three percent of the nation's lawyers and judges are African-Americans; only two percent are Hispanic. Between three and four percent of doctors, architects and college professors, to name some of the more common professions, are non-white. About fifteen percent of those in the traditional professions are women.

Most serious young radicals of the sixties, especially those being groomed for entry into these elitist strongholds at the nation's top universities, wanted no part of the professions. That kind of life offered just the rewards—money, status, prestige—they were *not* looking for. Working with and among the poor, the disenfranchised and, for the budding Marxists among them, the working class was the "profession" radicals imagined for themselves. There they could find the human rewards they sought: the fulfillment of helping people reach their potential, the satisfaction of working for social justice, the self-respect that comes from doing meaningful work. Throwing off the cloak of privilege that their parents had so painstakingly sewn, young radicals moved south to work with the civil rights movement, to blighted urban areas to assist community organizing, to working class neighborhoods to take jobs in factories and warehouses.

Although some recognized that "right livelihood" might be found within the professions, most felt that the compromises demanded by that kind of life would dangerously undermine their integrity. Being co-opted, selling out— these were the operative fears. Most believed that to get into the system, you had to cut your hair, dress appropriately (i.e., like everyone else in the system), speak the jargon and behave accordingly. And that was just the entrance fee. If you stayed at entry level you would have little chance of making an impact on the system. You had to advance; you had to pay a higher price by competing, learning and playing the game better than your colleagues, feeding the egos of those above you, socializing, fitting in. So the process of compromise went: You had to play the game in order to amass the power necessary to change the game. But the longer you played, the more real the game became until, years and rungs in the ladder later, your original values and priorities were unalterably eroded. By the time you rose to a position of power, you no longer wanted to create a revolution from within. You had now come too far and had too much to lose.

This sixties logic was simplistic, but in some cases, not far from wrong. Consider, for example, what happened to one strain of the women's movement during the past twenty years. Sixties feminist theorists began with a critique of male culture and the various institutions that emerged from it. Equating male or masculine with such ultimately self and societally destructive traits as insensitivity, hyper-competitiveness and lack of communication, they called for the end to male hegemony and the restructuring of institutions along feminist/feminine lines. Institutions could be sensitive to the needs of their workers. They need not be rigid and rule-bound but could respond openly to change, welcoming it rather than shoring up against it. Leaders could be empathetic; they could promote cooperation and collectivity of spirit. They could "empower" those below them. This was the vision, and it was revolutionary. The reality for many was something else.

To gain entrance to the institutions they wanted to change women thought, and perhaps rightly so, that they had to play the operative game, the male game—"the game your mother never taught you." The rules of this game were simple: act like a man. Thus most of the few women who were able to move up the ladder did so by mirroring corporate male appearance ("dressing for success" in navy blue business suits) and parodying corporate male behavior (enter the cold-eyed, stiff-upper-lipped turf-fighter). By the time they arrived at the positions that would allow them to "feminize" the institution, to humanize the workplace, they had become what they were originally fighting against.

Kathleen Dolan, ex-editor of the Los Angeles *Herald-Examiner*, wrote convincingly about this phenomenon in the early eighties. As one of the very few women top editors in the country, she promoted other women into positions of power and attempted to establish a new order in the newsroom. Several years later, she left bitter and disheartened, as she watched the women she promoted exhibit all those harsh, competitive qualities she had counted on them eliminating. In the sixties—or for that matter, in the eighties—fear of being co-opted was a fear grounded in reality. It acted as a powerful deterrent to participation in mainstream institutions and the professions.

Even if they believed themselves strong enough to withstand the pressures of compromise, most sixties activists were too impatient to consider working from within. They wanted change *now*, not in twenty years after enough of them had infiltrated to make a difference. Old Lefties, a smattering of seasoned New Lefties and some red-diaper babies may have had an inkling that the process of social and political change in this country was, even under the most advantageous of circumstances, extremely slow. But the legions of newly radicalized political innocents of the late sixties did not. There may be some truth to the accusation by today's sixties bashers that many student radicals were spoiled, middle class kids used to getting what they wanted, when they wanted it (and what they wanted was massive social change). But the energy and reckless enthusiasm of twenty-year-olds coupled with the passion of the times transcended class and color. Black Panthers, Brown Berets and AIM followers all wanted immediate, significant social change. As Jim Morrison sang menacingly in 1967: "We want the world, and we want it now."

What was the best way to make change immediately, to guard against selling out, to become part of the solution? The resounding answer in the sixties was: work from outside the system; create renegade institutions; create alternative settings in which to practice redefined professions. In doing so, you could retain your integrity and independence while you did important work. Most important, you could *live* the solution while you were inventing it. Thus activists who saw journalism as an important tool for social change didn't consider the traditional route of scratching for an entry-level job on a small newspaper, and over the years, working their way up to a position at the *New York Times*—so that they might, just might, have the chance to write a major article on a socially relevant issue. They created alternative newspapers. They wrote about the socially relevant issues right then. Those who saw the health professions as vital to the new society they were trying to build also criticized the traditional health institutions for their costliness, lack of accessibility and callous, patronizing attitude. They stayed away from hospitals and group practices to start or join the free clinics that cropped up in scores of urban centers in the sixties. Those who believed that the law could be used to empower the dispossessed didn't join fancy firms, they started their own legal collectives and law clinics.

One of the most dynamic counter-institutions of the sixties and early seventies was the so-called free schools. In book after damning book, from Paul Goodman's *Compulsory Miseducation* (1966) to Ivan Illich's *Deschooling Society* (1970), from Jonathan Kozol's *Death at an Early Age* (1967) to Carl Rogers's *Freedom to Learn* (1969), philosophers, psychologists and teachers denounced mainstream educational institutions. Instead of helping to develop intelligence, schools punish creativity and independence, compound social ills, induce alienation and educate for obsolescence, they said. As Jerry Farber, then an English instructor at L.A. State College, wrote in his famous 1967 manifesto, "The Student as Nigger": "School is where you let the dying society put its trip on you. Our schools . . . exploit and enslave students; they petrify society; they make democracy unlikely. . . . Our schools teach you by pushing you around, by stealing your will and your sense of power, by making timid, apathetic slaves of you—authority addicts." But if the problem was clear, so was the solution. Teaching could be a "subversive activity," as Postman and Weingartner wrote. Alternative schools, founded by disaffected teachers and parents, would allow creativity and independence to flourish while promoting critical thinking, involvement and action—the necessary components to a real working democracy. Hundreds of such schools were established in the sixties and early seventies.

But working outside the system had its drawbacks. It was possible to expend enormous energy and reach no one other than people like yourself. "Preaching to the converted" was the cliche, and it was apt. The readers of the alternative press, for example, were already true believers. Much of what they read was not news to them but a reaffirmation of their beliefs. Those who needed alternative information were busy reading *U.S. News and World Report*. Parents who sent their children to alternative schools had their criticisms of traditional education reinforced. The free school movement served the children of the hip, bolstering values they were already getting at home. The kids to whom these values would have been new weren't sent to alternative schools. Certainly preaching to the converted was not a problem unique to the sixties—just about every sociopolitical movement in the United States has suffered the same malady—but that didn't make it any less troublesome. Over the years, many of those working in renegade institutions and counter-professions began to wonder if their time could be spent more productively. They wondered if alternative institutions ultimately served to insulate and isolate them from mainstream society, diminishing the possibility of widespread change.

They also began to see that alternative institutions often suffered from the same basic problems as those in the mainstream. They learned that collective decision-making was tedious, exhausting work, and that at some point in the life of most organizations, it is more efficient to create a hierarchy. But once the hierarchy was in place, they saw that certain people gravitated toward the top. They were drawn to power and, once they had it, wanted to keep it. The institution itself, "counter" though it may have been, began to take on a life of its own. As an organism, its job was to stay alive and perpetuate itself. It began to insulate itself, to shore up its defenses. This did not happen within all alternative structures, but it happened to many. One day, the workers at the health clinic or the legal collective looked around and wondered what had become of the grand experiment they had been part of. They wondered what was so countercultural (besides the low salary) about the place they worked in.

Or perhaps, over the years, the counter-institution remained pure. Its members worked together in intense collectivity, usually at the expense of their personal lives and always at the expense of creature comforts and long-term security. Over time, the five-hour meetings, the endless self-criticism sessions, the years of scraping to pay the phone bill every month began to take their toll.

It's not surprising that, for a variety of reasons, many sixties activists ultimately moved from alternative institutions into the mainstream, from counter-professions to the professions themselves. Of course, some made the move compelled by the desire for a higher standard of living. Others were just worn out from years of swimming against the tide. But many made the switch for positive reasons. It was not because of a softening of their value system or a great desire for material goods but because they felt the alternative institutions were not the most efficient vehicles for social change. Alternative journalists took positions with the mainstream media, bringing with them the commitment that the media must be more than defenders of the status quo. The rebirth of investigative reporting in the 1970s is attributable, at least in part, to the redefining of journalism's role in the sixties. Alternative school teachers moved into public school teaching, taking their values with them. There they were able to reach a wider, more diverse student population, proselytize among the "unconverted" faculty and help make substantive changes in curriculum and policy. Creating the "open classroom," teaching from socially relevant texts about personally relevant issues, giving students some measure of control over their own classroom experiences, peer teaching and team teaching are all legacies of that time.

But there's no denying that the system eats people. The shift from outside the institution to inside can be the first step toward selling out. Even the most well-intentioned, "politically correct" people can be co-opted. They can tire after years of attempting to change the institutions and professions they've become a part of. The needs of their families can cause them to become more cautious. They can become attracted to power. They can succumb to the Zeitgeist of the times, the "me-first-ism"—at first contemplative, then truculent—of the seventies and eighties. So much can derail continued commitment to countercultural values that it is amazing so many sixties activists have come through with their ideals and optimism intact. It is perhaps one of the most positive lessons of the past twenty years. For many people, the core values are deeply seated and deeply felt. Neither fad nor fashion, they withstand not only the increasingly conservative political environment but the recent cultural imperative to "get yours and get it now." During the twenty or so years between their first intense political involvement and their current life, many have managed to find careers that mesh with their politics and lend themselves to expression of certain values. The people in this section of the book are prime examples. And, as a variety of studies focusing on the fate of sixties activists confirm, the people you are reading about represent many others who have made similar choices.

Sociologists who study what became of sixties activists all agree on one enduring difference between them and their nonactivist contemporaries: career choice. When sociologists Richard and Margaret Braungart tracked the careers of white leaders (including most of the Chicago 7, Mark Rudd, Joan Baez and Staughton Lynd) and black leaders (including Angela Davis, Jesse

Jackson, Stokely Carmichael and others) through the seventies, they concluded that the majority "did not retreat into drugs, therapy, or communes, join the Establishment or drop out of politics." In fact, wrote the researchers, "many have made politics their career or pursued jobs that allowed them to implement their political goals."

Leaders are relatively easy to track because of their media visibility. But what of the millions of followers, the rank-and-file sixties activists? Two Florida researchers, James Fendrich and Alison Tarleau, compared the lives of civil rights activists, student government members (nonradical activists) and apolitical undergraduates from Florida State University ten years after they graduated. What they found was a significant difference in career paths. Activists chose careers that offered the most opportunity to express creativity and work for human betterment. Their nonradical and apolitical contemporaries chose careers that offered chiefly monetary and status rewards. Only seven percent of the civil rights workers were employed in business a decade after graduation, compared to more than two-thirds of the apolitical group and close to one-half of the student government group. More than half the civil rights activists were teachers; almost a third were in social service and creative occupations. These two categories attracted a total of six percent of the apolitical students and sixteen percent of the nonradical activists.

In another study, California psychologists Alberta Nassi and Stephen Abramowitz contacted fifteen people arrested in the Berkeley Sproul Hall sit-ins eleven years after their arrest. They found that these former activists were employed in social service and creative occupations more than in any other job category. Job histories didn't indicate strong upward mobility, and the average income of the fifteen was less than what would be expected for people of their age, socioeconomic background and education. One of the same psychologists went on to compare a larger group of Free Speech Movement people with their nonactivist contemporaries and found, once again, quite divergent career paths, with the activists vastly over-represented in social service occupations. Another research team compared University of Michigan activists with nonactivist undergraduates, surveying them in 1969 and 1979. They found the 100 activists disproportionately employed in government (mostly in human services programs) and conspicuously absent from private business. They also found significantly more activists than nonactivists in law and teaching.

In a one-of-a-kind in-depth study, sociologists Jack Whalen and Richard Flacks, conducted extensive life history interviews with a small group of activists accused of burning the Bank of California branch near Santa Barbara. In tracking these people from 1970 through 1984, they found interesting patterns. During the seventies, the ex-"bank burners" attempted to create or join organizations that would help them integrate personal life and social change over the long haul. They participated in alternative institutions; they worked for radical causes. Toward the end of the seventies, there was a move toward more stable career paths, a move most attributed to the demoralizing aspects of chronic economic instability. But even so, as the researchers note, "vocations were chosen because they promised opportunity for social service and creativity." By the mid-eighties, even if they were married, raising kids, holding regular jobs and worrying about money, it was also likely that they were trying to be socially responsible in their work.

Finally, there are the results of a gloriously unscientific sample of members of the "Woodstock Generation" ten years after their radicalizing experiences. In true sixties fashion, the designers of the study mailed thousands of questionnaires to everyone they could think of: their friends, friends of friends, people they met hitchhiking, friends of people they met hitchhiking, etc. More than 1,000 people responded, some at great length. The results, consistent with the most careful social science research, indicated that members of the Woodstock Generation chose careers that were not particularly financially rewarding or competitive, and that they were more likely to work in areas concerned with human services than material products.

The people in this book, all well-educated men and women in their late thirties to early fifties, reflect that tendency. There are no corporate executives or mid-level managers, no bankers, marketers, financial planners, entrepreneurs, salespeople, insurance or real estate agents. Only one of them exists in the world of business (an environmentally conscious land developer). Half are in the human services and helping professions, including government work, law, medicine and teaching. The other half are almost evenly divided between the arts, politics and the media. In the general population, an average of forty percent of college educated men and women have executive and managerial specialties, and another thirty percent of the men are technicians and salesmen.

The men and women in this section of the book are established professionals who have been working in their chosen fields throughout the seventies and eighties. A few are making good money; most are not. All operate with a strong social conscience and with palpable connections to their sixties' selves. But few are busy congratulating themselves on their own integrity. In fact, just the opposite is true. Most regularly subject themselves to the "gut check," eighties style: Am I doing enough? Is my political commitment taking too much of a backseat to my personal life? What more can I do?

Some of the people in this section are using powerful mainstream institutions to communicate important ideas to a large public. Naomi Foner, one of Harlem's first Head Start teachers, is now an award-winning Hollywood screenwriter (*Running on Empty*) who strives to make films that question the status quo. Lowell Bergman started his career as an investigative reporter for the San Diego *Street Journal*, an underground paper known for its Black Panther and Brown Beret connections. Twenty years later, he continues to delve into corruption and the abuse of power as a producer for *60 Minutes*.

Several of the people in this section are working within mainstream institutional structures to help solve significant social problems. Judy Clavir Albert, a former Yippie and feminist leader, is the development director of a statewide alcohol and drug addiction program. Paco Mazo, who lives just down the road from Pete Seeger on the thirty acres of land that fulfilled his own immigrant parents' American dream, is a psychiatric social worker who counsels prison inmates.

Other socially conscious professionals interviewed here are working to change the very nature of their fields. Ken Doctor is a midwest newspaper editor who switched from alternative journalism to the mainstream media in the early eighties. He talks about "changing the face of journalism" by understanding the newspaper as a social tool that can set the community's agenda. Abe Peck, another ex-underground editor, is now a professor in one of the country's most prestigious journalism schools. He doesn't believe the press can ever be objective, and tells his students so. He thinks the university specializes in "power tripping" students and works to subvert that tendency. Shelley Washburn taught in an alternative school for nine years before moving into the public school system. Unlike many mainstream teachers, she has enormous respect for her students and regularly puts in seventy-hour weeks giving them special out-of-class attention. Chip Marshall, an SDS leader at Cornell who moved to Seattle to lead a worker-student alliance against the war, is now vice president of a suburban land development corporation. He has been instrumental in planning an environmentally conscious residential development that promotes rather than negates a sense of community.

Still other professionals have used their status in their fields to work for larger social change. Holly Cheever, a former Harvard anti-war activist, is now a veterinarian who uses her position to fight for animal rights. David Smith founded the Haight Ashbury Free Clinic in 1967 and continues today as its president and medical director. Over the years, he has done more than any single person to place drug abuse and treatment on the traditional medical community's agenda.

These people are, by and large, middle class and middle-aged. Most have children, marriages and mortgages. But they also have values, and they, like many others, have found ways to integrate these values with their professional work lives. Twenty years ago the equation looked simple: Join the system—lose your integrity—become the enemy. But two decades of experience has proven the equation wrong, not only for these people, but for the many others they represent. It *is* possible to care about a career without succumbing, eighties style, to "careerism." It *is* possible to find meaningful work that furthers social and political change. This is one of the most positive legacies of the sixties.

Charles Reich was a Yale law professor so taken with the promise of the sixties that he wrote what was even then an embarrassingly naive and optimistic treatise, *The Greening of America*. Two years later, in an introduction to a book about Grateful Dead guitarist Jerry Garcia, he wrote something that, despite the sixties patois, stands the test of time: "The point is to find a scene where you can put out energy and have your work, high and happy. To the straight world, there's a choice: unpleasant work or no work at all. . . . The real idea is to be a functioning human being, but in a way that is not alienated, not servile, one that is fulfilling of human needs." Today, many sixties activists continue to strive for this ideal.

S H E L L E Y   W A S H B U R N ,   3 9
1972: teacher, alternative school
1989: teacher, public high school

The daughter of two schoolteachers, Shelley was born and raised in Portland,
Oregon. She began college engaged to her high school sweetheart, who was
serving in the Navy, and ended radicalized by both the anti-war and feminist
movements. She never wanted to be a teacher, but took a job in an alternative
school in 1972 because she was at loose ends and had been too lackadaisical
about applying to graduate school.

"I did not want to be a teacher. My parents were teachers, and it looked
like a horrendous job to me. It looked exhausting. And also I was somewhat
rebellious, and I thought this is what my parents do, I don't want to do it.
But as soon as I graduated, a friend of mine who was working in an alternative school said they needed an English teacher. So simply on a lark, I said,
'Well, all right. I'll do that for a while before I go to graduate school. I'm sick
of going to school; it sounds like fun.' And this was a school for students having problems. This was the last step for these people. They'd been booted
out of public schools. I started out working with teenagers, and eventually
in my two years there worked with all age levels. And I was hooked. I saw
that we were making an impact on these kids.
    "Then I went to another alternative school, and this was the school that
changed my life. And that's the school where I stayed for nine years. It was
a private school, started in 1973 by five public school teachers who had
reached a consensus about their educational philosophy and decided that
they couldn't go on in the public school system, that they had another vision.
And they were marvelous people, still are. They believed that the main concern of the school should be the child, and that the education should give
the child the skills to function in today's world and hopefully in what we envision to be tomorrow's world. They believed that you freed the students when
you taught them to read.
    "I came to believe that what I was doing was the most important work
that a person could be doing. These were students from all over the place.
Many of them had very high skills, and their parents didn't want them in the
public school system, didn't feel they were being challenged. At the other end
of the spectrum, there were kids who were underachieving. There were all
kinds of students, and we were having a phenomenal success rate with them.
We had a small student/teacher ratio. The teachers were empowered; the students were empowered, and we were working together.
    "I guess it was one of the most important times in my life because I came
to be very clear about the culture I wanted to see. I was trying to educate
children for the culture I saw around me, but also for what I envisioned. And
it's an odd combination because I was trying to educate for the future, but

I was also trying to change the future and affect it. The vision was that these students would be empowered. We considered basic skills to be art and swimming and cooking and also using the community as a resource. We wanted students who would be able to go out and get their needs met and contribute to the culture. And so for me, it became an important place because I envisioned a world where people would be able to cooperate with each other. Nonviolence was one of our tenets—cooperation. I envisioned a world where people would not get their information solely from the television set, where they would have a dialogue with other people. I envisioned community.

"And I really believed it back in the seventies. I believed that we were creating a new world. I really believed it. I'm much more cynical now, and yet I still believe it to a certain extent, or I wouldn't be teaching. But back then I imagined a world where people were going to be able to work together, have respect for one another; where gender bias would eventually fade, and where we could teach students to problem solve and not resort to violence. I just saw a truly gentler world. I saw it working in my own school, and it worked beautifully."

Shelley taught in the alternative school for nine years. But in the early eighties, the battle for funding became too draining, and the teachers who had run the school cooperative decided to close it. "We just got tired," Shelley says quietly. For the past five years, she has taught English in the public school system.

"I have a list a mile long of the things that have sort of hardened me or made me more practical. And I regret that. Yet part of aging, or maturing, may be to leave behind some of those very idealistic dreams. I don't know, I go up and down about it. Sometimes I think it's realistic to expect less, and other times I think it's a cop-out and a 'dream deferred,' as Langston Hughes says. Within the public school system itself, the way the system is set up, teachers lack real decision-making powers, and because of that people begin to feel helpless. And it's passed on—it's a vertical kind of disempowerment. It's passed on to students.

"The students are very aware of a hierarchy as well, and that they have very little input at times as to what happens to them. In other words, the content and the method are not really up to students, and neither is it up to the teachers to make those kinds of decisions often. And I think that that's been discouraging, and I've gone around with myself on this, thinking maybe this is just the way it is in America, and I should accept the role of worker. Of course, I don't and I don't think I should, but it makes me cynical at times, makes me want to give up.

"These are some of the things that make me want to give up at times—the fact that students are packed into the classrooms. And so you have the student who's fading or disappearing or borderline psychotic, and you see him but you can't touch him because time constraints stop you, all the bodies in the room stop you. And it breaks your heart to see this person who desperately needs attention, who needs drawing, pulling out, and the bell rings, and the kid's gone, and if he doesn't come back after class, you never reach him.

"I used to have a dream when I taught in the alternative school, a very powerful dream, a nightmare. It was that I had about thirty students in a swimming pool, and I was trying to pluck them out of the pool because they were all drowning, and I was always saving them, saving, saving, and it was a constant battle pulling them out. What I find interesting is now I never have that dream. And when I analyze it, I think the reason I had that dream is that when I was in the alternative school, I actually believed or thought that I had the capacity or the ability to save them. And now that dream isn't even an issue for me. I can't save them all. I don't feel that powerful. And so I don't even have that dream.

"I think that alternative teachers bring with them a more humane teaching style. For example, they give students the respect that they are asking for, instead of coming in and demanding it, instead of treating the students badly and then saying, 'Now respect me.' I think that I bring to the institution a personal touch—and that is that I'm available after school, and kids can come and talk to me about their parents or about abortion, and I can give them suggestions for counseling or work with them on problem-solving. And I'm not the only one who does that. A lot of the people who have alternative backgrounds spend a lot of extra time with students.

"Some of the other teachers, especially the older ones, tease us. There's a teacher who says, 'Oh, you touchy-feely teachers. Oh, you old hippies.' I don't think that they really dislike it, but they sort of tease us about it, and ask us when are we gonna grow up. But the students need that. I mean, they can't talk with you in the four or five minutes between the bells. I'm somebody who cares, and I'm willing to stay until six or seven at night. And I'm willing to give kids my phone number. And I'm willing to spend time.

"I really haven't been involved in other political causes. And in defense, I would say that I worked on an average of twelve hours a day and then probably eight hours a day on the weekends, and I am not exaggerating. So my entire life has been taken up, especially at [the public school] with grading papers and lesson plans. And so no, I haven't done volunteer work. I consider my teaching volunteer work. Outside of teaching, I've had no life. I never had children. It was something I just couldn't bring myself to do, I guess because I had so many at school, and I just couldn't picture myself teaching and having a child. What I figured was I would have to quit teaching, and that it would be a choice between one or the other. And I chose teaching."

This year, Shelley is taking a leave of absence. "I'm exhausted," she says, "and I'd like to see what life is like outside the classroom." She is considering working on environmental issues and will probably assist her long-time partner, a cinematographer, with his documentary work.

"The drowning dream shows that I used to think that I could touch every one of those kids, and it was possible to send out thirty kids a year into the world who had a more cooperative world view. Now I guess I'm a little more realistic—maybe because of the constraints on my own energy and also just the reality of the public system. But now I'm happy if I hit a handful. And I have great hopes for them.

"This kid Eric who had trouble last year—now he's reading Yeats, and he gave me a book by Ursula LeGuin at the end of the year and told me that I'd really had an impact on him. And I thought, 'You know, this really feels good.' But now I don't take as much responsibility for Eric's success. He was gonna be cool anyway; he was gonna make it anyway. So now I'm more realistic about my role. I gave him a little bit of a push, or I gave him a couple of hugs, or I gave him some attention, and it just made his task a little easier. And so now I realize that I'm not gonna reach every kid. But I still believe that I'm having a positive impact on some people's lives. They tell me that.

"All I can believe in now is that each one of us takes our little corner of the world and tries to do what we can with it, to leave it better than we found it. And I guess I don't believe anymore that we're headed for a more ideal society. I guess that I've come to terms with the fact that every generation thinks that this is it. This is the end. Apocalypse now. And I teach anyway. I go on in the face of that, in the face of sometimes believing that things are getting worse. I teach anyway. And it's almost like money in the bank or a hope that someday my students will go out and they'll leave their little piece of the world in a better condition, and maybe I had some part in that."

DAVID SMITH, 50
1967: founder, Haight Ashbury Free Clinic
1989: medical director, Haight Ashbury Free Clinic

David was a very traditional medical student who says he exhibited "not a hint of activism" in his college years. He attended University of California, San Francisco, and lived in the Haight Ashbury district, like other poor students, because it was cheap and convenient.

After earning his M.D. in 1964, he interned at San Francisco General Hospital and did research in his specialty, biological psychiatry and psychopharmacology (the study of the effects of drugs on the mind). In June of the Summer of Love, 1967, David leased a few rooms above a nearby store and began operating the clinic in response to what he saw in his neighborhood: "All these young people taking drugs that I was sticking into animals in the lab."

"My original interest was in the chemical probe of the mind, the study of brain chemistry and adjunct psychotherapy and tools for understanding natural causation of psychopathology. Very academic. I remember the first thing that really impacted on me in terms of the counterculture was I observed that when people would have bad trips, like at a concert—there was a lot of high dose LSD-taking then for a religious experience—when they would have bad trips and really freak out, their friends would talk them down. And they'd have this whole thing with Timothy Leary's *Tibetan Book of the Dead*. And there was a whole lot of emphasis on setting, and a lot of nonpharmacological variables that were not taught in standard medicine.

"If the same kids had a bad trip and went into the emergency room, they were given high doses of medication. I observed that they did better if they stayed in their own natural culture. One of the early contributions of the Haight Ashbury Free Clinic was that we set up a Calm Center and developed a talk-down technique and really saved the emergency room and the hospital thousands of hospitalizations by using this talk-down approach. We really used a healthcare team. It wasn't just a medical team, but it was people from the culture that understood drugs. And this talk-down approach worked better than the hospitalization approach. And that really impressed me. There were a lot of interesting things happening in the drug culture, and in certain respects they knew better how to handle these drug reactions than did the medical community in the dominant culture.

"My first entree into the counterculture was the free clinic, but once I got involved with that, it all started happening at once. It's hard to say what came first. I mean I got involved in the free clinic, and I went from being very conservative to marching in anti-war marches and getting involved in civil rights. It's kinda like it all happened at one time. I went through a period of time in the late sixties, early seventies in which I had long hair and was described as a 'hippie doctor.'

"In terms of the free clinic, free is a philosophical concept that was in part born out of the civil rights movement and Martin Luther King's 'free at last, free at last, thank God almighty I'm free at last.' It was an alternative healthcare clinic. In the beginning it was primarily flower children, hippies, who were taking drugs and were not being taken care of. But essentially it was a civil rights type of thing in that we felt that the system did not have a right to deny care just because they disapproved of a particular lifestyle. And our original philosophy was—and still is—that health care is not a privilege, that people have a right to health care."

In 1967, the clinic operated on a shoestring, with donated medical supplies, volunteer help and David as the sole full-time physician. Today, thirty paid staff, including six physicians and fifty volunteers administer the clinic's five thriving sections: medical (with special attention to sexually transmitted diseases), emergency (delivering services to rock concerts), women's health, drug detoxification and alcoholism treatment.

"The clinic was originally very much considered anti-establishment. I know when I started the Haight Ashbury Clinic my malpractice carrier read about it in an article in *Look* magazine around '67 and he called up and said, 'I didn't know you were treating those weirdos.' And he canceled my malpractice insurance. So for a while we ran the clinic without malpractice insurance, which is totally unheard of today. We really perceived ourselves at that time as an alternative organization, as part of the civil rights movement, dealing with ostracized outsiders.

"Today about 85 percent of our funding is public and we're much more of a mainstream institution with stricter administrative procedure. There's extremely careful malpractice insurance. We've got a medical staff with risk management review, we've got a computer, a fax machine. All the stuff that's required to survive in the nineties.

"Our philosophy is that we have the values of the sixties and the technology of the eighties. You have to have the technology to survive in this very complicated modern world, and if we didn't adapt, then we wouldn't have survived. We still have our basic value system, our clinic philosophy's still the same. And we reaffirm the clinic philosophy—that health care is a right not a privilege. One, it should be free at the point of delivery for all who need it. Two, primary health services should be comprehensive, unfragmented, and decentralized. Three, medicine should be demystified, nonjudgmental and humane. Health care should be delivered in a courteous and educational manner. When possible, patients should be permitted to choose among alternative methods of treatment. And four, healthcare skills with an emphasis on preventive medicine should be transmitted to worker and patient alike. The essence of this is published in our earliest articles. These goals and objectives are reiterated at our clinic staff meetings.

" 'Health care is a right not a privilege' was perceived as very radical in the sixties. It was far less radical in the seventies. In fact, President Carter in his inaugural speech included it. But now, for two-thirds of the people in the U.S., the infant mortality rate, for example, is close to the best in the world. But for one-third of the population, the lower socioeconomic, mostly non-white population, the infant mortality rate is down with Third World countries like Haiti. So in the eighties, with this two-tiered system, our philosophy is becoming radical again. One of the reasons that we've held to our basic philosophies is to serve as an example.

"When I started, treating addicts was a very radical act. Now we have over 3,600 physicians in our national organization, American Society of Addiction Medicine. There's a well-established medical specialty of addiction medicine. In fact, I guess a sign of the times, I'm now an alternate delegate to the AMA [American Medical Association] in addiction medicine.

"I think the thing that keeps me optimistic is not so much changing the system but the community-based living and working and seeing people recover from life-threatening addiction or from serious health problems and being part of that process. I have my greatest optimism at the community and individual level. My forays into the national arena have been less than optimistic. The current healthcare system is in such crisis that I can't see how it can go on like it is. And yet I don't yet see a strong welling-up change. Some people have said that the only benefit of the terrible AIDS tragedy is that it will bankrupt the healthcare delivery system and force change.

"There are the problems of crack, cocaine, AIDS and the homeless. A lot of our patient population now is homeless. We see a lot of mentally ill patients who are dual diagnosis—addiction and mental illness. And that's a failure of the mental health system where they closed down the state mental hospitals and didn't provide adequate resources for humane mental health. It's kind of like the Haight Ashbury Clinic sees the system's failures. Whenever there's an economic downswing, and people lose their health insurance, then we see the unemployed. Or whenever a particular health problem is not being taken care of in the system, Haight Ashbury provides that service."

David has three children, all born and raised in the Haight. Twenty-three years after establishing the clinic, he is still its president and medical director. He also teaches, writes and travels to spread the word about addiction medicine, a specialty he has almost single-handedly pioneered.

"The experience of being a parent is very moderating. I'm just like every parent. I'm very concerned that my kids will experiment with drugs. I spend a lot of time with them around that. Family has become my most important thing, which means—I'm fifty now—if I'd had a family back then, I doubt I would have done this. I know I wouldn't have. I wouldn't have risked it. When you start a free clinic without malpractice insurance and work day and night, it's not just the time, but you absolutely risk everything. But that's the way things were then. There was a mindset of idealism and activism, people were going down and risking their lives in Mississippi.

"There's been this dissection of the sixties thing: 'Oh, it was just fun and games. People didn't really believe what they were doing then.' Well, that's just not true. We really did believe that we could change the system and end the war and end racial prejudice by the end of 1967. Terribly naive in retrospect, but it was a very passionate, idealistic time, and of course, things were going terribly wrong in the system. And then '68 came along with all the violence, which was very alienating, at every level—politics, war and everything. Speed hit then, and violence also entered the drug culture with speed. And then your values were really tested. I mean, mine were. A lot of people left. But other people, including myself, said, 'Look, if we really believed all this, then we have to stay even if the people we're taking care of are not the flower children any more.'

"I think I'm much more realistic and targeted now. My primary focus has been in the field of addiction medicine. And I'm more conservative, particularly about drug issues. Much more family-oriented, less risk-oriented. I'm still very committed in this sixties dream, but in a much more directed and targeted way. In terms of my own personal thing, I plan to live and die in the Haight. I'm not gonna move anywhere. I'm just going to try to keep this whole thing going."

JUDY CLAVIR ALBERT, 46

1968: Yippie/feminist
1989: alcohol and drug abuse program director

Born, raised, schooled, married and divorced in Toronto, Judy was a red-diaper baby who chose to study sociology because someone told her it was the best way to change the world. She came to Berkeley in the fall of 1967 for an American Sociological Association convention and fell in love with the whole scene: the politics, the mind-expanding drugs, the sun, a psychedelic house she stayed at in the Berkeley hills. The following year she met Stewart Albert and, during the summer of 1968, the two lived in the basement of Abbie Hoffman's "Liberty House" in New York, where they helped found the Youth International Party (Yippies) and plan the Chicago '68 demonstration.

"I was an anarchist because I liked to do things immediately, get immediate gratification and didn't see the need for any authority. I was always more fun-loving than the SDS. Less quote, unquote serious. That's not to say that Yippies weren't serious in the sense of wanting to get things done, which we did. But there was a sense that you could do it with a sense of humor, and have a good time doing it. I was never in SDS, ever.

"That summer we worked on the plans for Chicago, and then we went. And that was something else; my memories of that are both clear and vague at the same time. We spent a lot of time in the park, planning—I don't know if that word is actually real. It's certainly not real if you think of planning in the sense that we do today, where you actually think things through and have objectives and goals and stuff like that. It was not nearly as coherent as that. But I guess my most vivid memory is being in the park the first night and seeing Allen Ginsberg and a bunch of people sitting down and 'Om-ing,' assuming that their 'Om' would change the way that things were going. And then looking up and seeing the lights, tanks and in front of them a cloud of tear gas coming over the hill. It was just amazing, truly incredible. And of course we ran, because of the tear gas. I've never experienced anything like that in my entire life, in terms of its severity.

"I can't say that I remember Chicago changing me. But my guess is that it did because I don't see how it couldn't have. The popular thing to say is that it brought me to a level of understanding of the repressiveness of the police state or something like that. The truth is, I'm sure it did, but everything was going on so quickly that it was all part of a process."

Judy and Stew drove back to Berkeley after the Chicago convention, where they lived communally with Tom Hayden and became involved in the Berkeley Liberation Program and the fight over People's Park. Judy became one of the founders of the local women's movement, during which time she and Stew broke up. ("I thought he was an irredeemable sexist, and he thought I was out of my mind," she says.) She was a member of the first all-women delegation to visit Vietnam, returning home to travel around the country agitating against the war and for women's liberation. In 1972, Judy and Stew resumed their relationship. Five years later, on May Day, with a conservative rabbi, William Kunstler and a Universal Life Church minister presiding, they married. A month later, their daughter Jessica was born.

In the early eighties, Judy taught sociology and women's studies at Mills College, in the process co-editing (with Stew) *The Sixties Papers*, an anthology of movement speeches and documents. Now they live in Portland, Oregon, where Judy is the development director for a statewide nonprofit organization working to combat alcoholism and drug abuse. She also works with the New Jewish Agenda, the Peace Now movement, and the AIDS quilt project. Most recently, she helped found a state chapter of the Women's Foundation, an organization that raises funds and disburses them to various girl's and women's projects.

"One of the big changes that I've made is about drugs. In the sixties, we didn't know about addiction. Or we didn't want to believe it. We had a sense that drugs were liberating, and drugs were wonderful, and that was true for everybody. And there's no question that probably for the majority of the population a little bit of marijuana is like a little bit of wine, it can relax you, and you can have a good time and enjoy yourself and that's all there is to it. This incidentally is not my organization's position, it's mine. But what we didn't understand is that people get addicted to drugs. We had no concept of that, we really didn't. And in our promoting drugs, we didn't take into account that people got addicted. One of the things we did do in the sixties was make a differentiation between what we called life drugs and death drugs. And death drugs were—we didn't have crack in those days, but we did have heroin. And those can still be considered death drugs. But we had a much too cavalier attitude about it.

"Where my sixties values have remained the same on the drug issue is that I don't believe we should be pouring all this money into interdiction and stopping the supply of drugs, because really what people need is the ability to get into treatment and have recovery. And what we could do with a lot of this money that's poured into drug interdiction and supply is to have free or low-cost treatment centers, neighborhood treatment centers, that would really alleviate the problems. In the old days we talked about free legalized abortion on demand. At this point, you would want to talk about free accessible drug treatment centers. We have a foreign policy that supports dictatorships that are basically financed through drug dealing and through drug smuggling. And so really, if we want to alleviate the drug problem in this country we have to change the foreign policy and have a much more democratic, easily available access to treatment.

"I go to a lot of meetings with a lot of cops and a lot of supply-side people, and I get along very well with them, because one of the things that you learned in the sixties was to get along with all kinds of people even if you disagreed with their political point of view. It turns out that one of the people who works for one of the major treatment centers . . . and you know he'll talk about flag waving and so on. Well, he turns out to be the activist who was pushed through the plate glass window at the Hilton Hotel in Chicago in '68, and he's a real good friend of mine. So what goes around comes around. Basically my view is that if people are working to help people into recovery in whatever way, then they're working to help save people's lives.

"I have my ups and downs. I'm not a straight-line optimist all the time. I used to be. I used to be an optimist in the face of anything. Now I'm much more realistic. Certainly, Abbie's suicide affected me very deeply because you get a sense, well here's a person who was really committed out front to the old values, one of the few who carried on in the actual movement for social change and wasn't finding enough satisfaction in that life, therefore killed himself. So that was very upsetting to have to face that. He was a good friend. So I guess my family keeps me going, the desire to live a yuppie life and be surrounded by nice objects, which I've always had. I feel everyone should have the opportunity to live well. But then you contrast that with increasing homelessness, increased suffering of people, the increased division of society into the rich and the rest of us. And the very poor. It is really hard to live in a city where you're constantly being faced with the fact that people are really suffering. Men, women and children are suffering because they don't have enough to eat or because they don't have a roof over their head. And so I feel that in my work, in terms of addiction, I'm at least helping a little bit on that.

"You never know what the effect is of what you do. You find that you say something to someone and ten years later, they'll come back and say, 'You said this and this and it changed my life.' I think that in the sixties we had a more direct sense that what we were doing was affecting power and affecting the world. I think that now the sixties generation is poised to exert real power, and I think we actually do in a lot of ways. There are people in Congress, there are people in the newspapers, there are people in the media. There are people with the sixties values strategically placed in all walks of life.

And everything that they do affects people's consciousness. But I guess I don't have as much of a sense that what I do specifically is going to change the world the way I used to. 'Cause I don't see the avenue; and believe me, I tell you, I'd still like to be where the action is—if it existed, I'd be there. But for me, it doesn't exist. And that's not to say that the Nicaragua movements and all that aren't doing enormous amounts of good because they are. But that is not where I feel comfortable at this time.

"I am no longer a person who goes to extremes. I would call that aging. Mellowing. Today a lot of my energy is invested in my job and my family and my political work. I also think that the right-wing has essentially taken over extremism. So there's no market for it, there's no vehicle in which you can be an extremist and feel right. And also I think that we went too far in some instances in the sixties. For example, the uncritical view of Vietnam that we had, the sense that you had to work outside the system and not within it. I definitely work within the system now to change things. I don't know what it would mean to work outside the system.

"I have a lot of faith, and I say this from a very grandmotherly point of view, in the younger generation, I really do. I see Jessica [her daughter], and she's talking to me about the 'old growth forest' and this and that. She's unique because she has all these sixties characters in her life. You know, we all used to talk about the contradictions that would exacerbate and eventually bring about change. And I think that that's happening. Because you have young people with a lot of conscience today. You have people who are hungry and people who are homeless. And you have a government that's financially bankrupt and emotionally flat. And you don't know what's going to go on in five years or ten years. But I do know that if we get involved in whatever movements come along, we'll be probably be treated with as much disrespect as we treated the older people in the 1960s. We had our moment in the sun and whatever comes along, it's gonna be in the hands of younger people, as it was in China."

PACO MAZO, 40
1972: Peace Corps volunteer
1989: psychiatric social worker

The son of Spanish immigrants who fled during the civil war, Paco grew up in an eighteenth century farmhouse on thirty acres in upstate New York. He went to a small private college in Iowa and spent his junior year in Madrid, where he watched Franco's troops ride their horses through the corridors of the university, chasing students who were demonstrating against the Vietnam War. In the early seventies he joined the Peace Corps and spent two years in Guatemala, returning to earn two master's degrees, one in rehabilitation counseling and one in social work. In the late seventies, he worked in VISTA in California, helping senior citizens get legal assistance.

"I kinda grew up pretty politicized as much as I could be, given that my parents were pretty much illiterate immigrants. But my parents were totally opposed to the war in Vietnam. My mother used to sit and cry in front of the TV. She had twin sons who were draft age. And she had a brother who was put up against a wall and shot in Spain because of his political convictions. So she used to tell me, 'This isn't your war. Don't get involved in the war.' And they found me a girlfriend in Montreal when I was about twelve. They used to drive me to Canada, used to say, 'Go to Spain, go to Mexico, go someplace. Don't get caught up in this thing.' But then again, I had my own friends that were going to Vietnam. In the class ahead of me, a bunch of my friends went to Vietnam. Then three or four guys out of my class went to Vietnam.

"It was a real conflict. I felt that I didn't want to be any part of it, yet I felt that my childhood friends were there and I should support them. My first friend died in Vietnam September 8th, 1967, and that's when the reality of it hit. It's funny. My specialty is posttraumatic stress. And I've worked with Vietnam veterans for the Veterans Administration doing outreach programs and doing the Vet Center program and working up to being the coordinator of a unit for Vietnam veterans, one of the ten programs in the country. Maybe it was my survivor guilt about the war, the friends I lost in the war. Maybe it was my conviction to help those guys out, the underdogs that got caught up in the war. Anyway, given my background it's kinda crazy how I ended up working with them.

"So what happened was I got a job with the Veterans Administration in Santa Barbara. I was one of two social workers between L.A. and San Francisco. I traveled up and down the coast visiting veterans that were in either nursing homes or so infirm that they couldn't go out. Doing home visits. I had World War I vets who were hermits living up in the woods near San Francisco. And I had a Vietnam vet triple amputee who ran a ranch. Doing the psychiatric social work, I saw a lot of the problems, especially the readjustment problems of Vietnam veterans. Saw a lot of self-medication because of the inability to integrate back into society after having that experience. I saw their rejection by society, labeled baby killers and all, which was really sad.

"I still believed in the revolution then. I still believed in 'the people.' I remember May Day in 1980, it really opened my eyes. I was with a political group and they wouldn't give us a permit to have a May Day demonstration. We had to walk on the sidewalk. When we got to where there were all these big tall buildings, with no people, then the police hit us. They put people in the hospital. It was really warfare. I was there with my wife, who was pregnant, who was carrying our first child, and I was thinking that we were either going to jail or to the hospital.

"I saw a lot of people go down that day. And there was a lot of blood on the street. They didn't care whose heads they were breaking. I mean there were pools and pools of blood. There were helicopters in the air, and they brought in those huge batons and they were twirling batons with big shields. And they hit us. I mean they sealed off the entire area. I had been working with Vietnam vets, and I had been reexperiencing combat in my office in therapy. But this was real combat for me.

"So we got out of there. We moved back to Iowa. And this sounds like it's a story, but it's true. I was working in a neuropsych hospital in Knoxville, Iowa. I was driving home one day thinking about what had happened to me in the last year. Here I was in the desperate state of Iowa working in this neuropsych hospital. I had an Alzheimer ward, and I had the largest ward of Huntington's chorea. I'm coming home, I'm crying. I'm literally crying. There's a broadcast on about traveling minstrels, these people who were traveling from country to country, making music, saying there are no borders. They were just singing and walking through Central America, through South America. 'Don't tell us about borders, don't tell us about political things. We're walking.' And I'm crying. I'm thinking: Where has my life gone? What is going on right now?

"I can't say it was the same day, but within a few days, I hear Pete Seeger on the radio, and he's talking about . . . I guess the theme was: Your homeland was where you're from, you have to protect it. He was talking about this environmental stuff. And he said, 'What happens is, when some change comes into an area, people don't want to deal with the change so they leave. And when they leave, they leave the stewardship, they leave the responsibility to protect and preserve the land to the people that come in. And the people that come in have no idea of what's there because that's not their home.'

"And it was so true to my experiences. I had left my home in New York, you know. I had left the farm in New York. I had left this piece of ground, which was kinda sacred to me. And I tell ya, here I am in my '62 Volvo at a stop sign going 'Wow.' Listen to this. 'Cause you know Pete Seeger was never really anything to me. So anyway, here I am, and I get this flash saying we gotta go home. We gotta go and do something. We have to be someplace. 'Cause I felt as though I was in limbo in Iowa.

"So I got on the phone, and I think I found a job the same day. I called the VA hospital, and I called my brother and said, 'Hey, we're coming home to be on the farm.' We came back to New York, and I used to take the commuter train down to Montreux to the psych hospital, where I was continuing to work with Vietnam vets. And I was getting off the train one day, and a friend said, 'You want to go sailing?' I said, 'Yeah, sure.' So she said, 'Well, there's Pete. Maybe we can go sailing.' And there was Pete Seeger. It was really crazy. First that message from him on the radio that brought me back and then him, right there. He was a neighbor, and I didn't even know it. So I kinda fell into working on the crew."

Paco now works as a psychiatric social worker with Spanish-speaking clients in a nearby prison, and also runs a weekly group for children of alcoholics. He is an active volunteer with Pete Seeger's Clearwater project and recently coordinated a two-day music festival.

"I don't like to drop his name a lot, but I kind of look at Pete as an inspiration. I've never really asked him how he keeps going. But the Clearwater Organization keeps going. And four times a year we have festivals. And we have successes. We work together in all kinds of ways. There's no telling what the power of the people on the river can do. We get together. We have meetings. We share. We share potluck dinners and talk. We look at the problems and see how we can help and then we go for it. It might mean just cleaning up a parking lot, cleaning up a beach. But we get there, and we do it. We do it together. And we share that experience of making changes. That's very important for me. That's what keeps me going, because I can see that it can be done. And when it's real hard to keep going, I can draw on that experience.

"I think that right now I'm beginning to see how to integrate the parts of my life: of teaching my children, of being environmentally aware, of being politically conscious. I've had to accommodate my children, my responsibilities to them, and approach activism more like a lifestyle. I mean, if you're gonna continue doing it, you have to plan better and integrate it into your life so that it becomes more of a lifelong project. You learn how to be there for the long haul or else you burn out."

ABE PECK, 44
1968: editor, Chicago Seed
1989: professor, Northwestern University

Raised in a working class Jewish home in a Bronx neighborhood where "you experienced blacks only as apartment superintendents and Gentiles as people who would give you a hard time," Abe graduated from Bronx High School of Science ("Todd Gitlin–Stokely Carmichael Memorial High School"). He went to New York University to study aeronautical engineering but quickly changed his mind and became a history major.

"I knew some people in YPSL [Young People's Socialist League], but the idea of sixteen-year-olds arguing about Trotsky . . . I couldn't figure out what that meant, or why—especially since there was baseball to argue about.

But I had three interesting political experiences that led to my awakening. Actually I was a voyeur in all three. The first one, I think, was the Cuban missile crisis. I remember sitting in this guy's car listening to the radio and being scared shitless, listening to this guy who was kind of left, but I wasn't hearing the left part, I was hearing the 'this is the end, my friend' part. Then the second was going downtown once and seeing a picket at Woolworth's during the Freedom Rides. That really blew my mind. I responded to it very strongly. I had heard about what was going on in the South. But Woolworth's—God, that was like Disney or something, a symbol. The third thing was when Kennedy was shot. I had a liberal professor who insisted on holding class? And a friend and I walked out. It was like our disillusionment with liberalism. We walked out and went to my friend's house and got drunk. Which I guess is an inchoate political protest. It just seemed wrong. If you dug this guy, why hold class? Another similar thing was when I was in graduate school at NYU and there was a teach-in and I heard some people speaking out against the government. I thought that was really, really heavy. This was not Progressive Labor or anything, just statements like 'the government can be wrong.'

"I was just kind of dorking along. I was 21 or 22 at the time, working full-time, going to graduate school full-time—and both were failing. I had too much to do and not enough time or money to do it. I got a job at an insurance company because I thought I was going to get married, but that didn't go. I also joined the Army reserves because I thought I was going to get married. This was 1966, so there I was in a Green Beret unit because that's the only thing I could get into at that point. So the marriage went, school went, and I'm living on the Lower East Side, staying up all night Saturday, living a psychedelic hippie life and then going to the reserve meetings on Sunday. I was really spread out, a rubber band, living a lot of contradictions."

In May of 1967, Abe's reserve unit was called up, but his poor eyesight almost immediately got him a discharge. At loose ends, he trekked to San Francisco for the Summer of Love, thumbed back to New York and then took a job as a textbook salesman in Chicago. There he lived in a hotel for prostitutes, sold no books and took the company car to the Pentagon demonstration.

"The whole thing collapsed, and I started living in Lincoln Park with the guy who owned the head shop. Then I got involved with the Yippies. I wrote a letter to Paul Krassner because he had written a thing in the *Realist* about wanting to move out of New York. I knew a guy with a farm, so I wrote to Krassner volunteering the guy's farm, and I got a response from Jerry Rubin instead, who told me about the groovy festival that was going to happen in Chicago. So I went down to the *Seed* to write an article about it—and I stayed for several years after that. I was there for several years straight, then on and off through '71. I wrote my first piece in October '67 and kind of checked out for good in '71.

"So I wasn't a Freedom Rider, and I wasn't a red-diaper baby. I was moved viscerally by what was going on. I thought it was existentially correct to protest. I wasn't a Buddhist or an existentialist, but I thought there really was a thing like 'Right Action' and 'Right Behavior,' and that even though I was running around demented, a real freak, I really did have a moral sense. I was also firmly convinced that the psychedelic apocalypse was the way to go. We were at the dawn of new forms of relationships. So I could have been a candidate to go to the woods, because that's where a lot of those people went, but I didn't. I didn't because I stayed with politics longer than those people and because I found out that I like to write. I never thought of it as a career, at least not overtly, but I thought that I had a craft and I wanted to work on it. At the same time, I thought I had something to say.

"In '71 I was 26 years old, I was broke, and I had left the country because I was convinced that I would be jailed or worse, that I would hurt someone. I had been close to several illegal activities, and I just thought I had to get out of here. I really didn't like America. I didn't like who I was especially, and I didn't like big chunks of the revolution either. I was a bit of a casualty. I was burnt out. I didn't know what to believe any more. So I started writing."

Abe wrote for the *Chicago Reader* and reviewed left-wing books for the *Daily News*. He started a little post-hippie magazine in Chicago that didn't go. In 1975 he began writing for *Rolling Stone* —"a place to have a craft but not be in the mainstream"—first in San Francisco, and then in New York. In the late seventies, he returned to Chicago and began writing features and a weekly column for the *Sun-Times*. In 1980, he quit to write a book (*Uncovering the Sixties: The Life and Times of the Underground Press*) and begin what would become a teaching career. He now directs the magazine sequence at Medill School of Journalism, Northwestern University.

"You could take this whole resume and say this is my long march into the institution. You could take one look and say, 'This guy was a working class straight kid, who then had a curve of about four or five years—who, like many people in America, fell off the edge, but then got back in.' Or you could say, 'This is a person who was a mainstream kid, found something else, pursued it, discovered those utopias didn't work, and has tried to take parts of that back in with him.' What I don't like about either of those is that they're too mechanistic. I've never mapped out my life, which I think in some ways is very typical of sixties people.

"I think I've taken a lot from the sixties with me. I like being around young people, which is why I'm teaching now. I like to think I'm forthcoming. It's a legacy of the sixties that I don't want to power trip students.

"I'm much more open to alternate points of view. I'm a change watcher. I'm more respectful of inspired amateurism. I'm skeptical. I know there were times when I was wrong, and when the *Seed* ran stuff that was wrong, and when we did it deliberately—which was one of the reasons I left. So I think skepticism is part of the legacy. Also enthusiasm. I think one of the things about the underground press is it had a great zeal and a positive disrespect for institutions. I like to think I still have this.

"But my life is a lot quieter than it was, in part because I've got a seven-year-old and a five-year-old. I work hard; my wife works hard. In some ways, we're really middle-aged, middle class professionals, a two-career family with two kids, and that's one of the things that really defines our lives.

"I'm much more traditional than I thought I'd be. It's all very subtle. It's like, I don't know how I got from there to here. I'm not stunned, but I'm just not sure. I'm monogamous. I don't use drugs. I live in a nuclear family. I own a house. I have a job. I drive a Buick. But politically I'm to the left of 95 percent of the people in this country.

"I see myself as a pretty moral person. I like to think of myself as intellectually moral. I can't close off things I learned from the sixties about how the world works. Even if some of the lessons were painful, and even if some of the lessons were wrong, they weren't all wrong. I'm much less of an ideologue now. I guess my view now is that every extreme we took was wrong, in terms of 'Amazon Nation' and 'Doper Country,' but that doesn't mean you throw out the baby with the bathwater. It doesn't mean that you throw away some of the things you found along the way that were valid. I try not to have a sixties hangover. I hated last summer with all the [Woodstock anniversary] coverage. I thought it sealed off the period, and just made it into something we did when we were younger.

"I don't want to say I was burned by the sixties because that implies the sixties were conscious. But I've learned not to be a true believer. I'm a little more reluctant to commit, plus I have countervailing commitments—I commit to work, I commit to my family. But I just think certain sensitivities and sensibilities are different as a result of going through the sixties.

"People might say I'm putting icing on a compromised life. But I'm not quite sure what I'm supposed to be joining. I'm just not the person who's going to create that window, like [three-term socialist mayor] Bernie Sanders did in Burlington [Vermont], but I might be the person who climbs through if there was that space. And that's a change. I was an activist; now I've retreated to the second ranks. But I think when something comes along, I'll be interested.

"The thing is that people from the sixties have a different agenda. Maybe that's the fundamental legacy. I think sometimes that our lives would be easier if we could just look back at the sixties and say, 'That was some other guy, that was some other girl.' But we can't. And I can't."

NAOMI FONER, 43
1966: Harlem Head Start teacher
1989: Hollywood screenwriter

A 1966 graduate of Barnard, Naomi Foner was one of the first Head Start teachers in Harlem. Active in the civil rights and anti-war movements, she was also an early participant in the women's movement, joining a consciousness-raising group in the late sixties. In 1968, she began working for Children's Television Workshop, where, during the next ten years, she helped create much of the material that made the group's name synonymous with enlightened educational programming. In the late seventies she moved to Hollywood to begin writing screenplays.

"In general, back in the sixties I wanted the world to be a fairer place where people had an equal chance, where catastrophic differences didn't exist. If you got sick, there was a place to get medical attention; if you were a kid, you got the same fair education everybody else did; that we would eventually get to a place where the color of your skin wouldn't matter in attaining your personal goals; and that being a family meant some fair division of labor and pleasure among men and women . . . those kinds of things. And I still want all of those things.

"There was a rush during the sixties which made you feel you had more power than you did. I guess the moment I think of is when Johnson announced he wouldn't run for reelection which, at the time, made me feel like maybe we could accomplish everything we wanted to. Now I feel that it's a much harder thing to accomplish.

"This doesn't mean I'm pessimistic. I think this understanding is part of a general, organic process of growing older and seeing that things are more complicated. I think that, in fact, I feel more optimistic in the last year or two than I have in the last fifteen. People are waking up again. And either it's in direct relationship to having gotten old enough as a generation to have families and see what things look like from the position of parent rather than child or just because these things come in cycles. But I feel more hopeful than I have for a long time.

"I went, as many of that generation did, from being more directly, hands-on actively involved to doing things not necessarily defined as political, but political nonetheless. For example, I think of my work at Children's Televison Workshop as political. It was programming that was directed to a particular audience for a particular purpose, and it used the media in a way that I thought had integrity and purpose.

"You know, people in our business are paid way out of proportion to what they do. But a lot of people who have integrity and politics have tried to share what they have earned in some way or another. Norman Lear has set up this group called People for the American Way. He didn't have to do that. He could have bought himself five antique cars and two more houses. They're very concerned about the world they live in; they try to feed those issues into their work. The more powerful and wealthy they get, the more likely the work they do can be independent of other sources of money, and they can, in fact, get those things accomplished."

Among the dozen or so film scripts Naomi has written is the critically acclaimed *Running on Empty*, a film about two sixties radicals whose fugitive life is devastating their family. Nominated by the foreign press as one of 1988's best films, the movie focuses on a couple who, in 1971, blew up a napalm factory, leaving a janitor blinded and maimed. Fifteen years later, they still live on the run. Naomi named the characters Arthur and Annie after the parents of her oldest friend, a woman who went underground with the Weathermen in 1969.

A member of Hollywood Women's Political Committee and a supporter of a variety of liberal causes, Naomi's recent work includes the adaptation of Gail Sheehy's book about adopting a Cambodian refugee child and a screenplay about women homesteaders for Paul Newman.

"The media are terribly powerful. Most mainstream movies are political in the sense of keeping the status quo as it is. Those of us who are trying to make films with different points of view and get them out to as many people as possible are contributing toward having those ideas seen and heard. I think you have to be sort of circumspect when you're working in a mass medium that's meant to be commercial, and you have to find a way of walking the line and making a film that says those things without being threatening, making a film that says those things and is still entertaining, and making a film that's honest and fair and hasn't compromised what you started out to do. So it's a bit of a tightrope act . . . but to me it's certainly worth it.

"I'm right now in a position where I can choose what I want to do, and I am choosing projects that mean something to me. For a while, anyway, as long as I continue to be decent at what I do, I will probably be able to write things like this. Whether they get made and go the distance depends on whether other, much more important people also have a commitment to this kind of thing."

CHIP MARSHALL, 44
1968: regional traveler, SDS
1989: land developer

Chip grew up in what he calls "suburban Beaver Cleaverland" on the outskirts of Harrisburg, Pennsylvania. In this conservative town, his parents were the only liberals he knew and, in a straw vote in his first grade class, he remembers that he was the only one to vote for Adlai Stevenson. Nevertheless, his facility at sports made him "one of the guys." In 1963, he arrived at Cornell University as a freshman and immediately pledged a jock fraternity.

"Kennedy got killed that year, and I was watching the civil rights thing from afar, and getting demoralized. I remember walking into the student union and out of the blue, there was this table for VISTA and Peace Corps. I had just been elected social chairman of the fraternity and was going up to see about some party I was supposed to organize. And something in me was going, 'Jesus Christ, something's wrong here.' And I went over to the table and there were pictures of black people in the South and it just clicked in my mind. And I thought, 'Fuck it, something's wrong, I just can't go on with this fraternity life.' So just on the whim of the moment, I said, 'I'm doing it,' and I signed up. It was the end of my sophomore year, and I just dropped out."

He spent 1965 in Georgia doing community organizing and working with housing issues. During that radicalizing year, his commitment to civil rights deepened, and he began to feel vehemently that the war in Vietnam was morally wrong. By the time he returned to Cornell—sporting long hair and a single earring—he considered himself a radical. Back at school, he formed a group called Students for Constructive Foreign Policy that, a year later, merged with the campus SDS chapter. Chip became a campus SDS leader. After graduation he worked full-time as a regional traveler for SDS and served on the national committee.

"I used to travel around with Mark Rudd [the national SDS figure who led the student strike at Columbia] as his bodyguard on this tour of the campuses during the Weathermen days. And it was always the same thing. I would always be the one they'd throw up there when people started getting very antsy to say something to calm them down, and say something that they'd like. I remember standing in front of a crowd at Notre Dame trying to explain why it wasn't so crazy to believe that the Viet Cong were okay—with all these football guys, right? So basically, even when I was on the outs, I always thought that the system needed to be reformed not overturned. I believe that you have to have the majority or you're not going to make it. Vanguard strategies never ever appealed to me. I just never bought it.

"After a while I was sick of the campus thing and felt I should go organize in some city and should get close to the workers. I had always been considered the right-wing of the SDS, but by that time, the right-wing was getting more and more left. I had read a lot of Marx. We were this odd combination of, you know, LSD, Marx and Mao. We actually studied all the cities in the country to determine which we thought had the most revolutionary potential and decided Seattle was the spot because of its Wobblie [IWW, Industrial

Workers of the World, a radical union] history, its blue collar base, Boeing and high unemployment. So a bunch of us came out to Seattle in 1970 when everything was really going. There were about twenty of us from Cornell who came out, and we were all organizing full-time. We lived on food stamps, a little money we got from donations. In those days, whole houses were renting for 100 dollars, and if you had two T-shirts and a two pairs of jeans you were cool for the whole year.

"It was all very encouraging. The movement was much broader than just a few people on campuses. We got good reactions from people in factories. It really was a worker-student alliance. It felt like a mass movement. By the time Cambodia came, we had sixty, seventy thousand people marching and closing off the freeway. Clearly we were gaining at that point. We felt very good. But we also felt very threatened. I and a few other people were the only known national SDS people who were still above ground. We were right out there in the open. As it turned out, the two houses on either side of us were rented by FBI agents.

"Unlike some people back then, I really don't think I believed mass social change, the revolution, was imminent. I had always been able to travel with the suburbanites if I had to, so I think I knew at one level where it was at with the average American. I was very optimistic in terms of limited goals, in terms of Vietnam or social justice, but the revolution? No, I don't think I ever believed that was going to happen. I had studied history. I thought there was going to be change, but I think I had a more realistic view of what was going to happen. So I wasn't as demoralized as other people when everything started to fall apart."

Chip was indicted for his anti-war activities and spent some time in jail in the early seventies. When he got out, he traveled around the world on 600 dollars and came back to Seattle to work on local issues. He mounted an unsuccessful campaign for a seat on the Seattle city council.

"In the seventies, I needed a job. I lost for city council. I hadn't had an honest job and I was 32 years old. My hair was turning gray and starting to fall out. I was interested in housing so I went to work for a public corporation doing housing rehab, which was very socially rewarding on one level, but on another level, I became sick of it, sick of the public sector, sick of the bureaucracy, of not being able to innovate. I saw then that the Right was in ascendancy and that the public sector would be shrinking and shrinking. So what happens then is that everybody fights for the scraps and things get uglier and uglier. I thought I'd have a better chance in the private sector. Maybe it was just the spoiled, individualist attitude of the sixites, but I was sick of working under people in a system that fostered caution rather than innovation. And although the stated goal was to help people who were less fortunate, the real, practical result was that these social programs were a way for the middle class to stay employed. So I figured, what the hell, I am middle class, I might was well just do it—go into the private sector and not be fettered by all the bullshit.

"At that point, I felt very alienated from the liberal Left. I felt it had squandered its opportunity. In the sixties, we dealt with the issues that meant something to people, the war and civil rights. But I didn't feel that the Left had addressed the big issues of the seventies: the collapse of the family, economic dislocation as we go into an electronic society, crime, those kind of issues. I felt that the moral and economic issues that move people, that we were really addressing in the sixties, we failed to address in the seventies. And that's why the Right took over. I mean I can't blame people for voting for Reagan. I never brought myself to vote for him, but I basically stopped voting."

For the past ten years, Chip has been creating master plan communities in the Seattle suburbs that promote environmental concern and foster a sense of community. He is currently negotiating to build low-cost housing in China.

"In the grand scale of things, I feel pretty good. I feel a lot better now than I did in 1980. In 1980, I was pretty cynical and kind of demoralized by the whole thing. Now I feel I've actually been able to accomplish something that I'm pretty proud of. It's been very controversial. I mean, here I am a goddamn developer which is like one step above a child molester in the view of many of my friends. But I feel pretty proud of what I'm doing, and I think the world is going in a pretty good direction right now. It's never easy. But if you look at the situation of the world in 1950 and in 1990, you gotta say that things are a lot better. There's a whole new set of problems of course. But the fundamental problem used to be whether we'd be alive to have any problems at all. The fundamental problem was the possibility of nuclear war, and I think that's receding. The problem now is the environment in the broadest sense—whether the earth will be able to support 200 years of industrialization. But at least we have the opportunity to deal with that problem. So I feel optimistic.

"I'm far from rich, but I'm making a lot of money now, and it's something I'm concerned about. There's still part of the hippie in me. That's why I'm going to Asia. I realize that I'm in a position now where I could really let my values slide. I mean I sit on some boards of inner city projects and I'm into some charities. But I do worry about getting too comfortable. That's why I probably won't continue doing this for more than another year. So I'm going to go to Asia to build in China where they really need it, and where I can do some good—probably blow all my savings. But I'm used to living cheap. That hippie thing really stayed with me."

LOWELL BERGMAN, 44
1969: investigative journalist, San Diego Street Journal
1989: investigative journalist, 60 Minutes

The grandson of the founder of the International Ladies' Garment Workers Union, Lowell grew up middle class in Queens and Westchester counties. In the early sixties, he went to the University of Wisconsin on a scholarship, where, he says, he "met about 8,000 other Jews from New York." Involved in SNCC and early anti-war activities, he was also a brilliant student who caught the eye of one of Wisconsin's top sociology professors—who told him to go study with Herbert Marcuse. In the fall of 1966, he moved to San Diego to do just that. It was there, as one of Marcuse's graduate students, that he became involved in one of the better underground newspapers of the day, the San Diego *Street Journal*.

"I remember reading the Port Huron Statement when I was in high school, and my hit off of it was these were people looking for the truth, that there were contradictions in the way the world was, as opposed to the way you were told it was supposed to be, and that's what got me motivated in the beginning and motivates me now.

"In the sixties, I was motivated by a number of things aside from sex and rock 'n' roll. That time was really a sort of crossing of the paths of the civil rights and anti-war movements. I remember handling part of the logistics of the marches in Selma—I didn't go down there; I handled the moving of people there—that came just prior to the Gulf of Tonkin. Those were the kind of events that made people crazy, both politically and personally.

"There was a time back in San Diego when I was dealing with the military, with guys who had come back from Vietnam and other stations, and I got a taste of how disaffected they were. And I thought things might change very fast. There was a lot of turmoil inside, a lot. And militant people who were in the military were taking some chances that convinced me they were willing to give up their lives if they had to. You know, there were some major court martials in the military. There were riots in the brig at Pendleton, really brutal riots. They weren't covered by the regular media, but we went out and covered them. There was an incident where 800 black guys on the carrier *Ranger* shaved their heads. There were a whole bunch of things going on, and that's when I thought things might really start moving."

The San Diego *Street Journal* was in the midst of the action, publishing stories about military protest and the anti-war movement as well as exposés of the city's power elite, researched and written primarily by Lowell. But in the fall of 1970, hounded by the FBI and, like so many other underground papers of the time, torn apart by internal ideological disputes, the paper folded.

"Getting Carlos [a San Diego *Street Journal* commune member indicted for his activities as a Brown Beret] out of jail cost us not only all the cash we had but all the credit we had with all kinds of people. Then the bail bondsman split town with all the cash and all the pink slips on all the cars, and that just bankrupted us. That combined with the heat that was on us, and no money. And the women's movement claiming that I and this other guy were actually the bad guys. They actually came in one night and tore the newspaper up, tore the layout sheets. That was the last straw. When people inside our organization tore up our work, I know I gave up. I just decided that it wasn't worth going to jail for the rest of my life.

"So we packed everything up in a big convoy and went to Eugene [Oregon] where I lasted for about four months. Then one day the FBI and the local police came to a house I was living in—actually I was living in the garage. They came to the front door and this guy came running into the garage and said, 'The FBI and police are here, and they've got their guns drawn, and they have a warrant for your arrest.' So I jumped out this back window, ran over a hill and called this guy from a pay phone to come and pick me up. Within about three days I was in Vancouver where I stayed for maybe nine months. I was a cook at a suicide prevention center, you know, egg rolls for 300."

In the early seventies, Lowell lived quietly with other ex-*Street Journal* commune members along the Russian River north of San Francisco. In 1973, he moved to Berkeley and began his career as an above-ground journalist, first freelancing for a variety of magazines, then working as an editor for *Rolling Stone*, then establishing the Center for Investigative Reporting with David Weir. In 1977, ABC offered him a job as an off-air investigative reporter. Later he worked on *20/20*. Since 1983, he has been a producer for CBS's *60 Minutes*, identifying, researching and writing a variety of political stories.

"If I didn't have a critique of American society today, I'd run out of stories. Today we're not at war, we're not bombing a bunch of yellow people we can't see. We did not send troops into Nicaragua and we're not likely to. In terms of the amount of violence in the world that the United States is actively directing, there's a great improvement. I disagree with things like the Christic Institute lawsuit [against American officials for alleged interference in Central America] and other things I've seen thrown around because those things come from the perspective that the United States is always wrong, and that there are these conspiracies that are going on that are diabolical, Mephistophelean things. And that's not the way the world works, and it's not the way the United States works. So I think there have been great improvements in the way this country runs, many of them because of the sixties and because of Watergate.

"Now there are a lot of problems too. The racial problem is as bad, if not worse. And I think the problem of women's rights is worse, just the issue of abortion. And the other main crisis that I see that is worse than in the sixties is the turn towards incarceration. I think there are over a million people now in jail on any given day in the United States, which makes us the worst of any country in terms of locking up our own people, worse than the Soviet Union, as bad as South Africa. I see those problems, and that's where I do a lot of stories. I did something on the thirtieth anniversary of the Cuban revolution that was critical of Cuba but at the same time, the right-wing people are after me. And I did something on Costa Rica last fall, and I did a thing on the disability rights movement.

"So it's the same general stories. I haven't really changed my areas of interest. I would say that it's more difficult in the Establishment press, particularly in television, to do stories about people with a lot of money and power. The accumulated costs of libel suits, the increasing concentration of power makes it more difficult to take on one of them. There are fewer outsiders. Everybody knows everybody else.

"Sometimes my work is fun; sometimes I just need the money. Sometimes there's a story I'm real interested in. And I care about information. I like to be told the truth. I'm pessimistic and I'm optimistic. Pessimistic when I see some of the so-called leaders of the Left turn right-wing. It's not that it's disillusioning. It's that they were scumbags then, and they're scumbags now. So I'm pessimistic in the sense that people don't change much. And I'm optimistic only in the sense that the center of the world seems to be changing. It's more difficult to be in the United States and say that everything begins and ends here. And that gives me hope.

"When I think of a yuppie, I think of someone who has fancy suits, a sports car, you know. I have a 1980 Honda with 100,000 miles on it. I am the last survivor of the last commune in this house, which I rebuilt. I don't own any stock, except in a company that a friend of mine started. My kids don't go to private school. I know I'm the only employee of network news who works out of his own house.

"I'm an old hippie, basically. I'm not as crazed as I once was. And I'm making more money, that's true. But I haven't gone out and become a stockbroker like Jerry Rubin, and I haven't written a book on barbecuing like Bobby Seale. I mean, I could go down the list. I haven't become a right-wing reactionary like David Horowitz. I haven't gone out and gotten a job with an insurance company.

"On the other hand, I guess I accept certain limitations that exist within the institution of journalism, at least when you have a straight job. I don't go out and hold press conferences when I don't get what I want at work. I mean, I don't make it a secret that I'm unhappy at times, but on the other hand, I don't go running around saying that they're all part of some fascist, capitalist conspiracy.

"One of the things that I've learned, which I started to learn at the *Street Journal* and has become more and more important to me, is that you do more damage by being ideologically blind than anything else. And if there's a positive function to this profession, if you want to call it that, it's to try to paint in as many gray areas in the world as possible and to get people to think. I find myself trying to do stories that normally don't get in the Establishment press or to paint some gray areas in those that do. I mean, Mike Wallace has his hour with Ronnie and Nancy. You won't find my name on that one."

HOLLY CHEEVER, 39
1969: anti-war activist
1989: veterinarian

The child of Unitarian-Universalist parents, Holly grew up in a liberal, intellectual household. Her father was once a public affairs professor at Harvard (and taught Henry Kissinger) but was denied tenure and moved on. Holly was raised in Cambridge and then Pittsburgh. In 1968 she entered Harvard where, almost immediately, she was radicalized by a combination of the war and the university's ties to it through the campus ROTC program.

"It was an intense learning lab for that period of time. I started out on the periphery. I was not willing to go off and get arrested or get hurt. I just needed to be educated. I hadn't really gotten into the machinery of politics or the politics of groups, although I was certainly outraged by the war and came from this family that always thought morally in terms of world affairs. What got me very radical was first of all this whole confrontation with Harvard when the University Hall takeover occurred. That was on April 7th, 1969, and I was still a little on the periphery, still timid and learning. So I wasn't in the building, locked in, I was part of the first ring of people outside. I was not actually trespassing, but I was putting myself in line to confront police and to stand as a first guard and to be arrested if that came to pass. I felt completely intimidated by it, I might add.

"When the bust came, which was at four or five in the morning, I had gone to get some supplies, and I was not on the steps. I had climbed over the wall into the Harvard Yard area, right behind the police. So I watched it, and people were running off to help students, and there was certainly violence. Seeing it kicked me into the gear of being outraged."

Holly was an activist throughout college, joining a coalition of students, veteran civil rights workers, Quakers and neighborhood people who were involved in draft board sit-ins and anti-war civil disobedience. She was trained in and practiced passive resistance.

"I think the thing about coming through the sixties then was that you always felt money was easy. I knew I was bright, I had so many interests—I loved sports, I loved music, I loved social action and the social worker kind of stuff, I loved medicine, especially veterinary medicine, although I'd given up the idea of any more schooling because I was so burned out.

"So there I was; I didn't really know what to do. So I thought, why don't I do social work for a couple of years, and then I'll do voice for a couple of years, and then I'll teach women's lacrosse for a couple of years and just flit through life, enjoying myself. You know, you had that attitude in the sixties, despite the horrors of the assassinations and the war."

After Holly graduated (*summa cum laude*), she spent the next three years as a nurse's aide with a frontier nursing service in Appalachia. There she drove a broken-down jeep or rode a Tennessee Walking Horse into remote mountain communities, visiting her caseload of patients.

"It fulfilled what I realized I needed, probably directly from my father's influence, which was to do service to humanity. But I was so isolated—it was way the hell up these hollers—that I became very separated out from the political events in the rest of the country. I shifted my focus and concentrated on a small project, small piece of earth, small scope, small number of families, a tight community."

In the mid-seventies, she bounced around from job to job—tree surgery, cocktail waitressing, galloping thoroughbreds in Kentucky. Realizing that she couldn't be happy working for others, she decided to go back to school in veterinary medicine. At Cornell from 1976 to 1980, she says she had "no political existence." In the winters, her studies engrossed her. In the summer, she milked cows in Vermont. Halfway through the program, she met her future husband. They got married right after she graduated and had four children in quick succession.

"I struggled to be a veterinarian. My first boss, who was a douche bag, was someone who pulled me aside one evening and said, 'Dr. Cheever, do you know why men have lower sperm counts today than they did in the 1940s?' So, I said, 'No, tell me why.' I was thinking maybe tight underwear or stress or food additives, but he said, 'No, it's because of women's liberation, it's because of women like yourself coming into men's professional fields, it's intimidating.' Now, I'm five-foot-two, and tiny, by the way. I definitely have a gentle demeanor. And then someone says you're so intimidating that you cause men's testosterone levels to go down, and they can't produce enough sperm. Okay, what are you going to say? So this is the typical tenor of this profession, which needed to have women in it, especially women specializing in large animals. So I was the chutzpa kid for thinking I could be a woman and go into dairy.

"I started having my children. I lost my job, in fact, because of having children. But I got another, and I went back to work between babies. But I was doing less intense practice. I was home more and around Dean's [her husband] political environment. And things started resurfacing. So I picked up a little bit more in terms of getting more politically aware, and getting my engines revved up. And the form that it has taken over the last couple of years is to go into an animal rights movement, which can be either namby-pamby, little-old-lady-with-bird-glasses or it can be all the way to the animal liberation front, going right back to the violence of the sixties.

"I've been a vegetarian since 1970, but I support dairy products. I have my conflict here. I am a dairy veterinarian; I wasn't about to trash what I've been taking care of. And I don't feel that being a dairy cow has to be abusive if you're well treated and well managed. Of course, many aren't. But that doesn't mean you have to condemn the industry."

A member of a wide range of animal rights groups from the mainstream Humane Society to the radical People for the Ethical Treatment of Animals, Holly spends her off-time working on farming cruelty issues. She has been lobbying the New York legislature for veal calf treatment laws and was a leader in the fight to improve conditions for New York City's hansom cab horses. She also works as a lobbyist for the ASPCA. She and her husband, also an activist, live with their four children on a small farm near Albany, New York.

"I think I'm going to have the power to change some legislation here. Not single-handedly, but certainly as part of a wave of national awareness that is going to cause some protective legislation for all kinds of things in the next five years. When I look back at the '69 incident with Harvard, I took for granted the kind of power we had. We shut down that university for ten days and did effect change. I don't think that struck me as outrageous. It was the right thing to do. And in the seventies and eighties, the feeling of power seemed completely gone.

"So I felt very helpless in the intervening fifteen years, but now I'm beginning to feel pretty pumped up and effective, probably because I'm about to get a good outcome on a horrendous form of abuse. It's a minor issue, the carriage horses in Central Park. But it's a good issue for me, because I happen to be right, and it just might be recognized that we're right in the larger sense and that this movement I'm working with may, after several years, really get somewhere this year. So that does make you feel powerful.

"It probably has been helpful to have fifteen years off. I learned the skills young enough so that I was a follower, definitely not taking any initiative myself. Now I've really hit my stride. I'm realizing for the first time these last couple of years, because of my appearance—cute and pert—that I've always had people who would tend to dismiss me as that vivacious little blonde.

"Now they and I are learning that I can command respect, that I can outargue guys who are trying to tell me about farm economics. And they have to listen to me, and I can tell them to shut up, and it's a great feeling. Having been at the mercy of rednecks through sexual advances or employer-employee shit, it's nice to feel that power, and I wouldn't have been ready to launch on that until now. I had to go through having the babies, getting my head clear from that, and pulling out of motherhood. I really love that side of my life, and while I was having babies and all that, I couldn't really focus on anything larger. So now I'm ready."

KEN DOCTOR, 39
1969: anti-war activist/draft counselor
1989: associate editor, St. Paul Pioneer Press

Born in Hollywood, raised in Los Angeles and then suburban San Fernando Valley, Ken grew up with what he calls "pretty traditional, middle-class, second generation Jewish values: straight-ahead FDR Democratic politics and a lot of respect for education." Nevertheless, he hated high school and felt very much an alien there. "At seventeen, I had no idea what I wanted to be or who I wanted to be. I just knew I wanted to get out of L.A. and try something new."

"Something new" meant venturing north to enroll at the University of California at Santa Cruz, then a raw, three-year-old campus that had not yet awakened its sleepy coastal home. There he majored in sociology, joined the anti-war movement, trained as a draft counselor and met the woman to whom he is still married. Twenty years ago—thick, dark hair flowing to his shoulders, full beard and moustache—Ken was a part of a group occupying the administration building at UC Santa Cruz to protest then-Governor Ronald Reagan's decision to send the National Guard to the streets of Berkeley. Today—balding, corporately attired and the father of three—he is working to make mainstream journalism closer to the hearts and minds of readers.

"Santa Cruz was a place that encouraged people to be different at a time when we didn't need much encouragement. It was a bizarre place. In the spring of 1969 we actually got credit for not going to school and participating in any mass movement we wanted to. We had an amazing group of professors.

"At Santa Cruz I did a project where I studied the local draft board and got college credit for it. I investigated how the board made decisions and how it was arbitrary in giving its classifications, especially its student classifications and c.o. classifications. In fact, I testified in federal court about bias in the system. I made visits in Santa Cruz, which at that time was this little coastal town that was just becoming a college town—California wasn't the hip, expensive place it is now—and all the boys had beards and long hair, and we would go door to door and say to people, 'We want to talk to you about the war,' and some people would let us into their living rooms. It was an intriguing clash of world views.

"There's a critical moment that I remember. In fact, I have a photograph that captures it. It's of the Merrill College [part of UC Santa Cruz] strike center, which was in one of the classrooms freely given to student protestors by the administration. I remember there was a time when I walked into that office and I had a real clear sense that we were going to change the world. We were going to make the world the kind of place it should be, and we had no doubt that we were going to do it. That, of course, didn't seem to a twenty-year-old like a very amazing thing. To someone who is 39 now, it is real interesting to me that I—and we—believed it so strongly. In the intervening years we've seen such political and social apathy on college campuses and throughout society. There is such a sense of powerlessness. And even when there are good values—and there are pockets of good values in lots of places—there is still this feeling of 'gee, that's terrible, but I can't even begin to think about doing something about it.' That's the way most people respond.

"But back twenty years ago, not only did we think we could change things or that we should change things, we had no doubt that we were going to take over the United States government, and we were going to stop the war. We didn't know what we were going to do after that . . . but we were going to operate it in a humane way. That sense of power and the sense that things can be changed and should be changed is, when I look back on it, the most powerful thing I learned. And that's what's been lacking in the seventies and eighties."

On June 13th, 1971, Ken graduated from college. On June 14th, he and Kathy Francis, a fellow sociology student, got married in a meadow. Almost immediately, they drove cross-country to live and work in a Connecticut commune dedicated to nonviolent action. Later they worked with the rural poor in New Hampshire, helping to establish food co-ops and childcare centers. In the summer of 1972, they moved to Oregon and, after a long stint of unemployment and a year in journalism graduate school, Ken began publishing an alternative newsweekly.

For the next seven and a half years, the *Willamette Valley Observer* struggled on, presenting investigative journalism and leftist political analysis while putting Ken deeper and deeper in debt. In 1982—physically exhausted, in debt to the IRS, local creditors and his own staff, now the father of three small children—Ken closed the *Observer* and began a career in mainstream journalism. He was managing editor of a regional magazine and feature editor for a Colorado daily before moving to his current position in charge of features and art for a 200,000 circulation daily in St. Paul, Minnesota.

"Basically, there are now two spheres to my life. There's my work life, a basic 50 hours, and I'm always thinking of moving things along, changing things there. I'm still committed to work and to changing a major field. And the other sphere is family. There's an enormous amount of time and emotional support and intellectual support you need to put into your kids. I really try to talk to my kids a lot about the way the world is, about what's possible, about their roles and responsibilities. I do feel that there's something wider missing in my life, a wider role in the world that is beyond work. It's not something I think about constantly, but when I look at it, there's something that doesn't feel quite right there. I justify this lack by all the time I spend with my family and also that by the fact I think my work can be socially redeeming.

"People ask me now that I'm approaching 40, 'What are you going to do with your life?' And I tell them, 'I still want to change the face of journalism.' Newspapers should be a place of dialogue in the community, not just about the community's concerns about where to put a highway, but about who the readers are as people and what they want to do with their lives. I see a news-paper as a social tool, and I think that that's what most readers want it to be. It is the glue that can hold together a community, can raise a mirror to the community—but more than just reflect, it can set an agenda and it can do so openly, and it can do so without apology. The items on this agenda are not left or right political items, they are about good government, but they go beyond government to the social questions of who we are and what hap-pened to our values, of bringing together different generations and showing one what the other is feeling. Newspapers don't often do these kind of things very well. They are not in touch with people's feelings. What I've been able to do in five years is very much a beginning. But I'm beginning to understand how you can take something that is pretty much an unconscious manufactur-ing enterprise and turn it into something with some spirit that talks to people directly and is able to achieve something beyond manufacturing itself.

"The kinds of values I gained back in the sixties make a line—I guess a pretty crooked line—to where I am now, a manager at a paper owned by the second largest newspaper corporation in the country. The challenge for me is to see if I can maintain my values and at the same time do what the company would want me to do in a way that both produces the change that I want and also allows me to stay in the company. Curiously, I now think that's possible. Twenty years ago, I didn't think it was.

"A lot of people get into these kind of circumstances, and there's always the question of how much you change the enterprise and how much the en-terprise changes you. That doesn't scare me particularly because I do feel pretty secure that I know where the lines are and where I won't cross. I don't think we have done any real, lasting journalism at the newspaper. That doesn't surprise me. We have been able to do much more solid journalism, present material that people can read without feeling that it has gone through some filter of unreality. I think the kinds of stories I am assigning are closer to the heart of people, to what they really care about.

"The other thing I've done, through any means available, is to replace people who are not interested in thoughts, in ideas—in the idea that the world could be a better place—with people who are. This is part of my role as a corporate manager. It's not just what I can do personally, but putting good people in positions where they can do good. It isn't a guerilla enterprise—which probably two or three years ago I would have thought it would have had to be. It isn't like we're going to have this cell of people in the corporation who are secretly going to change the organization. It's very open; it's on the agenda. I talk to my editor about it. I talk to the CEO about it. This is what I want to do more of: put good people with good ideas in places where they can make changes.

"I know that our generation is not unique, although it certainly stands out in history. But I can remember being that kid who went into the strike office at Merrill College thinking that I was going to be part of the greatest change in the history of history. I know small groups of people in earlier generations also felt that, and to know that we are not unique is very comforting, very positive. It means that what we stood for was the product of much more than a demographic blip. So there are not only certain relationships among us because we're bonded by the sixties but indeed there are these bonds that transcend generations. We and the turn-of-the-century radicals share a millennial vision of the world: The world is not a good place; the world could be a better place. Their vision was ended by World War I. I don't know what ours was ended by. But I really do think this vision is going to reemerge in the nineties. A lot of these values are submerged. But we are, I hope, passing them on to our kids. Some of us are passing them on in the workplace. There's still a lot of us out there. I think we're a little bit more sophisticated than the days when we used to jump on top of police cars and yell, 'I'm gonna dance on your grave, motherfucker.' But the truth is, Ronald Reagan's generation is dying out, and it is up to our generation to create the world we want to create. I believe that's possible. I believe we are doing it."

COUNTER/CULTURE
IV

More than twenty years ago, Arlo Guthrie emerged as the quintessential sixties folklorist, spinning a (mostly true) yarn about his misadventures as a litterbug. "Alice's Restaurant" had it all: hippie communalism, clashes with authority, blind justice, anti-war activism, the collision of cultures, the cosmic goof. Today, at forty-two, skinny as ever with his now-gray hair longer and more exuberant than at Woodstock, Arlo continues to sing his eighteen-minute salute to countercultural values. And he continues to live his life according to those values.

The son of legendary folksinger Woody Guthrie, Arlo was born in 1947 in Coney Island, New York. His mother, Marjorie, was a former Martha Graham dancer. At thirteen, he performed in public for the first time—his "musical baptism," he called it—singing between sets at Greenwich Village's famous Gerde's Folk City. His father's friend and traveling companion, Cisco Houston, was the headliner. Houston died soon after, and, as Arlo later noted, "It did not escape my attention, that while one was going out, one was coming in."

Later that year, the Guthries hosted what one writer called "history's first and only hootenanny bar mitzvah." (Arlo's mother was Jewish. Woody, Protestant-born, was eclectic. When a hospital admitting clerk, filling out a form, asked him his religion, he replied, "Put down 'all.' " The woman said that couldn't be done. As the story goes, Woody shrugged and said, "Then put down 'none.' ") After a solemn religious ceremony performed in a Lower East Side dance studio, guests square-danced and then listened to a concert by Pete Seeger, the Weavers and others.

In his teens, Arlo was a student at a private school in Stockbridge, Massachusetts, where Alice Brock, the "Alice" of "Alice's Restaurant," was school librarian. In 1965 he began a very brief college career at Rocky Mountain College in Billings, Montana. He says he brought a guitar, a typewriter and some clothes—and used them in that order. The 1969 movie *Alice's Restaurant* portrayed Billings as a hostile cowtown filled with rednecks who hung around pizza parlors. But, as Arlo noted when he returned to Rocky Mountain College more than twenty years later to receive an honorary Doctor of Music degree: "They didn't have pizza in Billings in 1965." At college he and some friends began a tutoring program for local Indian kids but, as he later wrote with typically self-deprecating humor, it fizzled out when he realized he didn't know anything. He spent most of his time playing pool and playing guitar.

In 1967 he introduced "Alice's Restaurant" at the Newport Folk Festival, and his musical career almost immediately skyrocketed. In rapid succession, he signed with Warner Records, cut a first album that quickly became a million-dollar hit, charmed 300,000 people at Woodstock and starred in a semi-autobiographical movie directed by Arthur Penn. He also married Jackie Hyde, settled on a 250-acre spread in the Berkshire mountains of western Massachusetts and began raising a family.

Through the early and mid-seventies, he toured extensively and made six more albums. Steve Goodman's version of "City of New Orleans" was a top-ten hit for Arlo in 1972. But by the late seventies, his career was losing steam. His 1976 album "Amigo" didn't sell. It was his favorite album—he called it "almost perfect," adding that, "We had finally made a record I could live with, even though most everyone else lived without it." He continued to tour but instead of playing concert halls, he now played roadhouses and nightclubs. He made an album a year for Warner's but none of them did well, and the company lost interest in Arlo. In the early eighties, his fifteen-year recording contract ended, and during the next several years, he negotiated with Warner's to buy back the rights to his recordings.

Today he, family and friends run Rising Son Records from a guest house on the Berkshire farm. The company has re-released his old records, and there are plans for new recordings. To support the company, Arlo has started a cottage industry, selling tapes of his old recordings, T-shirts and incense. He puts out his own catalog, GET STUFF, as well as a quarterly newsletter sent to thousands of fans. *Rolling Blunder Review* is an off-the-wall, strictly homemade publication, slightly funky even in this age of desk-top publishing. In it, editor and writer Arlo offers lighthearted autobiographical sketches, concert schedules, ongoing tales of fictional characters, fans' letters (real and created), recipes by Alice Brock and articles with titles like "The World Comes to a Close" and "Fab Dad Goes Berserk at Home and Hits Road."

Arlo lives with his family—Jackie; Abe, nineteen; Cathy, seventeen; Annie, thirteen; and Sarah Lee, ten—on the same Berkshire farm he bought twenty years ago. The small house with a broad porch that used to be the family's home serves as Rising Son's office. Across the lawn is a larger, sprawling place with decks and dormers jutting from all sides. These days Arlo is sometimes on the road as many as ten months out of the year. But this is where he returns.

His popularity is on the rise now, spurred by the Woodstock twentieth anniversary fever of 1989, and his concerts are held in Carnegie Hall and at major auditoriums around the country. He is generous with his time, performing benefits for striking workers, health clinics, various environmental concerns, the homeless and other causes. He and family friend Pete Seeger often tour together. John Prine is an occasional road companion.

Arlo has known from the time he was seven that he had a fifty percent chance of inheriting the disease that killed his father. Huntington's chorea, which generally strikes between the ages of 35 and 45, is an untreatable degenerative nerve disease. Two of Woody's three children from his first marriage contracted it; one died in 1977. But Arlo says he doesn't think about it or live under its cloud. He sees life as valuable, regardless of how many years one lives.

"My father had Huntington's, but he lived not just a joyful life, but an important one as well—and not just for himself but for millions of people," Arlo once wrote. "I'm just glad I'm here now."

"I'm the kind of person who generally doesn't have a plan. I mean I have a plan for my interior life but I don't necessarily have one for my exterior life. That's not even true. I don't really have a plan at all. Buckminster Fuller once noted that when you have a goal you severely limit the range of possibilities for yourself. And although you may achieve that goal, you may discover that through some other route you could have gone even farther, and you could have come to another place. And he noted that the history of man seems to be people walking backward into the future wondering how they got there. I really take that to heart.

"I think he's absolutely right. People are generally very fearful of what will happen unless they plan for the future. In other words, the alternative to planning is seen as chaos. And I don't believe that. The alternative to planning is an unlimited future. It doesn't mean that you don't have to make right decisions. What it does mean is that decision-making shouldn't be feared.

"Making my living on the road may be what I do for the rest of my life. It's certainly one of the possibilities. One of the interesting developments of the last decade or so is that I'm beginning to see that this life is perfectly suited for me. It's kind of like God said, 'I've got a real life here, and I can't find anybody who can do it. Hey, look at that guy, he'd be perfect.' I feel like this is what I can do. It fulfills all the things I was brought up to believe I should be doing. It goes beyond any of the things my parents planned for me. It goes beyond the things I planned for myself.

"And I'm seeing now that it offers possibilities that I hadn't seen before, good things for me and my kids and my wife and everybody. One of the things that it allows me to do is to visit lots of people and not get stuck in one place for too long a time, not develop attachments to those people or those places that lead one down the road to thinking about security and those kinds of things. It forces you in a way to be detached from almost everyone else in the world. And at first that's very difficult, and a lot of people lose it at that stage. But I think that if you can get through it, the positive side is that you can work on yourself. You're not working so much on other people or using other people or places or things to support that interior part of yourself, which can then become free of all of those things. Because you're just traveling through.

"And it leads you to the inevitable belief that the same kind of discipline you need to be on the road is very helpful when dealing with your own life. When you learn to be detached from all those support systems, you find yourself inevitably wondering what it must be like to be detached from yourself. Because all of the things we're talking about are those typically impermanent things. It's one thing to think of your job as being impermanent. It's another thing to think of your environment or your spouse or even your kids as impermanent.

"It eventually leads you to think that you yourself are impermanent. So what is for real? If all of this stuff is just transient stuff, what's real, what's not going to change? And who am I? And who am I permanently, as opposed to who am I temporarily? Those kinds of questions get real interesting. And if you can find a lifestyle that allows you to think about all this . . . well, it's a wonderful opportunity to discover what's forever about yourself and therefore what's forever about everyone else and everything else. All I'm saying is that if these things are to be found out, this is one of the ways it can be done.

"I don't see the separation between what I do on the stage and what I talk about on the stage and what I do in my own life. I don't really have a political agenda. I'm not running for anything . . . or from anything. Politics for me is dealing with the society that makes decisions about itself. Those decisions are made based on what we think of as being within the range of possibilities for our own future. And whether that has to do with rain forests or health insurance—all the things that have to do with our way of life—I think it all boils down to what does it mean to me individually. And I think that's what my dad really made me aware of, not as a father but as a writer. He was able somehow to take all of these burning political questions of his time and make them personal.

"I have encountered lots of frauds out there. People who talk politics but who don't mean politics, people who talk about a better world but they're really assholes in disguise. As a group, we became pretty sophisticated about seeing through the disguises of our time. We saw through the political rhetoric of our own era.

"One of the reasons that "Alice's Restaurant" works, even today, is because—without there being any tremendous wisdom or foresight or insight into any of the dilemmas of our time—it's about a guy who escapes this massive barrage of stuff that doesn't make sense. It doesn't make sense that somebody can steal millions and millions of dollars and wind up in a residence in Hawaii, and some guy can smoke a joint and go to jail for twenty years in Texas. Something's wrong with that. We saw through those kinds of things back then. I think we still see through them, but we're not doing as much about it as we were back then. And that's because we're sort of sleeping through this time.

"But I think that's changing. And I'm real excited about that. There's a lot of young people coming to the shows who see through the agenda of our government system. And they want to make some changes in it. And I think those changes are for the most part changes that our founding fathers would have loved for us to be able to make.

"I think there's a fundamental difference between how kids are growing up today and how we grew up. And I think it's much more beneficial to us all the way it's happening now, which is in some ways more traditional. I think it's important for people to make mistakes earlier in life rather than later. And I think that a lot of the dreams we had we had too early in our lives, so that a lot of the possibilities of what we could be and who we were going to be and how the world was going to change—although these visions were popular and everyone could see that philosophically in some ways they were correct—they never materialized. We got in our own way to some extent. And that's because we had a lot to learn.

"When people, especially young people, ask me, 'What are we going to do, Arlo?' I tell them to pursue their education, make sure that they study things that will provide them with great jobs in great corporations so that they can make great salaries and drive great cars and have nice houses, and do all of those things that we as a generation rejected—do all of those things, but go after them first, do it all as quickly as possible, if they have an inclination toward that. So that if it then turns out that that's not where it's at, that it doesn't bring them the joy and pleasure they thought it would, they still have some time left over to look for things that do bring those joys and pleasures.

"Although we knew instinctively, and we were correct in rejecting all those things, the rejection of them alone isn't what brings all the things we hoped. It's good to get rid of them from experience and not to have to look back over your shoulder and say, 'Well, gee, all that peace and love stuff didn't work out. I wonder if I just shouldn't have gotten a job at the bank.' So I'm very pleased that a lot of young people are going out and in some ways rejecting the things that I think have value. Because they should be rejected until they are practical.

"All the peace and love stuff for me wasn't just some ideological dream. It was a very practical thing. I wanted to feel all of the things we were talking about. I wanted the world to change for the better in a practical way, not just ideologically. I'm one of the fortunate ones who was not only able to retain those dreams but make them real for myself. And now I'm in a position where I can help make them real for other people. And my instincts are, and have been with my own kids, to let them know that all of that is there, but you have to first of all go through the System, or the Establishment, words we don't use any more, to make sure that that's not the thing that you really want to do.

"I think that you don't need a lot of documentation to see that part of our generation is going back to those things we rejected twenty years ago. And it's too early to tell what the outcome of that will be because we haven't reached the stage yet where people are exhausted from being yuppies. We haven't exhausted that yet, and that's unfortunate. Because by the time you're forty or fifty you should have some idea of the direction you're going and hope that direction is leading to a place where you can do all of the things we dreamed about doing—which is sitting by a nice clear pond that's environmentally safe with a couple of happy kids all running around in a world that's not threatening.

"I think it's really positive that a lot of the people who come to my concerts these days are nineteen, twenty-year-old kids. There is a small core of people out there who either have the sensibility or the sensitivity, whatever it takes, to not have to go through the System first, not to bother with 'Arlo's Agenda for the Masses.' They don't necessarily reject all that stuff, but instinctively they don't take it all that seriously. And I think that's certainly the best route of all. Because there's more than being another victim of time and circumstance.

"In the sixties, we thought massive change would happen very quickly. But let's understand massive change *did* happen very quickly. Massive cultural change. We changed more in six months in America than the Chinese changed in two decades of a cultural revolution and with far less pain, and agony. The changes today may take a long time, but why exclude the possibility that they may happen tomorrow? I'm not saying that they will, but to think of change strictly as 'long term' and 'for the long haul' would limit us, and we don't have to be limited. It can happen very quickly. Certainly everything that went on in East Germany went on a lot more quickly than anyone would have thought.

"The world is changing very, very rapidly, and that's one of the fabulous things that we can't lose sight of. Things are happening to us now. And we're now coming to a point where we're going to see whether or not all of those people who shared the dream we're talking about are going to come through. Now that they are slowly achieving in positions of authority, will they abandon the authority? I don't mean throw it out, but detach from it. Or will they instinctively herd together and protect their vested interests from a fuller range of possibilities?

"Will we be looking into the universe again like we did two decades ago and just stare in wonder? Or are we going to say, 'Well, I'd like to do it, but I need to do it in my condo.'

"I don't know what's going to happen but I think some will be able to detach and some won't. But I want to tell you that I love them all. The guy who is afraid to give it all up is just as wonderful in his own way as the guy who is willing to give it up. A lot of times people forget that in order to really have an understanding we can't make judgments about each other. We just have to have the compassion that we dreamed we should have. We have to have the love we thought we should have in order to see the world we think we should see.

"I never wanted to see the dream. I wanted to see what was really happening. That was my personal goal, to see what was really going on. I'll see anything. If it's nasty, let me know. If it's love, let me know. I just want to know what's really going on. Now I'm beginning to see what's really going on. And it's not nasty and it's not evil and it's not the conspiracies of people working to make me feel bad. It's not those things. I see people who for very good reasons are afraid to let go of their own destinies. I see people who for very good reasons feel that they have to go out and make lots of money and do all of those things. And so I've become more reasonably compassionate.

"I'll never forget that I said a lot of nasty things about Lyndon Johnson when I was a young man. And then, right before he died, I saw an interview with him on the LBJ ranch. He had hair down to his shoulders, white flowing hair, and he was at peace. I just looked at that image, and I suddenly realized that this is who he really was. No matter what anyone else says, they cannot take that image away from me. I saw it for myself with my own eyes.

"For this man to look like he looked meant that all of the stuff I had said was about the wrong guy, ya know what I'm saying? You don't change. You grow into who you always are. You don't suddenly become a good guy. The good guy gets uncovered. He emerges. The bad stuff falls off like leaves in the wind in the fall. It's not that one day you're bad and the next day you're good. That taught me something really important.

"One of the things that's changed for me in the past twenty years is what I thought the world was for. Let's put it this way. Let's say that somehow we suddenly thought we were our own grandchildren, then waste dumps and national debts wouldn't be things we were passing on to other people but things we were passing on to ourselves. We would probably have a different attitude about it all. What I'm wondering is how can we understand even what the question is let alone what the answer is if we are so bound up in our own little lives that we never get to ask the right question.

"I wonder about that. All the 'why are we here?' kinds of questions, and 'what's going to happen to the earth?' Is it really going to get destroyed, or it is really going to get saved, or is it going to take some guy coming out of the clouds to do it? What's really happening here? To ask the right questions means that you have to be in an environment where those questions are being kicked around. And I don't see that happening right now.

"We kicked them around twenty years ago. I don't know that we came up with anything appropriate, but I know that we were kicking them around. And we're not kicking them around as much now. That to me is disappointing. But it also offers an opportunity so that those few who are kicking it around have an interesting environment in which to do it. It's not the fad that it was twenty years ago. The people who are kicking it around today are seriously kicking it around. It's not just the thing to do. And in that sense, I think that those of us who are still kicking these things around will maybe be able to come up with some good questions and even some answers because it's coming from our hearts.

"There are people who really care, and there are people who really don't. And I think the most important thing I've discovered is that these people are both sitting next to you and they are the bad guys across the street. They are in our midst as 'Us' and they are also in the midst of 'Them.' It cuts across Us and Them. And so my new agenda is to uncover that for us, and to in some way form a new coalition. And it's being done. It's being done by the Dalai Lama. It's being done by people who are sincere, whether they have religious sincerity or spiritualness or not. And I love it. Because it looks like the wheat is being separated from the chaff. And that's good.

"I am a yogi, and that's how I live. I live very simply. I live a real strict life. So I'm a veggie. I don't drink. I don't smoke dope or that kind of stuff. I essentially live the kind of life that any monk would be living. I'm a serious yogi. I'm not just doing yoga exercises or something like that.

"I think family is a fabulous thing. It may be the most fabulous thing, aside from what I'm doing right now. I count myself as extremely blessed that I am able to do both. Although I think that both is probably the most difficult thing I've ever done in my life. I have this fabulous opportunity to love them all and be a dad and at the same time not be so tied up in it that I lose the focus of who we really are.

"Who are we when we're here? Who do we have to be when we're here? What kind of fun can we have being that? And what kind of fabulous adventure are we really on? It's a wonderful thing to explore these questions with people you've helped to create. All of my kids live at home, and they're threatening to do that for a long time.

"I certainly didn't mean to be a folksinger or an entertainer, or a father or a husband or anything. I didn't have a plan. And I ended up doing all of this stuff because it was there. It became a reality. My inner instinct has always been to play it by ear. And I think the benefit of doing that for me is that it mirrors my instinct to be free. That's real freedom. When you are just simply being. You're not running around thinking about who you should be or what you should be or when you should be it.

"But to be really free you have to have a tremendous amount of discipline, and that discipline is not something you can make up as you go along. So there's the rub. Because undisciplined freedom only leads one to be sucked further and further into the world. Because it's all coming from one's own mind, one's own ego. Real freedom is the most disciplined thing in the world. When you ask all of the great guys, the Einstein guys or the wandering sages or the saints or the prophets they will tell you that it takes a tremendous amount of discipline.

"Back twenty years ago, we completely identified discipline with authoritarianism. That instinct was right. We were right to be wary of authority. The authorities were real creeps. But I'm talking about discipline from within. An inner fortitude, a real strength to persevere, a real unwavering faith that our instincts are right. That kind of discipline. It's really strength.

"It's that kind of discipline that's gotten me through. And one of the reasons I've been able to get through all this time with the same sort of unchanging sense of humor is that I've been helped by other people who have taught me or strengthened me. That's what we need to do for each other. That's what I try to do because that's what's been done for me, and it's been done for me free. There was no cost attached. There was no relationship demanded. It's all been for free. It's something that can't be bought. And although you have to pay to go to the shows most of the time, the stuff that you pay for isn't the stuff that has any value. It's the stuff that comes from the heart, that can't be bought. It's the stuff that has helped me, and hopefully that goes on through what I do with others.

"My gut feeling is that there are some serious hippies out there, but they don't have the same anti-authoritarian-ness that we had to have. They don't have to. They've taken the best of it—the desire to dance in the universe, and therefore be part of the creative part of that universe that says: 'This is sacred, let's treat it that way.' And that instinct is exactly right.

"Those of us who have kept alive that instinct are now helping the next generation. We didn't have a whole lot of people to do that for us. We rejected most of those people. Not all of them. There was my dad, he was one of the guys who didn't get rejected. And there were some heroes, whether they meant to be or not. But now we find ourselves in their shoes, knowing what they knew. And we have to grin and take it with a grain of salt, and help those of us who are coming along. And we can see that we are a fabulous family of people traveling together through history."

"Revolution is only very partially political," wrote an artist in the Chicago *Seed*, an underground newspaper that, more than many others, was sympathetic to both the political and cultural sides of the movement. "It must be poetic, sexual, total . . ."

Arlo Guthrie was one of those who gave cultural expression to political ideas. He was—and is—a hippie who not only sang about but seemed to embody certain principles. In the political sphere, principles were easy to see. The battle lines were clearly drawn, with the New Left first fighting the forces of racism in the South and then militarism in Vietnam. But the battle lines were no less distinct for those who approached social change from a cultural perspective, those who called themselves hippies, freaks or heads. Today those terms sound quaint or silly, but twenty years ago they had real meaning. "Hippies" were "hip" (black slang adopted by the Beats) to what was going on; that is, wise to the stultifying conventions of mainstream society and wise to new ways of living. They chose to live their lives as they thought true artists did—boldly, spontaneously, sensually, unconventionally. "Freaks" were self-made oddities, ostentatiously proud of being "abnormal"—for to be "normal" was to be part of what they saw as a sick society. "Heads" were concerned with the personal growth and liberation they felt would come from transcendent, often drug-induced, psycho-cultural experiences. Whatever they called themselves, those who fought on the cultural front were as important to the movement then, and perhaps ultimately more important to its legacy today, than their more respected counterparts, the "politicos."

Actually, hippies and politicos—or, as one chronicler of the time put it, "heads and fists"—had much in common. They shared a basic critique of American society, pointing to its violence, hypocrisy, aggressive competitiveness, racism, elitism and inequality. Perhaps most important in terms of the internal unity of the entire youth movement, they shared an aversion to American involvement in Vietnam. This anti-war sentiment, which became anti-war activism for many, forged a strong link between the two groups, which for a time at least made their differences seem relatively unimportant.

Many individuals had feet in both the political and cultural camps, and at least two highly visible groups made their dual loyalties explicit: the White Panthers and the Weathermen. The Ann Arbor–based White Panther Party attempted to unite rock and revolution for, as leader John Sinclair liked to put it, a total assault on the culture. "We breathe revolution," Sinclair wrote. "We are LSD-driven total maniacs in the universe. . . . Rock 'n' roll music is the spearhead of our attack because it's so effective and so much fun." Less fun-loving were the Weathermen who mixed Marx, acid, rock and terrorism. Commenting on the gestalt of the youth movement, Weather leader Bernardine Dohrn wrote: "People have been experimenting with everything about their lives, fierce against the ways of the white man. . . . People have purified themselves with organic food, fought for sexual liberation, grown long hair. People have reached out to each other and learned that grass and organic consciousness-expanding drugs are weapons of the revolution."

But for all the cultural-political overlap, there were some major divisions. At times the two contingents held extreme views of each other that, while overgeneralized and exaggerated, were based in fact. Hippies saw politicos as ego-tripping organization freaks who, with their meetings and manifestos, their anger and later their violence, bought into the system they were trying to change and thus were self-defeating, even counter-revolutionary. Politicos, on the other hand, viewed hippies as soft, useless, stoned, spaced out, flaky, selfish and sybaritic.

It is true that hippies were inherently apolitical. The various mottos of the cultural contingent—"Do your own thing," "Turn on, tune in, drop out" and "All you need is love"—suggest that the aims of the counterculture were personal, separatist and anarchic. In fact, freaks said they distrusted all political structures, believing that the capacity for change resided in the individual not the system. As politicos read Marx and Mao and looked to Cuba and China for inspiration, hippies nodded in assent to Gary Snyder's words: "All modern societies—communist included—are vicious distortions of man's true potential." Whether radical or conservative, politics looked like the same old game to hippies: positioning, manipulation, acquisition of power and ultimately, the creation of hierarchies. "Beware of leaders, heroes, organizers: watch that stuff. Beware of structure freaks. They do not understand. . . . Do your own thing," warned a San Francisco group in 1967. David Crosby put it more succinctly: "Politics is bullshit."

For the reality of today, you have to "go to the poets not the politicians," *Rolling Stone*'s Jann Wenner said (somewhat self-servingly) in 1970. And this is what the poets were saying:

> but don't get uptight: the guns:
> will not win this one, they are
> an incidental part of the action
> what will win
> is mantras
> the sustenance we give each other
> the energy we plug into
> (the fact that we touch
> share food)
> the buddha nature
> of everyone, friend and foe, like a million
> earthworms
> tunneling under this structure
> till it falls
>
> DIANE DiPRIMA
> "Revolutionary Letter #7"

While the New Left had little respect for its progenitors, haranguing with equal force the tired liberalism of the New Deal and the inflexible sectarianism of the Old Left, sixties hippies honored their cultural ancestors, the Beats of the fifties. When the two subcultures mingled in early 1967 at the first "Human Be-In" in San Francisco—not coincidentally the spiritual home of both groups—the mutual admiration was obvious. As more than 20,000 young hippies burned incense, passed out flowers and partook of the free Owsley acid distributed by the Diggers, Allen Ginsberg, then 41, led the throng in Hindu prayer while fellow Beat poet Gary Snyder blew an eerie accompaniment on a conch shell. Timothy Leary, then 47, delivered his famous "turn on, tune in and drop out" speech.

Certainly the Beats laid the groundwork for the sixties counterculture in many important ways. From the "old man" of the movement, Harvard-educated junkie William Burroughs, Jr., to its most breathless chronicler, Jack Kerouac, to the younger upstarts like Ginsberg and Snyder, the Beats attacked the sterility and conformity of bourgeois America while celebrating the exuberance of the moment, the "now-ness" that the men in the gray flannel suits had irretrievably lost. To the Beats, post-war America was in the throes of a spiritual crisis. "Moloch," the false god Ginsberg railed against in "Howl," was loveless and sightless with a mind of "pure machinery," blood of "running money" and a soul of "electricity and banks." In Kerouac's frenzied novels, thinly disguised replicas of the author and his Beat comrades escaped the straight-jacket of middle-class adulthood as they stumbled from basement apartments to jazz clubs and caromed across the country, rejecting jobs, comfort, security and conventional fidelity for a life open to all senses. Said Beat poet Gregory Corso years later, "the hippies were acting out what the Beats wrote."

The hippies' cultural critique of American society mirrored the Beats' to a large extent. But heightened by knowledge of the glaring inequities in the South, intensified by the war in Vietnam and later, enlarged by feminist sensibilities, the counterculture took on a life of its own. However, to both the sixties cultural vanguard and their Beat ancestors divisions in society seemed clear, sharp, neat, almost comforting. The nation (or the world) could easily be divided into "us" and "them." To the hippies, there was "America" and "Amerika" or "Amerikkka," the ks mimicking the Ku Klux Klan acronym in an indictment of the creeping fascism of mainstream society.

Their culture stood for:

Their culture stood for:	while the counterculture stood for:
war	peace
death	life
competition	cooperation
elitism	egalitarianism
racism/sexism	equality
bureaucracy	decentralization
conformity	individuality

WASP values	multi-cultural/multi-racial values
bigger is better	small is beautiful
spectatorship	participation
work	play

Furthermore,

their culture was:	while the counterculture was:
atomized	holistic
conservative	risk-taking
serious	light hearted
sexually repressed	sexually uninhibited
male/female divided	androgynous
"plastic"	genuine

The list went on. Their culture glorified "doing" while sixties counterculture stressed "being." Their culture was firmly rooted in science, rationalism and Judeo-Christian tradition; the counterculture steeped itself in mysticism, intuition, revelation, dreams, astrology, shamanism and Eastern philosophies. Their culture taught stoicism; the counterculture reacted with vulnerability. Their culture deadened pain and boredom with alcohol; the counterculture intensified experience with marijuana and hallucinogens.

In the late sixties, Yale University law professor Charles Reich attempted to codify the differences, arguing that the youth movement actually constituted a new consciousness. "Consciousness III," as he called it in the widely read *The Greening of America*, "sprouted up, astonishingly and miraculously, out of the stony soil of the American Corporate State." Its adherents lived in the moment. They sought a "wholeness of self" while creating a "sense of community." "Con III" found expression in every aspect of the counterculture, noted Reich, from its politics to its fashion, its values to its art. White Panther leader John Sinclair, a self-styled cultural revolutionary of the day, said it most succinctly: "Our culture, our art, the music, newspapers, books, posters, our clothing, our homes, the way we walk and talk, the way our hair grows, the way we smoke dope and fuck and eat and sleep—it is all one message, and the message is freedom."

Hippies were often considered (both then and now) self-indulgent drop-outs more interested in their own pleasures than in cultural transformation, let alone political change. And "programs" like the White Panthers', with it rallying cry of "rock 'n' roll, dope and fucking in the streets," did nothing to discourage the notion. But in fact, the counterculture represented a reasonably sophisticated and wide-ranging critique of American society (considering the critics were barely out of their teens), at least as sophisticated as the political critique offered by the ostensibly more serious politicos.

Of course there were those who were only interested in, to use the expressions of the day, getting high and getting it on. Of course there were "weekend hippies" who were cogs in the machine until Friday night when they grabbed their bellbottoms and fringed jackets from the back of the closet, found their well-hidden stash and, to use an eighties expression, partied. Fun was always part of the counterculture—in fact, it was one of its more important tenets—but for many there was more to it than that. There were also those sincerely interested in creating a new lifestyle (the word itself is a legacy of the sixties), and the variety within that group was impressive. There were back-country communards who strived to create their own self-sufficient communities. There were city freaks who did street theatre, beautified the urban landscape by painting murals and planting trees, created soup kitchens and hotlines and welcoming crash pads. There were traveling hippies, like the Hog Farm, who themselves were street theatre, but who also involved the communities they visited in various ecological projects. There were poets, pamphleteers, artists, activists, musicians and all manner of "drop-outs" who may have dropped out of mainstream society but were contributing members of countercultural society.

But more important than the groupings or the individuals were the themes that emerged from the cultural side of the youth movement, none of which were original, but all of which were given new relevance and significance. First there was the ancient idea that the quest for self-knowledge was a worthy one, more worthy than the quest for material goods or other measurable indicators of success. It was both a religious idea, especially Zen Buddhist, and a secular one. Plato had said it more than two thousand years earlier—"the life which is unexamined is not worth living"—but hippies gave it a modern twist with their use of mind-altering drugs to gain insight, their fascination with contemplative Eastern philosophies, their sensitivity training, their frequent "gut checks" and their sometimes interminable "rap sessions" to share and sort out feelings.

Fascination with the East and with indigenous cultures was itself a powerful theme reverberating within the counterculture. More than the standard liberal call for cultural diversity or respect for different philosophies, it was an excusably naive awakening to the knowledge and wisdom outside the Judeo-Christian tradition and, by implication, an indictment of the ruder aspects of modern Western existence. In the fifties, Kerouac had sought *satori* in Paris. In the sixties, the Beatles sought it in India with Maharishi Maheesh Yogi. Alan Watts, Allen Ginsberg and others searched for a place, philosophically and artistically, where East met West. Hippies dressed in the thin cotton garments of India. They listened to and ultimately created a new Western audience for sitar music. They tuned their bodies with yoga; they quieted their minds with meditation.

American Indian culture was also revered by the counterculture, but not as those in the nineteenth century had done when they rhapsodized about the "noble savage." Certainly hippies were guilty of over-romanticizing the native American, perhaps as an antidote to the "scalping redskin" media stereotype they had all grown up with, but they also respected and learned from the relationship American Indians had with the earth and its creatures. The traditional native American concept that land could not be owned by any mortal rang true. Tribal organization seemed far saner than suburban atomization.

To the counterculture, "us" versus "them" was more than the specifics of conflicting values or lifestyles. It was a glorification of outsiders ("us") that turned certain basic assumptions on their ears. "To live outside the law you must be honest," Dylan sang, echoing the idea central to sixties political protests (and, one might add, the Nuremberg Trials), that it took more integrity to disobey unjust laws than to quietly obey. It was not "America: Love it or Leave it," as reactionary bumper-stickers of the day proclaimed, but "America: If you really love it, fight to change it and make it better." In a related flip-flop, the "normal" world was seen as insane; those who were "well adjusted" to its insanity were themselves crazy. This was the premise of R. D. Laing's *The Politics of Experience*, on the bookshelf of every self-respecting hippie of the day. The corollary was that those who were defined by mainstream (crazy) culture as "insane" were actually saner than those defined as "normal." This was the message of *King of Hearts*, a cult movie of the sixties, as well as one of the themes of Ken Kesey's *One Flew Over the Cuckoo's Nest*.

Finally, there was a fascination with new ways of experiencing reality. Of course there were the drugs, from marijuana to mescaline, that opened, in Aldous Huxley's words, "the doors of perception." If the counterculture had a leitmotif, surely it was mind-altering drugs. Psychedelic themes ran through everything from novels to comic strips, from album art to what was inside. It is difficult in today's climate to say anything remotely positive about drugs. With daily revelations about international drug cartels, with crack and heroin devastating lives, with elementary school kids enlisted as pushers, the mood as we enter the nineties is unabashedly anti-drug.

But drugs meant something different in the sixties. The counterculture made a sharp distinction between "death" drugs like heroin and speed—highs to be avoided—and "life" drugs like marijuana and hallucinogens. (Crack didn't exist, and cocaine was so expensive few could afford it.) And, although many hippies used drugs as entertainment, a significant number used them thoughtfully and purposefully to enhance self-growth, promote insight and experience other realities. They used drugs to heighten reality, not deaden it, to celebrate life, not escape from it. Of course, not all trips were happy ones, not all highs descended smoothly. There were victims of bad drugs; there were overdoses and binges. There were users who ended up controlled by drugs instead of controlling them. But, unlike today, there was little talk of addiction, for neither marijuana nor hallucinogens, the hippies' drugs of choice, are physically addictive. (And at any rate, everyone—from hippies to physicians—was far more naive about the power of drugs twenty years ago than they are today.)

Once mind-altering drugs helped open the doors of perception, hippies began to experience nonlinear, nonrational life, and this experience then took on a life of its own. With practice, one could go through the door without drugs, by meditating, listening to music, hiking a backwoods trail or studying a piece of psychedelic art. "Reality" became "realities." There was the fragmented spontaneity of Rimbaud (a hero to both Kerouac and Dylan), the juxtaposing oddities of the surrealists (Dali clearly influenced Frank Zappa), the notion of synchronicity inherent in the enormously popular ancient Chinese book of readings, the *I Ching* (celebrated by no less a twentieth-century luminary than Carl Jung). There was attention to signs and omens, the portent of simple actions, the importance of dreams and hallucinations. "Reality is only temporary," sang a fleetingly popular sixties group, the United States of America.

The forms of the new counterculture were rich and varied. In fact, there seemed to be an alternative to everything in the mainstream, from architecture (Buckminster Fuller's organic geodesic dome rather than the boxy split-levels of the suburbs) to sports (Stewart Brand's noncompetitive games instead of the NFL) to humor (the manic surrealism of the Firesign Theater rather than the one-liners of Bob Hope). There were alternatives to mainstream food (granola instead of cornflakes, herbal tea instead of coffee), mainstream comic strips (The Fabulous Furry Freak Brothers rather than Li'l Orphan Annie), even mainstream advice columns (the counsel of the underground press' Dr. Hip[pocrates] on clitoral orgasm instead of the suggestions of Ann Landers on how to dress for a second wedding).

Countercultural film-goers of 1967 flocked to *Bonnie and Clyde*, a psychological study of misfits with shockingly realistic violence, while the mainstream escaped into the slick, glamorous world of 007 (*You Only Live Twice*) with violence so stylized as to be meaningless. To the counterculture, *The Graduate*, *Easy Rider* and *Zabriskie Point* were meaningful films. But *The Planet of the Apes*, *The Green Berets* and *True Grit* were what made it to the mainstream movie houses. While the counterculture read Kurt Vonnegut's dreamlike science fiction novel, *Slaughterhouse Five*, it was Mario Puzo's *Godfather* and Jacqueline Susann's *The Love Machine* that topped the best-seller list.

Fashion was probably the counterculture's most visible cultural statement—and it was boldly purposeful. Hippies revolted against the suit-and-tie/nylons-and-heels uniforms of the mainstream, which they saw as not only physically but also psychologically constricting. They revolted also against the "genderization" of clothing (an eighties word but a sixties concept) which created male and female "costumes" that further served to divide and alienate the sexes from each other. Instead, hippies—both men and women—wore comfortable, practical, cheap clothing like jeans. Or they wore fanciful, handmade clothing: tie-dye, batik, Indian prints. They experimented with ethnic clothing, donning the flowing robes of their favorite gurus or the fringed leather of native Americans or the embroidered muslin shirts of Mexican peasants. They played with history, wearing huge phantom-of-the-opera capes or brass-buttoned military jackets or turn-of-the-century tophats. Everyone wore sandals.

And everyone, male and female, grew long hair. It was a sign of rebellion, a "freak flag" (as Crosby, Stills, Nash and Young put it) to be flown proudly, a visible step toward androgyny. Mainstream society's sneer, "You can't tell the boys from the girls anymore," was in fact high praise. Countercultural clothing and grooming worked purposefully to obscure differences between the sexes as it worked overtime to create differences between hippies and straights. While fashion might seem to be a somewhat frivolous cultural expression, insofar as hippies' clothing and hair made a statement about freedom, playfulness, invention and androgyny, it was anything but frivolous.

Of course, there were the more traditional cultural artifacts created or popularized by the movement: literature, poetry, art. While it is debatable whether the sixties spawned great literature, certainly interesting, inventive books that tried to say something new about human experience or reworked old themes in new ways were part of the counterculture's literary diet. Eldridge Cleaver's searing *Soul on Ice* broke new ground as did the unsettling novels of Thomas Pynchon. Emerging writers like Ken Kesey, John Barth and the wildly lyrical Tom Robbins mixed social commentary with the construction of alternate realities. A new wave of psycho-cultural science fiction writers like Ursula LeGuin began to crest, taking their cue from Ray Bradbury's *Fahrenheit 451* and Robert Heinlein's *Stranger in a Strange Land*, both counterculture classics. Older works with particularly relevant visions, such as J. R. R. Tolkein's "Middle Earth" and Herman Hesse's psychological journeys, gained new popularity. Poetry ranged from the almost painfully hip ramblings of Richard Brautigan to the tough, revolutionary poetry of Diane DiPrima, Nikki Giovanni and others. Art came out of the museum and onto the street, with posters, murals and graffiti the major expressions of the day. Surrealists like Dali and Magritte found a new public. The visual riddles of the Dutch graphic artist M. C. Escher kept many a hippie entertained for hours. Psychedelic art, with its drug-inspired swirling, melting images, exuberant colors and fanciful trompe l'oeil, adorned record jackets, underground newspaper pages and concert posters.

But it was music more than any other form that was central to the counterculture. From the protest songs of the early sixties to the acid rock of the late sixties, music was more than entertainment, more than rhymed politics, more than art with a new twist. As it simultaneously chronicled and helped create the counterculture, music became the truest expression of its new vision. Wrote John Sinclair in the Ann Arbor *Argus*, "Music is revolution because it is immediate, total, fast-changing and on-going. . . . At its best, the music works to free people on all levels." Leni Sinclair, his wife, expressed the importance of music to the counterculture a bit more fancifully: "The turning point of Western civilization was reached with the invention of the electric guitar."

Overstatement notwithstanding, music did provide one of the few continuous themes that defined and held the counterculture together. If other generations had the Depression or World War II to give them an identity, the counterculture had Dylan, the Beatles, the Stones. "Music gives us the community that politicians never have given us," said Ralph Gleason, one of the very few mainstream music critics to treat rock 'n' roll seriously. "Music in this age has become not only the entertainment, but the religion, the educational system, the community, a network of electricity linking people together by invisible chains of sound." That was also the conclusion Charles Reich came to in *The Greening of America* when he wrote: "The new music has achieved a degree of integration of art into everyday life that is probably unique in modern societies."

This was certainly no news to the millions of people in the sixties who worked, played, marched, got high and made love to the music. The words spoke of their struggles, their passions, their revelations. The sound moved them, not just physically but emotionally, even spiritually. With or without the addition of mind-altering substances, music had the seemingly contradictory ability to both create an all-enveloping "now" and transport its listeners to another reality. Sixties rock concerts were tribal gatherings, communal celebrations, often rites of passage. People didn't just sit back and listen, they participated: singing, dancing, banging tambourines, clinking finger cymbals. The bands played in parks for free. Even hippies who slept on second-hand mattresses on the floor had decent stereo systems.

Through the sixties, as music expressed political ideas it forged a vital link between hippies and politicos. Early in the decade, Malvina Reynolds's "Little Boxes" commented on the stifling conformity of suburban tract living, while harder-edged songs like Phil Ochs's "Talking Vietnam" began to take America to task for its overseas involvement. Sang Ochs in 1964: "Sailing over to Vietnam/ Southeast Asian Birmingham/ Well, training is the word we use/ Nice word to have in case we lose/ Training a million Vietnamese/ To fight for the wrong government/ And the American way." Ochs's album, "All The News That's Fit To Sing," was one of the best examples of topical political folk music, with its songs about the Cuban missile crisis, the murder of civil rights activist Medgar Evers and the plight of William Worthy, a man who dared disobey U.S. travel restrictions by visiting Cuba. Ochs, himself a civil rights and anti-war activist, mixed dark humor and anger as he cast a skeptical eye on America. A television announcer, in "Talking Cuban Crisis," says: " . . . here comes the President/ But first a word from Pepsodent/ Have whiter teeth/ Have cleaner breath/ When facing nuclear death." Country Joe MacDonald's "One, two, three/ What are we fightin' for?/ Don't ask me, I don't give a damn/ The next stop is Vietnam" was obviously tied to the moment, while Bob Dylan, also a master of the folk protest genre, created songs less rooted in particular events. "How many times must a cannonball fly/ Before they're forever banned" (from "Blowing in the Wind") was an anti-war sentiment pertinent to all wars. And when Dylan sang, "I ain't gonna work on Maggie's farm no more," in 1965, the emerging youth movement understood exactly what he meant. Berkeley Free Speech Movement leader Mario Savio had said the year before, "There is a time when the operation of the machine becomes so odious, makes you so sick at heart, that you can't take part."

In the late sixties, many hard rock lyrics were explicitly political. The Rolling Stones sang "Street Fighting Man" as a paean to youthful demonstrators while Marty Balin of the Jefferson Airplane wrote: "Look what's happening out in the streets/ Got a revolution/ Got to revolution." The Detroit MC5, the musical arm of the White Panther Party, pulled no punches with its "Up Against the Wall, Motherfucker." But it was the Airplane's Paul Kantner who wrote the anthem of the day—cocky, self-satisfied and angry: "We are all outlaws in the eyes of America . . . "

What happened to the counterculture? As early as 1970, Todd Gitlin asked plaintively whether "the youth culture will leave anything behind but a market." His fears were well-founded, for the superficial forms of the counterculture were quickly and easily assimilated by the mainstream. It was perhaps five years between the playing of a Dylan record on a new free-form FM station and the Muzak version of the same song piped into an elevator. By the mid-seventies, one strolled the aisles of the local A & P or Safeway to a jazzed-up Beatles tune. Jeans became a designer fashion. Businessmen sported paisley ties and collar-length hair.

The counterculture's symbols, stripped of their meaning and context, were "commodified." Values became jingles. Multi-culturalism and international peace became a Coca-Cola commercial, with people of all ages and races intoning, "I'd like to teach the world to sing in perfect harmony." The value of a simple life in tune with nature was transformed into a host of "natural" products, from chocolate-covered granola bars to cosmetics that, in true *1984* newspeak, promised their wearers a "natural look." Women's independence became a marketing ploy to sell cigarettes ("You've come a long way, baby"). The sexual revolution was co-opted by *Playboy*. "Every revolution starts in the streets" was, in 1989, a slogan for selling Audis.

Ironically, it was the richness and diversity of the counterculture that made it so easy for the mainstream to assimilate its most visible symbols. There were so many alternatives, so many outward manifestations of cultural change. While politicos who wanted to "smash the state" failed to suggest what would take its place, hippies offered a whole way of life. At its root, this life—with its noncompetitive, anti-consumption, anti-private property beliefs—was antithetical to the American capitalist tradition and could not be absorbed. But the outward trappings of the life could, and American marketers soon discovered that there was a ready public for hippie artifacts (as long as they were divorced from their real, threatening, anti-capitalist meaning). The counterculture itself, the true believers, weren't buying, but others were, spurred by America's obsession with youth and newness.

The counterculture's heroes, the rock stars, also proved a disappointment. A rock 'n' roll band was supposed to be "a working model for post-revolutionary life," according to the White Panthers. And for a few years, for a few groups, there was truth to that. The Grateful Dead and the Jefferson Airplane lived communally and gave free concerts. For the MC5, politics always came first. Joan Baez and a few others regularly courted jail sentences for refusing to pay the part of their taxes that went to support the war. But mostly rock stars were rock stars. They may have been singing about street fighting men, but they themselves were busy amassing fortunes. "Limousine liberals in a billion dollar business," is what Abe Peck calls them in his book about the underground press.

But even as the counterculture was commodified, it began to affect the mainstream. Androgynous fashions, organic food, holistic health and spiritual growth were all "sold," yet as people bought, they began in some ways to change. Multiculturalism, mysticism, the feminist revolution and the sexual revolution all might be used as marketing ploys, but they were also vital ideas that not only continued to be important to the way the counterculture lived but also began to make an impact on the everyday lives of mainstreamers. Native American symbols might be used to sell margarine (made from "what my people call maize"), but the essential idea of living lightly on the earth was translated into curbside recycling in the suburbs and a powerful national ecology movement. "Natural" might become a meaningless grocery-store buzzword, but in fact, America's dietary habits changed drastically. Twenty years later, "hippie food" (rice, beans, yogurt, fresh fruits and vegetables) is officially promoted by the medical establishment. Women's new roles might be used to sell everything from pantyhose to perfume but that does not negate the fact that women indeed have new roles.

The counterculture itself still survives in many of the places it thrived twenty years ago: Berkeley, Boulder, Madison, Austin, Eugene. More important, it infused America with new ideas, and it left a legacy of people who embody those ideas, people like those in this section: Joan Holden, the San Francisco Mime Troupe playwright; Dan Einbender, the eco-activist musician; Saphira Linden, the visionary artist—all of whom have managed to meld art and politics; June Millington, the sixties rocker who still rocks; Terence McKenna, who keeps alive the Timothy Leary tradition; Steve Itano, who continues to live the sexual revolution; Jan Diepersloot, who finds more meaning in tai chi than he did in political activism; and Trim Bissell, the poet-turned-Weatherman-turned-poet, who is proof that an examined life is very much worth living.

JUNE MILLINGTON, 41
1969: rock 'n' roll guitarist
1989: rock 'n' roll guitarist

Head flung back, wild, black, silver-streaked hair falling across her face, long, graceful fingers playing hot licks—June's stage persona is as formidable as her talent. A rock 'n' roller for almost 25 years, she hasn't slackened her pace. Half Filipino, half English-Irish, she lived in Manila until she was thirteen when her family immigrated to California. There she and her younger sister Jean lived double lives: "By day, we were straight-A students. By night we were rockers in pantyhose." In high school, the sisters founded the first of several all-girl groups they were to be a part of, the Sveltes.

"We just had this incredible urge. I think it was sort of our destiny to be in the first all-girl rock band to make it to Hollywood. Of course, we were all placed in the position of having to prove that we could play like guys. That was the deal. That was the whole deal back in those days. Of course, I had no idea at all of what feminism was about.

"I was just trying to survive. Just to play electric music in those days was really a big deal. And to just keep it up and somehow keep getting the gigs and learning the songs, and ignoring the fact that we were just regarded as chicks. Like, 'Hey, not bad for chicks.' That was the highest compliment in those days. We were just trying to do it as women. And I suppose the act itself was very political. If you had sat me down and asked me what I thought about politics, I'd have told you I distrusted the establishment, I distrusted the newspapers, I distrusted politicians—all I wanted to do was really just get off. And not be what society told me that a girl was supposed to be. To get married and go live in the 'burbs and raise kids—that to me would have been death.

"So, we were just following our hearts, following our inner voices and our muse—which was just an overwhelming feeling that we wanted to play music. It was our link to the world. We were suffering from the effects of racism, having moved from the Philippines, being half Filipino and half white, and music was really our lifeline. I think it was just we were so lucky to move to California at a time when that whole music scene was exploding."

In 1969, after playing professionally for six years, June and her sister Jean signed with Warner Brothers, and their band, Fanny, became the first all-women's rock band on a major label. With June as the lead guitarist and Jean on bass, Fanny produced four successful albums and toured Europe and the U.S. extensively. Then, in 1973, June left the group.

"Fanny did not break up. I had a nervous breakdown and quit the group. In the beginning the inner drive was enough. I had that inner drive to be one of the first women guitar players to be recognized. To express myself. And to hopefully make it big. I did want to become a rock star, I did want to have those hit records and make a lot of money and all that kind of stuff. But then that all fell away. When I had that nervous breakdown, Fanny was so close to being over the top, and I realized it was a joke. 'Cause I had no inner life."

She retreated to Woodstock, New York, to focus on song writing and her own spiritual development. In the mid-seventies, she became involved in women's music, touring with Cris Williamson and playing on "Changer and the Changed." Later she produced albums for Williamson and Holly Near. She's since recorded several solo albums on her own label and is the founder of the Institute for Musical Arts, a multi-cultural, non-profit teaching and performing arts organization based in Oakland, California. Its primary purpose is to support women, especially women of color, pursuing careers in music and the music business. June also continues to tour and is currently working on her autobiography.

"I started getting into the world of prayer and the world of surrender and realizing through Buddhist practice that we really are in a world of suffering, and that if you can just surrender and get behind it, and let the spirit speak through you and have an attitude of prayer, that's really where the strength comes in. You're not doing it, it comes through you. So I spend a lot of time just trying to remember that. It's such a simple little paradigm shift: If I can just remember that I'm not the one who's doing it, that I just try to, you know, eat well, for example, get enough sleep, and have that attitude, that prayerful attitude. Then the rest kind of takes care of itself, and I'm so grateful to have gotten to that point where the strength comes not just from my ego, but from the universe.

"I think it would be great fun to be on top again, I really do. I think I could handle it now. Before, I wanted it but I was scared stiff, 'cause I knew it was bigger than me. But now I am protected. I know that my guardians are right by me. I can feel my allies. And it's time for us to really pull it together. It's time for us to really be here in this world, present. And music is a great way for us to remind each other of that. I have to tell myself every day, 'Just relax. It's all happening right now.' Mother earth is doing it right now. We don't have to do a thing but just be present for it. And the greatest gift that we can do for each other is to just remind each other, 'Just be here.'

"Music is such a great medium for that. And that's what I want to do with my music, have it be an awakening tool for consciousness. I use music as sort of guerilla warfare because I do a lot of music in that sort of top forty mode, so you can get seduced into the groove, into the beat, that rock thing or that funk thing, that reggae thing. And I think that's really wonderful, because, if you want to you can not listen to my lyrics and just get behind the beat, the feel.

"But if you listen to the lyrics, then it's a package deal and I find a lot of people who say, 'You know, the first time I listened to your album I really liked it a lot, but then I realized I had to play it over and over and over again, it's like a really nice mantra.' To me that's the highest compliment. And I've had people tell me that some of my songs have helped transform their life or given them the strength to give up drinking or leave an abusive situation or get through a winter in Glasgow. So music really serves on a lot of levels. And that's what it's about, service. That higher ground.

"Boy was I ranting and raving in my teens and twenties, you know, to pull off the straightjacket of racism and so forth. I was really very much in denial of the effect of racism on me. It wasn't until I was in my thirties that I started to really come to terms with it. Writing "Brown Like Me" was incredibly painful because I realized through doing benefits for the native American movement and meeting native American women that this is the real thing, the elders, they've really got it, they know, the elders know, there's no question about it. They've got that wisdom that I've been searching for; it's embodied in them, they are living it. And meeting women from South America, you know, Latina women who are coming here and Mexican women. Their strength is just incredible. Women who are single mothers taking care of their children by themselves. It makes me proud to be a woman when I see that.

"But to write a song about that, I had to come in touch with all those layers of shutting down so I could just be in the world. If I had been in touch with all my pain starting in the sixties when I was trying to do music, I think I would have just been cowering in a corner and could not have done it. I had to put on this rock persona. 'Yeah, I can get into it. Oh, yeah.' Just kind of blast off. 'I'm taking off now, see you guys later.' I needed to do that. But then I also needed my little periods of falling apart. Those little nervous breakdowns were very useful because bottoming out got me in touch with that other vital stuff.

"The Institute for the Musical Arts is sort of a thank you to my own karma. 'Cause even though it has been very difficult for me to do what I've done in the last twenty to thirty years, in a lot of ways I've been really lucky—to be in the first all-girl band, to have gone to Hollywood, to have picked up an awful lot of information, never having taken lessons. In the sixties, there was no place for me to learn anything. I always had to ask guys—and there was always a little of that, you know, 'What does she *really* want? Does she want to learn the licks, or does she want to learn THE LICKS.' And there was no music school. So the Institute is a way for me to give back. It's a way for me to share my experience and my energy. And it's a way for me to sort of feed that fifteen, sixteen-year-old kid in me who had no place to go for information. It's full circle once again.

"I have this conviction that in my next lifetimes, especially this next one, I'm going to be reborn as a musician, and I'm going to be attending IMA, [Institute for the Musical Arts] so I'd better take very good care to plant these seeds right now. 'Cause I don't want to go through this again, I really don't. I want to have a place to go where I can learn to take care of my own business when I'm fifteen or sixteen, to know what it is to get into a publishing deal, to know what it is to sign a management contract and get an agent and so forth. If I would have known all this back then I really would have felt a lot better.

"But I have no regrets. I'm learning every day. And I feel so empowered. I feel so lucky to be alive in 1989 and still be part of that forward moving crest. And I'm empowered by all the changes I see in the world, and the growth in women that I meet everywhere. It's just really tremendous. It's happening. It's definitely happening. We have lost not one minute.

"You see, I have no choice but to do what I do. This is what the creatoress has told me to do. This is what I'm supposed to do. And it's a full-time job. And I really feel like I'm sort of a guerilla out there with my music kind of weaving in and out of the different scenes. It really has been fascinating, but I guess my biggest frustration is that I feel like I'm always slightly ahead of the times. So my biggest challenge is to try to be patient. To keep doing what I'm doing as full-tilt as I always have while realizing that a lot of people are just still learning how to be in the world.

" A lot of the practices I learned were from the Dalai Lama, who I think is just one of the greatest beings on this planet. I remember when I had the initiation in Madison, and there were days of teachings before that to prepare you. And I remember when he took questions from the audience, somebody asked him, 'It seems like it's almost impossible to reach enlightenment. How come we even bother to try?' And the Dalai Lama said, 'Because you have no choice. You have to try. Even though you might be a little bit discouraged, you have to try every single day.' And I feel that way. Hearing that sort of resonated with me, because I feel the same way about doing music and doing what I do—I have no choice. And we all have to do it."

DANNY EINBENDER, 39
1969: Meher Baba follower
1989: musician/environmental educator

A Mt. Vernon, New York, red-diaper baby, Danny Einbender continues to live his politics as fully at 39 as he did at 19. Two decades ago he was a playwrighting student at Northwestern University, involved in music, radical street theatre and the creation of an on-campus coffeehouse collective. Today he is an educator for the *Clearwater*, a Pete Seeger boat that travels the Hudson teaching environmental consciousness and respect for the river. His resume for the intervening years reads like a lesson in countercultural commitment: He helped start a food co-op, managed an alternative community arts center, cooked at a vegetarian restaurant, played music on the streets and worked as a music therapist with emotionally disturbed kids.

Danny's personal quest has been part political, part spiritual. During his sophomore year in college, he dropped out in search of a guru. "I grew up without any religion at all, so when I finally heard about God, I sort of went into it with a great deal of vigor," he says, laughing. After spending time on two Meher Baba communes, he returned to graduate in the winter of 1972. Soon afterwards, when he thought the campus coffeehouse he helped start was becoming too commercial, he moved to an upstate New York commune, where, for a few years, he "made music, grew food, got high and went to rock festivals." But the West Coast beckoned him.

"There was this idea of community, a defined alternative community, that brought me to Eugene [Oregon]. It drew me like a beacon. It was a pretty amazing time. I was pretty much a street musician for close to three years. I played at fairs and festivals and just on the corners.

"And, for the first eight months of its life, I was the director of the Eugene Community Center for the Performing Arts. The community that came together to make it happen was awesome. There were hundreds of people, and an enormous amount of energy. For the months I was working there, I was lucky to get 25 dollars a week. I was living on stale donuts and 25 bucks a week, but you could in Eugene. I mean it was easy enough. I was also a total dumpster hound. It was living off the land. Some friends and I would drive around Monday morning in a pickup truck and go around to all the dumpsters at the big supermarkets. My housemate was a very charming fellow. He knew all the produce managers by name. He knew their kids' names. We would go out there Monday morning and come back with literally a truckload, with more food than we could ever use. So we used to go around town distributing it to various places. It was a great lifestyle. We had food dryers in the kitchen that we kept going all the time. We·recycled cardboard. We picked blackberries. I think it was the purest lifestyle I've ever lived."

When the community arts center bogged down in bureaucracy, Danny left to take a CETA job as an artist-in-residence, playing music at a school for emotionally disturbed kids, a senior citizens' clinic and a childcare center. The work appealed to him so much that he decided to become a music therapist. In 1977 he moved to Manhattan to study at the now-defunct Turtle Bay School while simultaneously working with emotionally disturbed kids and apprenticing with a metal sculptor. Then something happened that changed the direction of his life.

"When I was living in the city, I was in a pretty dark place in my head . . . a very unhappy relationship. I went to a concert in my neighborhood to see Pete Seeger, who I'd been aware of all my life. I'd been going to see him since I was four years old. I took my first guitar lesson from him when I was seven at a camp. I used to send him letters from wherever I was telling him what I was doing. Somehow I felt like I knew him. He's the ultimate kind of father figure.

"So I went to see this concert. I hadn't seen him in years, and he was setting up the chairs for the concert. I just sat down and watched him setting up all these chairs for people who were going to come to listen to him, and it was an amazing moment. I felt drawn to where he lived, not really consciously, but in the back of my mind. Pete is amazing. If he wanted to, he could make a few phone calls and give a concert tomorrow and make 20,000 dollars. Yet he's still wearing his father's suit, you know. I wouldn't hesitate to say that the man is a lay saint. He's even better than I imagined him to be, much as I imagine God would be. He's a pure, loving teacher."

In 1980, Danny became involved with Seeger's famous boat, the *Woody Guthrie*. A few years later, he signed on as cook for another Seeger-inspired boat, the *Clearwater*. Now he is an above-decks educator on the *Clearwater*, teaching kids about the environment through music, discussion, demonstration and puppet shows. He is also one of 20 Americans who sailed from Leningrad to New York with 20 Soviets as part of a joint citizens' peace initiative.

"In my work today, there's a very clear connection between my music and my politics. I've become a musical teacher, not a music teacher, on the boat. I'm the one who does the music with the kids. I've also been involved in writing songs. It's a way of reaching the kids. I mean, there's a lot of technical information they get in a five-hour session, but information that's coded musically, they seem to retain. They may have been exposed to an enormous amount of stuff, but the thing they end up remembering after a week is: 'Animals need water/ People need it too/ Keep it clean for me/ And I'll keep it clean for you.' And that's okay.

"So music is part of the job, and it's personally satisfying to me. It satisfies my creative needs while doing something more. In a way, it's a compromise, a way to keep making music, keep working on my craft while earning some kind of a living. I've got one real hot tune right now, it goes: 'It really isn't garbage 'til you mix it all together/ It really isn't garbage 'til you throw it away/ Just separate the paper, plastic, compost, glass and metal/ And you can use it all again.'

"I wrote a song about the peace sail, too. I don't expect it will have a very long half-life. It's very topical. 'We're all in the same boat/ Sailing on the same sea/ And if we sink or if we swim/ It's up to you and me/ In the same boat/ There's no room for enemies/ This is just a commercial for cooperation/ This is just an advertisement for peace.' And it goes on with lots of grueling details about the power of the media and financial priorities, the reality of the six-minute time frame on the Pershing missile. A lot of the songs I've written are, I think, a bit heavy-handed.

"There are still quite a few people writing essentially from the evening news broadcast, carrying on that tradition, writing songs without any possible hope of any kind of financial remuneration. The songs have a purpose other than making money or entertaining. But I try to do both myself. I want people to dance to the music I write. You know, 'If I can't dance, I don't want no part of the revolution.'

"People come from all around the world to sail on the *Clearwater*, and they take back the idea to wherever they're from. It's really a good idea, using the boat as a symbol for what the river could be or what it used to be, changing people's attitudes about the river—from thinking of it as a sewer to thinking of it as a beautiful river. That's what we did with the peace sail, we tried to create a symbolic statement that drew people's attention to cooperation between the two peoples. 'We're all in the same boat' is the motto of the sail, and that pretty much says it.

"Twenty years ago, I thought there was going to be a revolution in the streets. I knew people in Chicago who had bazookas and were planning on destroying tanks. But at the same time, the notion was that we would radically change things, redirect the priorities of our parents, direct their attention to the obvious hypocrisy. I don't think I've really changed from that position. I still think our generation has the capability to act. People have yuppified to a great degree, it's true, but just lurking beneath the surface is a force that can still be tapped. I've written songs to that effect. But I understand that the problems that face us are enormous and it's easy to be overwhelmed. That's part of the problem.

"When Pete talked about *Clearwater*, he said we needed an issue where we could win. We needed to start small and then let it grow and accomplish more. I think it's a very hopeful time. Gorbachev and the Russian people are becoming much less of a threat to us. The media taught us to fear the Russians and now they're reeducating us, teaching us not to fear the Russians, which is great. And if we can do that, we can change the way we appropriate our resources, we can still make this world into a fantastic place. We have the technical ability, if we can use it right. And we've infiltrated; we just don't know it yet."

STEVE ITANO, 41
1968: California communard
1989: freelance motion picture cameraman

A third-generation Japanese-American, Steve grew up in one of Los Angeles's tougher neighborhoods, where his parents owned a mom-and-pop grocery store. He excelled in school until his father died and his mother moved the family to a lily-white Orange County town.

"I remember walking into school the first day, like, wow, where am I? I remember walking into class, all eyes on me, all the kids, they have blue eyes, red hair, freckles. The teacher looks like June Cleaver. Then the teacher says, 'This is the new student Steve Eye-tano.' And she tells me what the class is talking about, and immediately, I'm like totally lost. So I spend the next three months with my head on my arms buried in my desk trying to be invisible. By the time I was a senior, I was in the cellar. I grew up thinking I was stupid.

"I got to junior college, thinking oh great, I'm out of fucking high school. Wrong. It was just the same only a bigger place. I ended up flunking out. Big time, big time. I flunked every single class I signed up for. So I'm very bummed out. I'm a cook at a greasy spoon. I hate my life. The draft is on everyone's ass, and I have friends who are enlisting, friends who are getting drafted. So someone told me I could go volunteer for the draft, you know, get it over with. I was tired of all the waiting. So I went down to the draft board. At this point, I was really, really bummed. I just wanted something to change. When I was in the draft board signing up, there was this commotion outside. All of a sudden these two guys fall through the door laughing and wrestling on the floor. Everyone just stares at them. Then I realize that I know them. They are these two guys I know from high school who graduated the year ahead of me. I hadn't seen them for almost two years. And they say, 'Steve, what are you doing here.' And I say, really befuddled, 'Well, I'm here to sign up for the draft.' And one of them says, 'What? You're doing what?' They told me to come see them. So I went and saw them, and they said, 'Why are you volunteering for the draft?' And I said, 'Well, you know, I want to get it over with. I want to go to 'Nam and see what all the shouting is about.' And they say, 'You wanna go over there and kill people?' And my reaction was, 'Ah come on, don't give me all that faggy, commie, pinko shit.' But we started talking. And they had a whole lot of information I didn't have. They had a whole new perspective. They were very witty and very sharp, and they cared. They gave a shit about me and about what was going on. This was 1966. It was my introduction to politics. All of a sudden, my life started to get a whole lot better, a whole lot more interesting. I was starting to wake up. I was starting to learn things."

Steve managed to extricate himself from the draft and returned to school at Long Beach State. There he joined up with a group of people doing anti-war and community work and living communally. He also met Joan, with whom he soon had a child. They never married nor did they live monogamously within the commune.

"This idea that monogamy was just not for me was already in my head. I'm not sure where it came from. I mean I had my first serious girlfriend, when I was twenty. I would have died for her. I didn't want her to go away.

I wanted to marry her. And that's why she left. The other thing that might be connected is about my father. When he died, I remember saying to myself: I'm never going to let myself get hurt like that again. I don't ever want to feel this kind of pain again. So maybe I decided not to get that close to any one person again, I don't know.

"What's kept me committed to non-monogamy after all this time is I've seen so many of my friends get so totally fucked up. I've seen some of them kill themselves over it, because their true love never really showed up. I think the way I live is right. I think it's a civilized way of living. I mean the results of the whole process of Western monogamy have been so pathetically poor that I've kinda gone, wait a minute, this can't be right. I mean I just don't believe in monogamy. I've never had to stop fighting this fight about how I live. A lot of friends ask, 'When are you going to grow up?' I say, 'Well, I thought we had a good idea back in the sixties,' and I still believe it.

"I'm not a whole lot different than I was back then. I still consider myself a socialist, but I was never a disciplined political person and I'm still not. But I don't mean to say that nothing has changed. It has. For example, I'm not as cocky as I was back then. I still think I can change the world—but maybe not today. But I do think I can have an impact on the world, slowly, piece by piece. I mean there's Destiny [his daughter, now a film student at UCLA]. She is a really, really good kid, very well balanced, extremely intelligent, very creative. It's very personal, very small, but it's something."

Steve was a photographer for an underground newspaper in the late sixties. For several years, he stayed at home raising his daughter. Since then, he has helped start an automechanics cooperative, worked in a print shop (where he was elected shop steward and became a union activist) and produced training videos. Most recently, he has begun a career as a freelance motion picture cameraman working on Hollywood and TV movies. For the past five years, he has lived cooperatively with more than a dozen artists in a renovated warehouse north of downtown Seattle.

"We have people as young as eighteen. I'm the oldest person here by ten years, and sometimes at a meeting or something, I can cut through the crap and use my experience to make this scene better. The people in the building, they say I'm important to the cooperative. And that makes me feel good.

"I've done very little total schlock work. Even when I did videos for corporate television, a lot of what I did was human relations stuff, anti-racism, anti-sexism. I worked on a pioneering video project for the Seattle bus system, which was to develop a hiring test on video. You know they would test people on paper to see if they wanted to hire them as bus drivers, and all the 30-year-old white guys would test real high, but they were making lousy bus drivers. They would test high because they knew how to take tests. So we developed these scenes on videotape that would test how people would react to the various real life situations, to see how they would handle being a bus driver. That was years ago, and they're still using it.

"I'm really just getting established as a cameraman. Give me something with real meat to it, something with a social conscience. I mean doing movies for illiterates is a great way to make a living, but I don't want to do it. I've been very lucky in that by and large most of the things I've been involved with have some substance. I've worked on Robert Altman's *Caine Mutiny*. I've worked on this screenplay called *Birthright* which is about individualism, about battling authoritarianism. I worked on a David Lynch made-for-TV special which was kind of like David Lynch meets "Knot's Landing." And at a couple of points, I was saying to myself, 'Gee, I don't know if we need more stuff like this.' But it's David Lynch, and it's good for my resume. I mean, you sacrifice some things, you get some things back. I'm not as perfect as I used to try to be, I'm not as politically correct."

SAPHIRA LINDEN, 45
1966: co-founder, experimental theatre company
1989: visionary artist and organizer

Raised by strict parents in Detroit, Michigan, Saphira—who changed her name from Barbara fifteen years ago to reflect her Sufi consciousness—received both her undergraduate and graduate degrees in theatre from the University of Michigan. In 1966, she moved to Boston and, with another woman, founded an award-winning experimental theatre group that still exists today. Like Saphira, Theatre Workshop Boston (now known as Omega Theatre) has gone through many incarnations.

"We started out as a political theatre, hitting people over the heads with everything that was wrong, which is what you did in the sixties. It was a time to shake things up, and that's what our theatre did. What we discovered as time went on was that you can only do that for so long, and then people become paralyzed, audiences become paralyzed, as do the actors themselves. You cannot be dealing with all that negative energy and not have it finally have its effects. Bottom line, we did what we did in the sixties, and then suddenly as the early seventies came it wasn't working anymore. Audiences weren't responding. So we now had to find another way. And what happened is out of this need and out of what was going on—it was very organic—we began to create much more. People needed to be healed, and so we got into a lot more psychologically oriented stuff and personal stuff. At a certain point, that became limited too. It was like it became: me, me, me, I, I. We were obsessed with the I-ness, and there was something else that needed to happen. And this paralleled my own spiritual journey that ended up really connecting up with the need to be larger than ourselves. And that's when I entered the metaphysical realms, in the early seventies, and began my own spiritual growth in terms of taking initiation with a Sufi teacher. So it went from this heavy duty political stuff through more social and personal, psychological healing stuff to more metaphysical and spiritual.

"In '72 or '73, the first day at my first meditation camp, I had a vision. I just went into an altered state, and I didn't know what had happened. I had this whole vision of the glory of the heavens is all I can say, and I came back to my theatre company with this incredible vision of what I was being asked to do through theatre. And it was like suddenly knowing that I had had all that early success very fast to give me credibility to do the real work. And the real work was to bring a vision of some of these spiritual values through the theatre, to use the theatre as a medium to spread a message, and the message was about the awakening of the consciousness of humanity to the divinity in every human being. It was a vision of peace and harmony and love, but not in a goody-two-shoes way."

In 1973 Saphira started rebuilding the theatre from the ground up, finding people with compatible spiritual values and training them as actors. She created a major production for the U.N.'s 1975 spiritual summit conference and, during the 1979 World Symposium on Humanity, she coordinated arts festivals in three cities. From this work grew the Omega Arts Network, an organization Saphira founded to help hook up so-called visionary artists. More recently, she helped organize events in the northeast for the Harmonic Convergence. She also maintains a psychotherapy practice that integrates meditation, the arts and psychology.

"Visionary, transformational or sacred art is basically an instrument for change and transformation. Those words are used interchangeably, but all of them mean people not just into self-expression, but into a larger purpose and channeling something through that's gonna help humanity. And people do that in their own ways. So it's political and it's social. But it demonstrates the possibilities. It can deal with all the negativity but it doesn't end there. It always somehow leads toward something that is the potential of what humanity can do or what the world can be.

"I feel that art really does have the potential to turn things around—and has in other societies in other times. And I think now with the kinds of resources we have, with the computers and databases and the technology, if people were more connected, that collectively we can really create a vision of what's possible. So I call it art for a positive future because I feel we could be on the brink of disaster. The positive future would be ultimately transcending the them/us syndrome—that the government is bad, all the people in power, everybody's bad. The real idea is that *we're* in power, that we put those people into power, that we can create the world we want if we can envision it. And the world we want is a world where we break down the distinctions and differences that divide people, where people are tolerant of differences in races, religions, backgrounds—a world of peace, not destruction and nuclear suicide. I think it's just essential. And I think we have to shift our consciousness. But we have a lot of work to do, and I think we have to feel empowered to do it, and to try to make the difference rather than waiting or feeling hopeless. And I feel the role of art in all of this is crucial.

"What keeps me going is a very strong dedication to my purpose, which I feel very clear about. And I feel that at the deepest level that's what everyone is looking to find—what's their purpose, why are they here. I feel that people, once they get past their mother-daddy issues and their conditioning, are really looking for meaning in their lives. And purpose. The purpose for me is believing fervently that in our time there's a crucial spiritual message that needs to be conveyed on lots of levels: that God or the divine or the ultimate potential is in each person, and if we could really connect with that in ourselves and in other people, there wouldn't be any wars. And if we stop seeing ourselves as different from each other, as all part of the same fabric, the world would be in much, much better condition as a planet. So I would say my purpose is about continually finding ways to express this—and the arts seem to be my particular major vehicle—to communicate. And I feel like it's not just coming from me. It's bigger than any person.

"So whatever role I can play in contributing to that consciousness feels like part of my purpose. And the other is to create art that reflects these messages without it being pedantic or goody-goody. Because the truly spiritual integrates all of that and doesn't just work with sweetness and light. It works with the total reality of what's happening but points the way to the future in a way that inspires rather than knocks down. If you create a vision of what's possible, then you begin to move towards it. If you create a picture of the negative side of reality, that's what you reinforce. So you just have to decide what you want. That doesn't mean that you deny or you leave out all these awful things that are going on; in fact you include it all. But you do it in such a way that inspires people to move through it and go beyond it—to see what's possible."

JAN DIEPERSLOOT, 48
1968: founding editor, San Diego Street Journal
1989: t'ai chi and mediation instructor

Born in Holland in 1941, Jan immigrated to the U.S. when he was fifteen. Settling in southern California, he went to San Diego State University and, in 1965, began working toward a Ph.D. in linguistics at the University of California, San Diego. In those days, Jan wore wire-rimmed, rose-tinted glasses, a handlebar moustache and a limp blond pageboy. His trademark was a big, green embroidered coat that he wore everywhere, in all weather. Tall and very thin, he was half hippie, half European intellectual. At San Diego he encountered Herbert Marcuse, the radical philosopher, began attending his seminars and became one of a core group of Marcuse disciples.

"Marcuse got a lot of flack because he was a left-winger in a right-wing place. Everybody was coming down on him very hard, with lots of threats. So a lot of us started talking about what we could do to counter it, and we decided that the best way was through the written word. So we started this alternative newspaper called the San Diego *Street Journal*.

"It was purely out of political motives that I got into journalism. I never had any formal training, although I had always written and I still write. The politics of the situation just seemed to demand that I do this at that point. It seemed to be the most efficient way of getting out into the community and making our views known, to propagate our values.

"We were very radical and very experimental and a lot of people got hurt in those experiments. Basically a lot of sexual freedom and experimentation was going on, and we weren't sensitive to the hurt we were inflicting on others while we were engaging in those things. Definitely, I got hurt. I know that I hurt people. But I think the growth and the satisfaction outweighed the pain. The pain was the price we had to pay for it. I learned from it. I would never go about my business now as I did then, but I learned profound lessons.

"I think we did a lot of damage to the power structure down there at the time. But in the final analysis, I don't think it mattered one whit. I'm pretty skeptical about journalism, especially about the investigative branch. I see a lot of people turning very cynical because they are just so overwhelmed with the crap of our social system that it's difficult to maintain an optimistic point of view. So I don't know. I think that my own development came to a point where I gave up that approach [journalism] because I realized that if I wanted to change the society that I really had to change myself before I did anything else. To me that involved going inward and finding out what was stewing in there.

"The *Street Journal* disbanded . . . we sort of got run out of town, really, the pressures got very heavy from all sides, from the paramilitary right-wing to the FBI and the city cops. Those external pressures together with the internal things that were going on, basically the whole feminist movement, with those two things together, the center couldn't hold. We broke up. I wound up in Berkeley and then northern California in the countryside, part of the return to the land movement that was popular at the time. I continued to do political work but in a much more covert way, not as public, helping a lot of draft dodgers and anti-war people. And I continued my studies, not in any formal sense, but on my own. I started reading a lot of psychology and psychoanalysis to try to get a fuller understanding of human nature.

"I did all these investigations into the political structure and found all this incredible corruption that existed, and I came to the conclusion that the old saying was right: Power corrupts. At that point, I started to do more psychological investigations into what makes people want this power, what are the underlying drives that make them go for it. Then I realized that as far as the political structure in this country, the electoral system, that it mirrors the economic system we have. It is designed to get people in positions of power who have that drive and who will tend to be corrupted by the process itself. I believe basically that whoever goes into politics these days, whoever finds it their calling, has a certain lack of something else inside of them.

"In 1972 I did my last overt political project. I did a documentary on Nixon and his ties to organized crime, a video. It was basically a no-budget thing, very primitive. But it was a very interesting experience. After Nixon got reelected I continued to study him from a psychological angle, and I wrote a book about him which never did get published. I was involved in Berkeley politics for a while but I really started to get disillusioned with the process. I saw that all our hopes and dreams were really fading away quite rapidly. I guess I suffered a burnout. It was a very heavy and stressful life we were leading."

By the mid-seventies, Jan had come to a crisis point, both physically and intellectually. As he later recounted in his book, *The Tao of the Species: Investigations into the Psychohistory of Western Man*, his ardent optimism had turned into deep pessimism. His health was poor. Smoking a pack-and-a-half of cigarettes a day, suffering severe migraines, becoming dependent on tranquilizers and painkillers, it occurred to him that "I, myself, the would-be savior of humanity, was in more desperate straits than the humanity I wanted to save." Then, in 1975, a friend took him to a t'ai chi class.

"I was immediately bitten by the bug. I realized that while I had been reading all of this theory about the relationship between mind and body, about human sexuality, that here was a discipline or practice that had been around for thousands of years that really put it all together for me. When I was reading [Wilhelm] Reich, I was always saying, yeah, that's right, yeah that's really great. But the problem with Reich was that after you read him, you were left thinking, okay, what can I do? How can I live my life? Those questions were really answered for me in the theory and practice of this art.

"Like all forms of meditation, t'ai chi seeks to quiet the mind and restore the body to its natural functioning. I really feel it delivers on the promise. Now you may say this is just a function of aging, but I'm a much more balanced person than I was in those days.

"T'ai chi has liberated me from competition, the pursuit of ego or power or status—all the things we were rebelling against at the time. I've found it is a way of being yourself and developing your potential, physically, mentally and creatively. I look at meditation as an art form. I guess I consider myself an artist. The creative thing is what's most important to me. I believe that if everybody was able to liberate their creative potential, then the world would be a heckuva lot better place, a lot less frustrations around."

Today Jan operates a t'ai chi and meditation school in Walnut Creek, California. Short-haired, clean-shaven, bulkier but infinitely healthier than he was twenty years ago, he says, "I kind of like where I am now."

"One of the things t'ai chi has done for me is that by nature I am a very impatient person, or I was. So maybe it was my karma to end up doing something that is very slow and to teach other people to do the same thing. So I have developed a great deal more patience than I ever had before. The process of slowing things down for myself and showing other people how to slow things down, thereby aligning both their minds and their bodies—this is what I see as one of my goals, my calling. So the ego is there, but it is very different from the days when I was organizing radicals and trying to get on television to speak for all these groups. That, I would say, was a lot of ego involvement on my part. I have no desire to be in that position again.

"I see the danger of narcissism in what I do. I guess I'm in the New Age, although I shudder to say it. I do think narcissism is a problem, and I don't see an easy way out of it. I have told people not to be so concerned with themselves. I think a lot of sickness stems from a neurotic concern with oneself. I just think there are different ways of being concerned with yourself.

"I mean, you have to be concerned with yourself on some level. The people in the political protest movements who push everything personal aside "for the greater good" are losing parts of themselves. By the same token, I see people who are so much into the personal growth syndrome that I don't think that's balanced either. Certainly I am still vitally interested in what's going on. I haven't lost my concern or my awareness. It's just my perception of what I can do, where my role fits in, that has gotten quite a bit smaller.

"I think the sixties changed the country in very profound ways. I don't think it's been the same since. The values that we were talking about and expressing are still percolating, and people are still pursuing them, although in less fanatical ways. In my own life I feel I am in a deep way still committed to these values because I always thought that it was the liberation of the human spirit that was at the core of it all, and that's what I am striving to do in my own life."

SILAS "TRIM" BISSELL, 47
1969: Weatherman
1989: poet/writer

At 47, Trim has already lived three rather complete lives: one as an award-winning poet and college teacher; another, using the alias Terry Jackson, as a soft-spoken physical therapist who painted for a hobby; and briefly, in between those two personas, Trim Bissell the revolutionary, the member of the

Weather Underground who tried to bomb the ROTC building at the University of Washington—and spent the next seventeen years as a fugitive.

Born to a family of upper class activists (the Bissells won special achievement awards for their civil rights work from the NAACP in 1959 and 1960), he at first deliberately shunned political activity in favor of his own artistic and intellectual growth. But, he says, the horror of the Vietnam War compelled him to act. In the summer of 1967, he and his wife Judy were living in Detroit, where he was writing and teaching at Wayne State University. They knew there would be a race riot that summer and left the city to stay with friends in Ann Arbor. For a week, they sat glued to the TV set watching the riots.

"When gradually the riot began to phase out, I found myself very disappointed. I wanted that riot to go on, and I wanted them to get to the suburbs. Later that summer we were traveling around the country and seeing the sights, visiting friends, and in the midst of a conversation about the war, I said what countless other people had said, I said, 'The only way this war is gonna be stopped is if people start doing some bombings, because they're not gonna listen to the protests.' And then I listened to myself and thought about that for a while and realized that I was sitting there hoping that somebody else would continue that riot in Detroit, but I wasn't out there doing it. And I thought that this war was an atrocity and that somebody needed to do some bombings to stop it, and it just seemed like my number had been called in the moral draft lottery.

"Well, I didn't run right out and become active. In the best academic tradition I spent another year thinking and reading and talking to people, planning, with the notion that after I finished that next academic year, then I would become a full-time activist. It was my plan from the outset to do bombings, and that would have been where I would have most likely started had Johnson not abdicated. I still felt that the bombings would be necessary, and I had no illusions that the war was going to stop with the end of Johnson's term, but I also saw that at that point the public perceived the war as being so identified with Johnson that bombings during this interval of time would be counterproductive, so I decided to go ahead and do above-ground activities and wait for the time to be right.

"I was a poet who came from a family of activists and who resisted activism for a long time and who became active only out of a sense of moral necessity—because of the war. And a good part of why I went to Seattle rather than staying in Detroit where I'd been living is that I knew instinctively that I was going to commit myself to this new activity, that I had to make a physical break with my artist-writer life. One of my fears was that I would try to be a poet type of activist. I had been to readings by various poets who were writing political stuff, and I found that very often they seemed guided by their egos, and they wanted to have some unusual idiosyncratic theory of the personality to explain history so that they could make interesting poems about it and be an interesting personality on stage. And I did not want that route for myself, so I in fact stopped writing. I wanted to do something that was directly involved with the Vietnam War."

He moved to Seattle in the summer of 1968, joining a local radical group that soon affiliated with SDS. Later, when SDS split, Trim's group allied itself with the Weathermen faction. On January 18th, 1970, he and his wife placed a bomb under the stairs of the U.S. Air Force ROTC building on the University of Washington campus. (The bomb failed to explode.) The Bissells were almost immediately arrested by campus police. Both jumped bail and went underground.

At first, Trim attempted to hook up with other radicals to continue direct action, but after a "lonely, miserable, isolated" year-and-a-half, he settled into a tame, quasi-countercultural life in Eugene, Oregon. He went back to school—beginning with earning a GED under the assumed name he was to use for the next seventeen years—and became a physical therapist. He was one of the mainstays of a local food cooperative. He made new friends. He lived with a woman. Then in January of 1987, the knock on the door finally came. Trim pled guilty to the 1970 charge and served seventeen months of a two-year sentence before being released. He returned to Eugene last fall, where he is supporting himself by doing temporary office work while he edits his prison poetry and works on his autobiography.

"[The bombing] is not a decision that I regret. Absolutely not. If you do something right, you have to expect to be punished for it. I actually expected things to come out much harder for us. I had a very pessimistic view of what our personal fate was likely to be, and at one point during the preparation for the bombing, as we discussed whether to continue, I said to Judy that it was in my view really probable that we would end up either getting killed or spending the rest of our lives in prison if we went this route. So I went into it with my eyes wide open, not happily, but out of a sense that that's what I needed to do. I didn't do it out of anger. There were times when I was angry, but my actions were based on a sense of moral responsibility. I think that what I did came more out of a sense that I had this life, that I'd had pretty good opportunities already, pretty good advantages, and there were many other people whose lives were being destroyed, and I might make a difference in that. And so it was time to trade some advantages.

"I still believe in what I was fighting against, but I no longer believe in what I was fighting for. I think we all naturally assume that there has to be a better alternative to whatever the wrongs are that we've confronted in our lives. I was one of many people who called themselves revolutionary communists. And so that says a lot about what I hoped would change the world. But I don't have that faith in revolutionary communism any more, and I don't have that faith in people any more. Let me put it another way: If human history were the history of any species besides humans, human beings would look at human history and they would say, 'Aha, human history is a description of how human beings behave and what they are. You look at history, and you see what they are.' But because human history is our own history, we look at human history and we say, 'Ah, this is an aberration, this is how humans went wrong,' because of whatever—sin, capitalism, whatever. And our true natures will be revealed, and we will be the humans that we truly are if we then follow this other 'ism'.

"I've come to believe that there is nothing that will save us from ourselves. Regardless of our ideologies, we're still going to be human beings. We're stuck with ourselves. And that's not a pretty picture, and it's not an optimistic picture. But I've always tended to be philosophically fairly pessimistic, but in behavior fairly optimistic. And I've become more pessimistic philosophically with time.

"I still believe that a lot of the overt part of Weathermen, the overt politics, was correct. And I think that the bombings contributed greatly to the end of the Vietnam War. And I think that even my own failed attempt at a bombing contributed substantially to the end of the Vietnam War. Not because of a single act, but as part of that whole process. What happened physically with those bombings was minute, but it was the perceived effect that they had then, because the American people began to believe that the society was coming apart at the seams. In fact, it was nowhere near coming apart at the seams. This society was rolling along merrily. But that perception of what we were doing was major, and caused people to put pressure on their congresspeople to vote that war to an end. So, for all their craziness, I don't condemn the overt politics of Weathermen. But Weatherpeople were just like other people, and when there was a chance for people to grab power and misuse other people for power and sexual advantage or any other advantage, there were people who damn well did that—and in the name of the highest ideals.

"Being a fugitive made me regard my life more intentionally, more consciously than I probably would have regarded it otherwise. And I don't mean just for those issues that are obviously related to being a fugitive. Being a fugitive forced me to think fundamentally about what my life was all about, and what I wanted my life to be. Before I became a fugitive, I began the process of formulating rules of survival, which I continued to do as a fugitive and afterwards. And one of the earliest principles I formulated was that there was simply no point in being a fugitive if all I accomplished by that was to avoid being arrested, because my life would still be defined in a sense as a prisoner. And so I decided that the only reason to be a fugitive would be if I could make my life a worthwhile life. And so I very deliberately set out to find out what was the most fulfilling and useful and happy life that I could make for myself.

"When I was arrested, it was my physical therapy more than anything else which was proof that, aha, I had remade my life and I was a good guy. Yet the truth is that part of me has always regarded that as a sellout. From early on, before I became an activist, when I was trying to determine the course of my life, one of the courses I considered was medicine, or more specifically, physical therapy. I had the sense that going the medical route was a sellout, because I knew that those who had dedicated their lives to evil in the world were going to be maiming people at a rate far in excess of what anybody else could go around and heal those bodies one by one. If I was really going to make a difference in the physical world, it was not going to be through medicine but by trying to affect the larger shape of things. And if I wanted to know that I was a responsible person, and not just make myself feel better, then I'd better not go out there and just patch up a few bodies, I'd better go out there and do something about all the shot-up and napalmed bodies before that happened.

"I had a dream just a few nights ago that fascism had come to America. And it was a very frightening nightmare. When I woke from the dream, I felt again, as I had not felt for years—I'd lost touch with a vivid awareness of how that war was not simply unjust, as we so blandly put it now, but that indeed it was a terrible atrocity committed against so many people in that country. And that it was an atrocity committed by policy, systematically. And for all that the GIs were victims too, they also became willing executioners and fascists. And they did things that are just horrifying, there's no way around it. And they didn't do it just because they were under pressure; they did it because they had that in them, as all people do—and that part of them, that fascist part, prevailed. They did it because they had the opportunity to do it, not only because they were forced by circumstance.

"I had lost touch with just how deeply appalling that was. All the talk about healing the wounds and welcoming the soldiers back is not being done to make the GIs feel better. It is being done so that people will accept the same brutalization, which has always been part of not just American history but world history, so that we can do it in Central America and anywhere else that greedy power-hungry people damn well choose to do it. I'm not one that tends to get into saying, 'this society of ours,' because I don't think that it's particularly American society or capitalism that's the basis of it. I think that it has to do with who's in power, but it also has to do with human nature, because the people in power really could not get away with it if they couldn't in some way or another get the populace to go along with it. But I do believe that the worst of us, with rare exceptions, prevail. And there's a good reason why that happens. People say power corrupts. And there's truth to that, but power corrupts the already corrupted. It's the evil who live for power and greed who devote themselves, drive themselves for power and wealth. And we'll never match their energy.

"I would like to be one of those who says, 'Yet, in spite of it all, humans shall prevail.' Or something else stirring like that. We like things to end on a triumphant note. We like the yea-sayers. I'm really not one of the yea-sayers of life. But I also do feel some responsibility for what I do with my life, even if what I do with my life makes no great difference in the world, it matters to me that I live decently. But you won't get the rousing huzzahs from me.

"It's important to know that we aren't good guys or good gals; we're just human beings. And maybe we do things with our lives that are good, and because those are the public things, those are the ways we are defined in the public arena. But we are every bit as human as those people who went over to Vietnam and killed babies, although it's not fashionable to talk about that. And we're every bit as human as those people who made the policies and still make the policies that send the soldiers over there. We don't do ourselves any service to believe that 'superheroes of the sixties' version of ourselves."

TERENCE McKENNA, 42
1967: hippie expatriate
1989: psychedelic philosopher

Raised in a small cattle-ranching town in western Colorado, Terence transcended his surroundings at an early age, reading Aldous Huxley at fourteen and subscribing to the *Evergreen Review* and the *Village Voice* as a high school sophomore. The summer before he entered Berkeley—which he says he chose specifically for its countercultural environment—Terence took LSD for the first time. He found the experience "quite stunning."

After two years at Berkeley, studying in an experimental program and becoming increasingly active in anti-war protests, he decided to leave the country. "Everything was just too screwed up here," he says. He traveled for more than six months, trekking across Europe to Israel, Africa, India and the Seychelles. He arrived back in Berkeley in the spring of 1968 in time for a number of major anti-war demonstrations. Tailed by plainclothesmen after fighting in the San Francisco State strike, he decided that his career as a political activist was over, and he once more hit the road. For the next three years, he wandered the globe as an expatriate hippie, supporting himself by capturing butterflies for collectors, exporting art and "some casual smuggling."

"We felt like we struggled for a long time. I mean these street riots were getting wilder and wilder. First they were peaceful marches, people carrying banners, then they were all about running and shouting and overturning stuff, and then Molotov cocktails, and then the other side brought in the Army and the National Guard. And Berkeley became the sixth military district at one point. Every twelve feet there was a kid with a bayonet on a rifle. I mean it was surreal. I became quite cynical, and I remain cynical. That's where I learned my politics. I think anybody who wasn't there doesn't understand.

"Like this Tiananmen Square thing. I had that figured months before it came apart, because it's just a simple fact that all revolutionaries learn, that the state does not relinquish power gracefully. It doesn't care how many million people you can put out in front of the party headquarters or whatever it is; when push comes to shove, these guys always go for the gun. I mean there is no dialogue with power. It is ultimately corrupt. And ultimately it's not going anywhere that it isn't shoved. And you see . . . I guess this is what being old means, you can rave like this, and say, 'Those kids, they should have known. Why didn't they ask me. I could have told them.'

"I was just being formed when I was first traveling, you know, that was the crucible. And my God, these cultures were so bizarre, and I was fleeing from my own. And, yes, the stage was large. The canvas was large. You could think of yourself as the hero and you could be a hero, and you could wander among dusty peoples.

"I was looking for different things. In India I was trying to understand the psychedelic experience. In Indonesia I had gone back to trying to understand nature, to looking at tropical nature and following in the steps of Darwin and Wallace. For me, it was always a kind of philosophical thing. It was a search for spiritual bearing, essentially, which didn't really bear fruit until I got to the Amazon, to the shamanism that was plant-based, and hallucinogen-based."

Terence became a student—and later, a teacher—of shamanism and the ethnopharmacology of spiritual transformation. He's authored several books, created an interactive computer software program and regularly gives lectures and workshops at New Age stomping grounds like Esalen and Ojai. He calls himself a "psychedelic philosopher" and sounds much like the Timothy Leary of decades past: the same riveting combination of surrealism and scholarship, even the same slightly nasal tenor voice.

"My critique of American politics . . . I just thought it was preposterous. I mean I did, and I still do. It's more serious now because the amazing thing is that these right-wing types have actually been able to get their agenda back on the track when it seemed like a lost cause during that extremely creative period of the sixties. So in the present situation we're having to fight battles that we thought were won twenty ago. And of course, there is no Left, because the whole Marxist thing has now shown up to be just preposterous. And the whole world is going over to mall consumerism and beige capitalism, beige fascism of some sort. But all the issues that were raised back then remain legitimate: abuse of state power, abuse of wealth, misuse of propaganda, the interference in people's right of free expression and so forth.

"My metier is raving about the evolution of culture into a kind of mental dimension that was foreshadowed and anticipated by psychedelics. I really see psychedelics as the hidden culture-shaping factor in all this. The direction of this new culture would be de-emphasis of materialism, but at the same time, a deeper retreat into electronic simulation. What's coming is a technology for realizing the imagination that will be a perfect mirror of the psyche, the mass psyche. And so I suppose for some people it will be bondage flicks and shoot 'em ups and for other people it will be the sublime and the transcendent. And that technology has this weird neutrality about it. It makes possible the expression of the lowest and commonest denominators of the cultural dreams.

"But this is what I see. I sort of follow the French sociologist who said, 'There are no political solutions, only technological ones. The rest is propaganda.' And in the broadest sense I believe that. But I think that we're gonna have to do some really radical cultural rewiring. Either that or we are actually going to realize this fundamentalist apocalyptic scenario and just stew in our own juices downstream thirty years or so. There has to be change—global reorganization, which means the sacrifice of a whole lot of nationalist and political sacred cows that have been carried along.

"I don't know if we're up to it. It'll be exciting, that's for sure. I'm hopeful, but I don't put my faith in wisdom-laden white men managing great institutions. It's coming from a deeper level than that. I think something extraordinary is happening on this planet, and that we are not out of or against nature; we are somehow pivotal to nature's plan. I mean that sounds a little hokey, but something is going on on this planet. The incubation of an information transforming ontology of some sort, of which we are just a part.

"Drugs and computers are migrating toward each other. Technology and hallucinogens are going to create a shamanic dimension for culture. It will be done in media somehow. And this will be a major cultural breakthrough analogous to the invention of printing, but it will restructure our self-images because it will be much more intimate. I'm a neo-McLuhanite, I guess.

"A lot of the sixties stuff has never been called into question by me. I didn't recant, and I don't have a complicated apologia to make, because I still think all this stuff. I mean for me, it stood the test of time. Jung, McLuhan, Whitehead, all of the ideas that I associate back then are still the working models for my creative thinking.

"I guess I'm a psychedelic philosopher. I mean it's become that. I'm simply educating people about this psychedelic option because, strangely enough, no one else is talking about it. And I think that it's central. I've carried out a reasonably thorough examination of the culture and its literature and underpinnings and so forth, and as far as I can tell, the psychedelic thing is absolutely big news. It's as bizarre as having a flying saucer land in your front yard. But nobody's talking about it, apparently because of the cultural trauma of the sixties. But it is repeatable, accessible to ordinary men and women and just the strangest game in town. And I don't think people realize it. We're not talking about twelve years of doing yoga here or having to go off and live on the side of a mountain. This is here and now, friends. And there is not a peep in the culture. I mean I don't know what's going on. It's really freaky to me that such an astonishing cultural artifact, cultural phenomenon could be raging and, you know, everybody's tied up in Jim Wright's book deal.

"Obviously, today the well of language has been polluted on the drug issue. So I go out and try to point out to people that this is a birthright. These experiences are as profound and complex as human sexuality—and as basic to who we are and what we're doing. And to go from the cradle to the grave without having these experiences just outrages me. I mean it's like virginity or something. It's just weird to choose to be that narrow in your contact with life.

"I've spent a lot of time in the Amazon and seen shamanism in action in these societies. And I just think it's the most confounding mystery on the planet, and I went into it as a skeptic. I am not to be identified with crystal gazers, friends of fallen Atlantis, or any of that malarkey. I'm pretty hard-headed, vulgar even. And I'm telling you, this psychedelic thing, there is something going on there that is the confounding of science, Western values, rationalism, and all the rest of it. It's pretty strange stuff. It's repeatable, and you can choose to do it on your own terms. And it's not magic, and it's not dependent on finding the right lineage or any of that. It's actually real. I see the human potential movement of the seventies as basically a flight from psychedelics because of their effectiveness. I mean the motto of the New Age seems to be 'We'll try anything as long as it doesn't work.'

"I'm cutting down on my dosage, but I continue to have psychedelic experiences. I think psychedelics always hold up your values to inspection, and maybe as you get older you get less comfortable with that because it will take more energy to undo some of it. But I do psychedelics several times a year, always these plant hallucinogens, the ones people have been doing for thousands of years. I'm not big on synthetics at all.

"One of the things I've come to see in watching it all over the world is it takes courage in all situations to really go to the depth, because it does challenge the existential nub. It's hair raising, this stuff, it's really between you and it. You don't have *Time* magazine or *Scientific American* running interference on the sidelines. It's you out there in the tall grass, and there are real lions.

"Life is so strange; it's so much like a work of art. It's so unexpectedly artful that I'm puzzled. That's what drives me to continue with the psychedelics. I feel like we're part of a tale of some sort, a story. And I would like to know where in the story we are and how it all ends. And I just keep digging. And I'm just amazed at the complexity, the richness, the plotted artifice of being. And beauty, I mean, these things are tickets to really titanic realms of the unexpectedly beautiful, really the astonishing beautiful side of the other. So, all that motivates me. I love the weirdness of it, the magic, the confounding of it.

"People are so ready to watch the tube three hours a day and completely atomize themselves into mass values. Because they underdefine their own worth. That's what it's all about. And that's really what the whole cultural struggle has been about. The primacy of experience, it can't be taken away from you. And these drugs focus you on the primacy of experience, the here and now, what is happening right here, right now all around you. And it's rich. People's mental lives are rich, their imaginations are rich. They undersell all this, and then they feel politically disempowered.

"I think I understand why psychedelics are illegal. They're illegal because they dissolve fidelity to group values. They are true deconditioning agents. If you dabble in psychedelics it just shows you the relativity of all belief systems, and that's really politically potent stuff. It's like a generalized virus against institutional loyalty."

JOAN HOLDEN, 50
1967: playwright, San Francisco Mime Troupe
1989: playwright, San Francisco Mime Troupe

A native of Berkeley, Joan says she was "born on the Left" and grew up surrounded by family and friends who fought in Spain and visited Moscow. "There was never any question what side my family was on," she says. She attended Reed College in the fifties and came home to Berkeley for graduate school, dropping out just before the Free Speech Movement began. In 1964, when her brother and cousins and everyone she knew went to Mississippi, she went to France to become a writer. Two years later she returned, sans the Great American Novel, because "we heard about the anti-war movement, and it seemed that history was being made in the U.S. not France." In the spring of 1967, she wrote her first play for the eight-year-old Mime Troupe. Twenty-two years, dozens of plays and three children later, she's still at it.

"The Mime Troupe has been through a lot of changes. We went through our collectivization and our Maoist period and our working-class period, and now we do it in a different way. I mean our business is much more professional; professionalization—that's another phase that these kind of institutions went through, if they survived, in order to survive. You know, hiring a staff and getting your graphics to look slick and sending out your booking materials on time and going to the booking conferences, being realistic about the business. And getting grants. We've done all those things. So we're now in this paradoxical position of being a venerable institution that's still part of the counterculture.

"These are very hard times for theatre. Really hard times. And much more mainstream, middle-of-the-road, what are called mid-level theatre companies are going out of business all over the place. So there's no question that if we hadn't gotten our act together we'd be off the map. We had to get our act together. And that means not doing certain kinds of things that we used to do. Like we don't do demonstrations a lot anymore. We don't have time.

On the other hand, we do open a new political satire every single summer in the parks and perform it for free. And while we perform in big theatres all over the world, we also perform in very grassroots communities. You know, we go to Mendocino and Nevada City and Point Arena and Ukiah and perform for 1,500 dollars. We've made a decision to play both sides of the street. And it seems like we're able to do it.

"Compromise used to be a dirty word to me. Now it's interesting. It's recognizing reality. You know, when we play for grassroots groups, we're pretty much preaching to the converted. When we play at the Kennedy Center, we're reaching a new audience. And I think those things are important to do. You know, there's always a question every time I do an interview with the daily press, it's, 'Don't you feel you're preaching to the converted?' And I say, 'Well, if you insist on using that metaphor, part of any evangelist's job is to do revivals, to keep the faith alive. You spread the word and you keep the faith alive.' And they're both part of the job. So I don't feel guilty about preaching to the converted, but if that's all I did, it would be depressing.

"So our structure may have changed, but what hasn't changed is that the inspiration for all our plays, for everything that I've ever written, really, always comes from the same place, which is: Who's the enemy? What's the injustice of the year? What cries out? What should be changed? Where should people direct their energies? What's wrong?

"In the last three years we've done one play about radioactive waste and the government coverup of the problem of radioactive poison. One about *Rip Van Winkle*, about the hippie activist who slept for twenty years and wakes up in the eighties, but it's really about what values have been lost, between the sixties and the eighties. So while the play satirizes some errors of the sixties, it celebrates the spirit. We did many silly things back then, and we thought many things that weren't true. The idea that the revolution was two or three years away is now a very funny idea, but the willingness to take everything on, that energy of 'we can change the world,' which was the energy of the movement at that time, is still a little flame in a lot of people that's waiting to be stoked up again, and it's a beautiful thing, a great thing, and it is that spirit that changes the world.

"I realize that there's a continuing theme in our plays, which is that very, very often the central character is someone struggling with the question of whether to be active or not. Not just living for themselves. Rip's girlfriend, who didn't go to sleep in *Rip Van Winkle*, realizes that all her friends are moving up. They've got nice houses, they've got nice apartments, they've got nice cars, and she's been doing benefits and trying to be a good person, trying to work for social justice, and now she's forty, and she has nothing except an ungrateful child.

"I started noticing that since the middle seventies I've been writing central characters who were tempted, who were tired of struggling with what seemed to be intractable problems and telling people things, proclaiming news that people didn't want to hear. You know, when you've been trying to make people think for years, and you feel that you're not making any progress, you do ask yourself: 'Why don't I go to law school and start making 60,000 dollars a year?' So we've probably written ten plays with this as the issue of the hero.

"There's always a topic, but the real subject of our plays is what choices to make, what values. You know, whether to devote your life to the public good or to your own. These characters are us, you know, we're all forty or fifty years old with no retirement plan, suddenly middle-aged, who've been in the movement for twenty or twenty-five years.

"What keeps me going is that it's fun. It's also a kind of puritanism. There's a kind of morality that I was raised on and a political consciousness. Social conscience is just part of my culture. And personality, I guess. I would feel guilty if I weren't doing something useful. I have to be useful. But I can't claim any nobility for that because the work that I do is extremely enjoyable. It's just not very profitable, doesn't make you rich.

"But, the life of an artist, if you can make a living—even a bad one—is an extremely privileged one. I haven't felt once since 1967, that 'I don't want to go to work today.' I've felt tired, and taken the day off, but not, 'Oh, god, do I have to go in there for eight hours?' My life is integrated, and it's happy. What I do is I make my living doing my political work. I couldn't lead three lives—as a worker, a political activist and a parent.

"I'm optimistic about the future, yeah. But if you asked me why, if you asked me to defend it rationally I'd probably have a hard time. I think it's just my nature. Why do we do comedy as opposed to tragedy or a dark kind of realism? It's really an optimist's art form. Comedy celebrates the life force. And possibility. Everything's open. People all over the country and all over the world are struggling to make the world better against gigantic odds. And as long as they keep doing that . . .

"I'm long past the point where I think there will be a revolution, and then everything will be fine. History is a struggle. And there are many setbacks and many terrible things happen. The thing that makes me optimistic is that people keep coming back. They're never permanently suppressed.

"The thing that depresses me the most, actually, is the paving of California. This is the visual stifling of life. Places that I remember in the Santa Clara Valley or the Pomona Valley, places that were all orchard when I was a child, are now endless shopping malls and subdivisions. Those are the things that make my heart sink. But leave concrete alone for two years, and grass starts to grow through it. That's the same thing I feel about the human spirit. It does break through. It always breaks through."